The Visitor's Guide
to
THE NORMANDY LANDING BEACHES
Memorials and Museums

SWORD BEACH, QUEEN White Sector ⇨

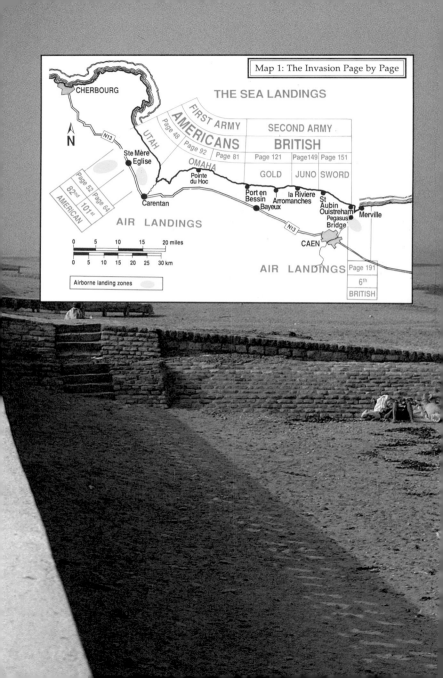

Map 1: The Invasion Page by Page

THE SEA LANDINGS

FIRST ARMY
AMERICANS

SECOND ARMY
BRITISH

CHERBOURG

N13

UTAH

Ste Mère Eglise

OMAHA

Pointe du Hoc

Carentan

82nd AMERICAN

101st

Page 52

Page 64

Page 48

Page 92

Page 81

Page 121

Page 149

Page 151

GOLD

JUNO

SWORD

Port en Bessin

la Rivière

Arromanches

St Aubin

Bayeux

Ouistreham

Merville

Pegasus Bridge

N13

CAEN

AIR LANDINGS

AIR LANDINGS

Page 191

6th BRITISH

0   5   10   15   20 miles

0 5 10 15 20 25 30 km

Airborne landing zones

THE
VISITOR'S GUIDE TO
NORMANDY
LANDING BEACHES

Memorials and Museums

Tonie and Valmai Holt

MPC

British Library Cataloguing in
Publication Data:
Holt, Tonie,
   The Visitor's Guide to the
Normandy Landing Beaches
   — (MPC visitor's guides).
   1. France. Landing Beaches —
Visitor's guides
   I. Title II. Holt, Valmai
   914.4'04838

Published by:
Moorland Publishing Co Ltd,
Moor Farm Road,
Airfield Estate,
Ashbourne,
Derbyshire DE6 1HD
England

ISBN 0 86190 301 3 (paperback)

Published in the USA by:
Hunter Publishing Inc,
300 Raritan Centre Parkway,
CN 94, Edison, NJ 08818

ISBN 1 55650 191 9 (USA)

Colour and black & white
origination by:
Scantrans, Singapore
Printed in the UK by:
Richard Clay Ltd, Bungay, Suffolk

Cover photograph:
Churchill AVRE at Graye-sur-Mer

The authors and publisher would like
to thank the following for the use of
illustrations:
Portsmouth Tourism Office, pp 35,
37; Centre Régional de Documentation Pédagogique de Caen , p42;
Calvados Tourisme Office, p133,
134; Imperial War Museum, pp137,
172; Emris Morgan, p226; Musée
Mémorial de Caen, p232.
All remaining photographs were
taken by Tonie and Valmai Holt.

The Authors:
This book is the only Normandy
guide written by authors whose
company specialises in conducting
battlefield tours to many parts of the
world. Together they have written
fourteen books, most with a military
history theme, including four
battlefield guides.

CONTENTS

INTRODUCTION

E ach year, especially since the important fortieth anniversary in June 1984, the numbers of visitors to the war museums (some of which prefer to be known as 'peace' museums) in Normandy increases steadily.

Each year new memorials and plaques to divisions, regiments, even to individuals, are dedicated to those who took part in the D-Day Landings and the Battle for Normandy.

Still, each year, veterans and war widows are welcomed at ceremonies of remembrance and friendly '*Vin d'honneurs*' by Normans, faithfully grateful for their liberation. That their liberation was won at the expense of fearfully high civilian casualty lists and ruined towns and villages does not diminish the warmth of these gatherings.

Nowhere more than in Normandy are the *Entente Cordiale* and good Franco-American relations alive and well. Nowhere does the flame of remembrance burn more brightly. The visitor to the areas of the Landing Beaches will be met with a wealth of interesting things to do and see as he or she studies the world-shaping events of June 1944.

Museums range from grandiose and official (like the new Memorial Museum at Caen) to well-intentioned private and amateur collections (as at Surrain). Elements of Hitler's Atlantic Wall defences are in some places extraordinarily well-preserved (for example the batteries at Longues, Crisbecq, etc). Shell holes still pock the landscape (as at Pointe du Hoc). Remnants of the brilliantly conceived Mulberry Harbour can still be clearly seen (at Arromanches). The main sites and memorials are well maintained, marked and signed (with *Circuit du Débarquement* road signs), by local councils and the Comité du Débarquement (qv).

It is not only the veterans who visit Normandy. More and more young people (who have perhaps studied the Landings in their history lessons at school) and family groups tour the area, interested to see where dad, or grandad, fought or where history was made.

To add to our own extensive researches, many veterans and local

6

civilians who experienced the events of June 1944 have kindly given us their personal, vivid accounts. Their words will bring those events alive, whether they be heroic, mundane, fearful, amusing, or simply human. Such is warfare.

When following the battlefield tours in each chapter, the visitor will be going through one of the most beautiful regions of France — the *départements* of Calvados and La Manche. To help you to make the most of their varied attractions and delicious local specialities, comprehensive tourist information is given. We hope you enjoy your visit to Normandy as much as we *always* do. And if you are an armchair traveller, we hope this book will add to your knowledge of this fascinating campaign.

Tonie and Valmai Holt
Sandwich, Kent

Acknowledgements

The authors would like to thank the following for their help in preparing this book: M. Raymond Triboulet, OBE, Ancien Ministre, Président Comité du Débarquement; Mlle Geneviève le Cacheux, Keeper Documentation Centre Memorial Museum, Caen; Valentine de la Provote, Service de Presse, Memorial Museum, Caen, for kind permission to reproduce illustrations; Joseph P. Rivers, Superintendent, US National Cemetery, St Laurent; John R. (Bob) Slaughter, Veteran US 29th Division; Madame Bouvier-Muller, Franco-American 9th USAAF Airfields in Normandy Association; Arlette Gondrée-Pritchet; Régine Turgis Khalla, Comité Départemental de Tourisme du Calvados, for unfailing good humour and the loan of photographs; Daniel Mariette, Monsieur Laroche, directors of the Novotels/Mercure at Caen and Bayeux for making our 'recces' a pleasant experience in their hotels; Monsieur Noel, Curator Arromanches Museum; Brigadier Peter Young, DSO, MC, MA, FSA, (who sadly died 1988); Mr Roger Dalley, Director of Information Services, the Commonwealth War Graves Commission for permission to reproduce from the CWGC's *Guide to the Commonwealth War Cemeteries and the Bayeux Memorial. Normandy June-August 1944*; Mr. Henry Brown, Commando Association; Major Jack Watson, Airborne Assault, Normandy; Mr. E. S. Hannath, Normandy Veterans Association; Portsmouth Tourism Office; and Vivien, for — yet again — an 'above and beyond' feat of deciphering and typing.

For their moving, vivid, sometimes amusing, sometimes sad 'Memories of D-Day', our heartfelt thanks to the following (with their 1944 ranks):
Lt Laurie Anderson, Paratrooper Les Cartwright, Sgt John Clewlow, Gunfitter Harry Cooper, Lt Cdr Rupert Curtis, Major Tony Dyball, Aircraft Engineer John Ginter, Trooper 'Goody' Goodson, Major John Howard, Lance Cpl P.L.M. Hennessey, Piper Bill Millin, Brigadier Nigel Poett, Major Pat Porteous VC, Pte Lee Ratel, Lt 'Tod' Sweeney, Lt J.J. Whitmeyer, Captain John Winckworth, Lt D.J. Wood.

HOW TO USE THIS GUIDE

Most people who visit the area of the D-Day Landings want to see places which featured prominently in the accounts of the actions. Therefore the battlefield tours in this book are designed to enable the visitor to see the maximum amount in the minimum time. They are as compact as is possible, giving a representative view of what happened without the danger of becoming too detailed and hence incomprehensible.

There is no doubt that a better picture of what happened on D-Day, and why it happened, can be obtained from a general understanding of the background to the invasion. Therefore, the traveller is advised to read the brief introductory passages before setting out on the tours.

If You Want to Tour A Particular Beachhead
Consult the map 'Landing Beaches Page by Page' on page 2. This shows very clearly how the text relates to the Landing Beaches. You can select the beachhead and turn directly to the appropriate page.

If You Want to Visit A Particular Memorial or Place
Use the index at the back of the book.

If You Just Want 'To Tour The Beaches'
The beaches invaded by the Americans start on page 47 and those invaded by the British or Canadians start on page 116.

The Battlefield Tours
The tours need not be taken in any particular sequence, nor travelled in the directions given in this book, though it will ease navigation if they are.

Each tour is both preceded, and accompanied, by an historical account which should be read en route. Broadly the tours relate to the five Landing Beaches, though for both geographical convenience and in order not to make too long a touring day, some airborne operations have been incorporated into landing beach tours. Nevertheless, by using the sketch maps, which show the exact route of each tour, travellers can mix and choose the sections in a manner to suit themselves.

The times stated do not include stops for refreshments or visits to museums

Maps

A number of clear and simple sketch maps are provided in the text. These should be used in conjunction with the maps recommended at the start of each section. Without these maps it is difficult to grasp what happened. It is also difficult to navigate. It is a good idea to mark the battlefield tour route on the recommended map before setting out.

The best overall map which covers the whole area is the Michelin Carte 54 1/200,000. It is essential.

Museums

All the museums worth visiting have been included in the battlefield tour itineraries and, where they add significantly to the understanding of what happened, they are placed at the beginning of a tour. More museums spring up every year. It is best to visit only one or two, since the major benefit to be gained from being in Normandy is visiting the battlefield.

ABBREVIATIONS

Abbreviations used for military units are listed below. At intervals the full name of a unit is repeated in the text in order to aid clarity. Other abbreviations and acronyms are explained where they occur.

AB	Airborne
BEF	British Expeditionary Force
Bde	Brigade
Bn	Battalion
Can	Canadian
Cdo	Commando
Com Deb Mon Sig	*Comité du Débarquement Monument Signal*
Co	Company
CWGC	Commonwealth War Graves Commission
Div	Division
DZ	Dropping Zone
Inf	Infantry
LZ	Landing Zone
Mem	Memorial
OP	Observation Post
PIR	Parachute Infanty Regiment
Regt	Regiment
RM	Royal Marine
RV	Rendezvous
Sqn	Squadron

1

BACKGROUND TO NORMANDY

It would not be appropriate in this guide, which is first and foremost a guide to the D-Day Landing Beaches, to include a comprehensive account of the province's rich history and culture. However, as the visitor will pass through areas redolent of its eventful past and productive present, he or she deserves at least a brief background to Normandy's history, geography and culture, the better to enjoy the tour. It is also an area of outstanding natural beauty and delicious food — neither of which should be neglected.

Historical Resumé

Pre-1940

The name 'Normandy' derives from the Norsemen who invaded the area in the ninth century. The land they occupied was known as *Neustrie* (Kingdom of the West), one of three Frankish Kingdoms founded by Childeric in 567. It was inhabited by Celtic, Iberian and Gallic tribes who had already been conquered by the Romans in 50BC. The warring tribes were subdued by Roman rule and an uneasy peace, broken only by the warring Francs and Carolingians, reigned — until the Norman invasion.

The story of the most famous Norman of all, William the Bastard (also known as 'the Conqueror'), is charted in the famous Bayeux Tapestry — a *must* when visiting Normandy (page 148). When William invaded England in 1066 it was with the greatest invasion fleet and force the world had ever known. The fleet and force that invaded, in the opposite direction, in 1944 was also the greatest invasion fleet and force the world had hitherto known. The irony of the conjunction of these two historical landmarks is recorded in the Latin inscription on the Bayeux Memorial: '*Nos a Guilelmo victi victoris Patriam liberavimus*' ('We, once conquered by William, have now set free the conqueror's native land').

After the Normans it was the English who were to be Normandy's next invaders — during the 100 Years' War. As in 1944, the proximity of Normandy's fine beaches to the English coast attracted invaders, such as Edward III and Henry V. The last battle of the 100 Years' War took place in 1450 in Formigny (on what is now the N13 behind OMAHA beach). It is marked by a splendid memorial that was knocked over by a Sherman tank in 1944, but now once more proudly dominates the town's crossroads.

From then until the German Occupation in 1940, the province flourished. Its temperate climate and good soil fostered successful agriculture and dairy farming. Its plentiful seas offered a rich harvest of seafood. The province's reputation for rich gastronomy encouraged tourism, which developed in the 1890s with the rail link to Paris and the burgeoning of smart resorts like Cabourg, Deauville and Trouville. For Normandy it was truly the beginning of the *Belle Epoque*, and royalty, high society and the artistic *monde* savoured its clear air, beautiful sandy beaches and fine Romanesque and Norman architecture. It was to remain so until the Fall of France in 1940.

The Occupation 1940-44

For the four years until June 1944, the phlegmatic Normans by and large evolved a comfortable *modus vivendi* with their German occupiers. The quality of the German troops during the occupation was generally poor. There was a high percentage of under or over age soldiers and convalescents. Many of them were non-German. Most Normans settled for a quiet life with them — glad of the money they could make by supplying much appreciated dairy produce, cider and Calvados. Underneath the sleepy surface, active members of the Resistance worked by day and, more often, by night. Forbidden radios, tuned to the BBC picked up the message which was to announce the Allied Invasion.

This message was the first verse of Paul Verlaine's *Chanson d'Automne* (Autumn Song). The first three lines,

Les sanglots longs,
Des violons,
De l'Automne   (The long sobs of autumn violins)

was broadcast on 1June. On 5 June, the next three lines,

Blessent mon coeur,
D'une longueur,
Monotone   (Wound my heart with a monotonous languor)

followed. It signalled that the Invasion would take place in 48 hours.

From 6 June 1944

As a reprisal, and in a certain amount of panic, when the Germans realised the scale of the landings, they executed (by shooting) all the male Resistance workers in Caen Prison except two — a youth of only 16 and a man whose name was wrongly recorded by the Germans, who thus did not call him out to be shot. The killings started on the evening of 6 June and continued the next day. Over eighty men were executed.

The Normans certainly paid dearly for their liberation. As well as these Resistance executions, thousands of civilians were killed over the next seventy or so days in allied bombings and bombardments and the fierce fighting between invaders and occupiers.

In Caen alone, starting with an incendiary bomb raid on 6 June and continuing to its liberation on 9 July, at the very lowest count 2,000 (and it could have been as many as 5,000 as records were impossible to keep in those fearsome days) civilians were killed. Thousands more were injured and made homeless.

Lives were lost, homes were destroyed, albeit on a lesser scale, all along the landing beaches. Valuable farm land was scarred and pitted. Livestock was killed in profusion. One of the most vivid memories of many D-Day veterans is the pathetic sight of bloated cows, their legs up-turned, and the dreadful stench of rotting animals. Yet today, the French welcome returning veterans with genuine warmth.

'At one of the wine receptions', wrote John Slaughter, veteran of the US 29th Division, returning to Normandy in September 1988 for the unveiling of his Divisional Memorial at Vierville, 'many of the locals would shake hands and say, "Thank you for what you did". This is after we tore hell out of their homes and villages. After three years of living under the Bosch iron boot we were their liberators. I now have a different perspective of the French.'

Memorials are on the whole well maintained, ceremonies well attended, by local people and Resistance workers and Free French standard bearers, delightfully out of step, standards sometimes less than rigidly held, beret and Gauloise both at a jaunty angle, but with the heart in a very correct place.

Although of only small significance, there was another side to the coin. There *was* an element of collaboration during the occupation. Some British veterans recall being met by fierce sniper fire, which turned out to be from young Frenchmen. After the invasion many female frater-nisers had to be ignominiously shaved, tarred and feathered. Returning German veterans are still sometimes greeted with more than cordial enthusiasm in some households — notably, it is reported, when mem-bers of 12th SS Panzer attended the burial of Oberstürmführer Michael Wittmann in La Cambe German Cemetery in May 1983.

But these were rare cases and the spirit of remembrance and gratitude fostered by the unceasing efforts of the *Comité du Débarque-ment* (cf page 246) and its chairman, ex-Minister Raymond Triboulet, and by individual French men and women seems as strong as ever.

Great Anglo/American/Canadian-French ceremonies are held every fifth year. But each 6 June and on the successive days into July that mark their liberation, small French communes and private individuals (like Bernard Saulnier, the Amfréville farmer who still holds 'open house' each year for British commandos) welcome returning veterans. *L'Entente Cordiale* is alive and well and manifest along the Normandy battlefields and beaches.

Norman Architecture

The routes one must follow to visit the Landing Beaches and Dropping Zones of the D-Day Invasion take the visitor past some outstanding examples of ecclesiastical, agricultural and manorial architecture.

The predominating style (many superb examples of which, thankfully, survived the fearful battering of the invasion) is known as Romanesque. The Normans created their own brand of Romanesque, which in Britain is known as Norman, and which can still be seen in many churches in Southern England.

It was a harmonious, geometric style, with zigzag decoration, square towers and narrow windows, which retained the rounded Roman arch. William the Bastard's Abbeys at Caen (L'Abbaye aux Hommes and L'Abbaye aux Dames) are High Romanesque, but the style was modified when, as the Conqueror, he carried it over the Channel to England.

On a simpler scale, the churches in many rural and littoral villages are fine examples of the style, eg at Secqueville en Bessin and Ouistreham. The distinctive, tall, wedge-shaped, tiled roof surmounting a square tower can be seen on old farmhouses and churches, throughout the Bessin. With their courtyards enclosed by high walls and turrets, the farms, still in daily use, seem like living pages from history books.

The restraint of the Romanesque/Norman period gave way to the exuberant, ornate Gothic era. Again, the Normans had their own version — Gothique Normand. The most glorious example in Calvados is the cathedral at Bayeux, but more modest churches are to be found at Bernières, Langrune and in many smaller towns.

The Renaissance left its architectural mark, principally on the church of St Pierre in Caen, with interesting examples of statuary and furniture scattered throughout the surrounding district.

Of the scores of picturesque *châteaux* in the areas covered by the Landing Beaches (most of which were used as German, then Allied, command posts) that of Fontaine-Henry, with its beautiful Renaissance wing and high, pointed slate roofs, is probably the most architecturally interesting. The local villagers sheltered in its cellars during the bombardments covering the invasion. Creullet Château, where General Montgomery pitched his caravan (page 144), is not open to the public, but is perfectly visible through the ironwork gates, and it is very close to Creully, whose sprawling, multi-period *château* was used by Allied broadcasters after the invasion (page 145). Their broadcasting tower can be visited by appointment with the town council, whose offices it now houses.

The beautiful creamy-coloured Normandy stone, quarried from the Caen area, and which was exported by the Normans to build their new castles and churches in England (notably Canterbury Cathedral and the Tower of London) is the building material used for many Norman towns and villages, even today. Some of the delightful villages bear a strong resemblance to Cotswold villages.

The most characteristic Normandy style, however, is the half-timbered, lath and plaster façade, akin to the English 'Elizabethan style'. It is much reproduced in modern pseudo-Norman buildings. It is the image that the visitor will most likely retain from his visit to Normandy.

The philosophical Normans approached the destruction of their buildings (an estimated 200,000 were damaged) in a practical way during the reconstruction. Many towns, in particular the devastated city of Caen, were rebuilt with wider roads more fitting to today's modern transport, better housing and office buildings and pleasant parks. Modern architects were able to leave their mark, too, on this ancient countryside. The new university building at Caen is considered an important example of modern style.

The most recent building of note in the area is the impressive new Memorial Museum at Caen (page 229). It was designed by architects Jacques Millet and Philippe Kauffmann, with artistic designer Yves Devraine, and was inaugurated on 6 June 1988 by President Mittérand.

Geography and Economy

The old province of Normandy is divided into administrative *départements*, two of which include the sites of the June 1944 Landings.

CALVADOS (bordered by the River Vire to the south, the Eure to the east and by the *Département* of La Manche to the west). Its capital is Caen. It includes the area of the British action at Merville, the airborne landings near Ranville, GOLD, JUNO AND SWORD beaches, OMAHA beach and Pointe du Hoc.

Calvados got its name in the 1790s, when the old provinces were divided into *départements*. Resisting the description *Orne Inférieure*, the inhabitants preferred the suggestion of a Bayeux lady, who proposed that they should be named after the rocks lying off Arromanches — *les Rochers du Calvados*. They in turn had been called after one of Philip II of Spain's Armada ships, the *San Salvador*, which was wrecked on them.

Départements are further divided into *pays*, from the Gallo-Roman *pagi*. Those that concern our itineraries are:

Plaine de Caen. A rich agricultural plateau, that grows sugar beet and grain, famous for its stone. Caen is now the eighth busiest port in France, especially since the new Portsmouth to Ouistréham ferry has been in service.

The Bessin. Bayeux (city of the Bacojasses) is its main town, Port en Bessin (where the British and American sectors met in June 1944) and Grandcamp are its main ports. Arromanches on the tiny river Arro, is its most important resort, due now mainly to the remnants of its Mulberry Harbour (page 131) and its museum. The ruggedly beautiful Pointe du Hoc, where the US Rangers landed (page 92), is its most picturesque site.

The Côte du Nacre (The Mother of Pearl Coast). This runs from Ouistréham to Courseulles (SWORD and JUNO beaches) with beautiful sandy beaches, where today it is difficult to imagine the terrible drama that was played out in June 1944. The small holiday resorts are very popular in the summer for their excellent seafood restaurants and water sports. The new Brittany Ferry route into Ouistreham has increased the port's importance.

LA MANCHE (bordered by Calvados to the east — between Carentan and Isigny — and to the north and east by the English Channel, which gives it its name.) The area which interests us mostly comprises the near-island of the Cotentin Peninsula.

La Manche includes UTAH beach, Ste Mère Eglise and the US airborne drop zones and Cherbourg, its main town and port. Cherbourg was provided with a hospital and a church by William the Conqueror and was often of importance during the 100 Years' War. Vauban recognised its potential as a large port but the main port was not opened until 1853, seeing its first transatlantic ship as late as 1869. It was taken by the Americans on 26 June 1944 and in late August its PLUTO (page 127) was in operation. The taking of Cherbourg had been crucial to Montgomery's plan. Today it has an attractive pleasure port and is an important ferry terminal. The *département* is famous for its thoroughbred racing and trotting horses.

Gourmet Products and Specialities

Both *départements* share a climate similar to the south coast of England, although somewhat milder and sunnier. Their moistness contributes to their fertility and to the lush pastureland which feeds the cattle, which are the *départements'* greatest asset. There are some six million head of cattle in Normandy, whose pedigree is proudly guarded. Dairy products include milk, cream and fabulous cheeses like Camembert, Petite Ste Mère Eglise, Livarot and Pont l'Evèque. The cream forms the basis of the rich *sauce normande*, served on seafood, chicken and pork chops.

The apple is also important in Normandy as it is the basis for its scrumptious cider (look for *cidre bouchée* [mature bottled] or *cidre fermière* [home brewed on the farm]). To drive through Normandy in apple blossom time is a visual delight. Calvados, distilled apple brandy, is the famous *trou normand*. This sharp liqueur is drunk in gulps between rich courses to clear the palate and then as a *digestif* finale to a good meal. Make sure your Calvados has been aged for 15 years, or it will take the skin off your throat — as many an Allied soldier found to his cost, sometimes fatally, in 1944. Other local specialities are: *Tripes à la Mode de Caen* (tripe cooked in the Caen style) which is an acquired taste, Courseulles oysters, Isigny mussels and caramels.

Crêpes (pancakes) make a superb lunch-time snack. Savoury pancakes are called *gallettes*, usually made with whole-wheat flour and come with a variety of delicious fillings: *Vallée d'auge* (with cream and mushrooms), ham, cheese, onions, tomatoes, bacon etc. They are sold in *Crêperies*, often simple but attractive establishments. A *gallette*, tossed green salad, crunchy *baguette* (long French loaf), Normandy cheese and a glass of *cidre bouchée* make a perfect mid-day meal.

TOURIST INFORMATION

ATTRACTIONS OF THE AREA

Visitors to the Normandy Landing Beaches are coming to an area which is full of other attractions. There are safe, sandy beaches, casinos, tennis, horse-racing, fishing, sailing, wind-surfing, water-skiing, golf, horse-riding, delicious food and drink, fascinating history, culture, architecture from Romanesque to modern, handicrafts and beautiful, varied scenery — from the ever-changing coastline, to the open wooded areas of the famous 'Bocage' (high hedges and ditches enclosing small fields, which were a great hazard to glider landings and tank progress in the battle for Normandy), the pretty villages, the colourful apple orchards.

You may come to Normandy to study the D-Day Landings and fall in love with the country and its people.

BEFORE YOU COME

All these attractions add up to a very popular holiday area—not only with British and American veterans, but also with French holiday makers, especially from Paris, which is a short, easy journey away. It is, therefore, very important to book hotels or camping sites in advance during the busy summer season, which lasts from June to early September. These are the steps to take before travelling:

1. *French Government Tourist Office*
Obtain a copy of their current *Guide for the Traveller in France* from the French Government Tourist Office (178 Piccadilly, London, W1V 0AL, ☎ (01)4917622, or 610 Fifth Avenue, New York, NY10020, ☎ (212)757-1125). It contains up-to-date practical advice on *everything* the visitor to France needs to know. A few vital points are summarised here:

2. *Passports/Visas*
A valid passport (or visitor's passport, available at Main Post Offices for UK citizens) is needed. Non-EEC residents require a visa, obtainable from French embassies.

3. *Driving Documents/Regulations*
A valid driving licence, car registration book and insurance are needed. Caravan owners will need the caravan log book and Green Card endorsement. Red warning triangles are compulsory in case of breakdown and seat belts must be worn. A country of origin plate is necessary.
Tolls. Remember to budget for tolls (*Péage*) if you are approaching the Landing Beaches area by the *Autoroute de Normandie* from Caen. Having the right change ready will speed the process.

4. *Medical Cover/Insurance*
Travellers should take out comprehensive travel insurance to cover all medical and loss contingencies.
Reciprocal medical treatment is available to EEC citizens who must have Form E111 with them to qualify for treatment or refund.

5. *Currency*
Banks will change travellers' cheques or Eurocheques, as will most hotels although they are slightly more expensive (passport needed). Credit cards (especially VISA — *Carte Bleue*) are widely accepted.

6. *Maps*
The Michelin Map 54 (1:200,000) which covers the whole area is

recommended . IGN (Institut Géographique National) produce more detailed maps (1:100,000 and 1:50,000) of the Landing Beaches.

HOW TO GET THERE
The Normandy Landing Beaches are now *very* accessible.

From Paris
The A13 *Autoroute de Normandie* toll road goes all the way and takes just over 2 hours. Fast trains leave frequently from the Gare St Lazare.

Ferries
Brittany Ferries   Portsmouth-Ouistreham.
                   ☎ Portsmouth (0705) 827701
P & O   Portsmouth-le Havre/Cherbourg
                   ☎Portsmouth (0705) 827677
Sealink   Portsmouth-le Havre/Cherbourg
                   ☎ Portsmouth (0705) 75511

Services are not so frequent from September to May.
Some night crossings with cabins or reclining seats are available.

Flights
Direct flights from London, Gatwick to Paris, Caen (Carpiquet), Cherbourg and Deauville. Some operate only in the summer.
Air France ☎ (01) 499 9511 or British Airways ☎ (01) 897 4000.

Motorail/Train
London Victoria to Dieppe, Dieppe to Caen.
British Rail ☎ (01) 834 2345. SNCF Motorail ☎ (01) 409 3518.

IN FRANCE
1. *Opening Hours*
Banks: 0900-1200, 1400-1630/1700 weekdays (some close Mondays).
Post Offices: 0800-1900 weekdays. 0800-1200 Saturdays. Stamps are also available at *Tabacs* (tobacconists).
Shops: 0800-1200/1230. 1400-1700/1800
Larger shops may close on Sunday and even Monday. Small food shops normally open Sunday morning.
Restaurants: often have a weekly closing day (eg Sunday evening or an arbitrary day early in the week).
Churches: Normally not visitable by tourists during services.
Museums: Many shut on Tuesday. Smaller museums have restricted opening hours from October to Easter. Generally open weekends.
Public Holidays: New Year's Day, Easter Monday, May Day (1 May), VE

Day (8 May), Ascension Day, Whit Monday, Bastille Day (14 July), Assumption (15 August), All Saints Day (1 November), Armistice Day (11 November), Christmas Day.

2. *Telephoning*
To phone the UK, dial 19, wait for change of dialling tone, dial 44, dial the area code omitting the first '0', followed by the number. You may have to dial a preliminary digit to get an outside line if phoning from a hotel. To phone France from the UK, dial 010 33 followed by the number.

3. *Electricity*
Mostly 220-30 volts. Two pin, circular plugs. An international plug adapter is recommended.

4. *Metric Measurements*
1 kilo = 2.2lb. 1 litre = $1^3/_4$ pints. 1 gallon = 4.5 litres. 1 kilometre = 0.6 miles.

Tourist Offices

Known as *Office de Tourisme* or *Syndicats d'Initiative*, they are to be found in all towns of any size. Follow 'i' for information signs. Useful tourist offices for Landing Beaches tours are:

Calvados Departmental Office. Place du Canada, 14000 Caen.
☎ 31 81 9477.
Caen. Place Saint Pierre, 14300 Caen. ☎ 31 86 2765.
Bayeux. 1 Rue des Cuisiniers, 14400 Bayeux. ☎ 31 92 1626.
Cherbourg. 2 Quai Alexandre III. ☎ 33 53 1110.
These tourist offices will make hotel reservations, give information on local restaurants, events (eg festivals, sporting events, concerts, shows), places of interest (eg museums, markets, Calvados distilleries), guided tours and 'Routes'; *du Fromage* (cheese); *du Cidre* (cider); *des Moulins* (mills); *des Trois Rivières* (three rivers — l'Aure, la Drôme and la Tortonne), etc, all with well signed itineraries.
Note that tourist offices usually close during the French lunch hour.

Accommodation

Lists are obtainable from the national or local tourist offices (see above). Book well in advance for busy holiday periods and in September when the Caen International Fair (*Foire de Caen*) takes place — check the precise dates with the tourist office.

Hotels. The area is rich in hotels, which are graded as follows:
*plain and basic, often known as *Auberge* or *Pension*;

**can be quite comfortable, especially if in modern chain like Ibis, Urbis, Campanile, Fimotel, which have private bathrooms, but small rooms;

*** good quality hotel, with private bathrooms, often with lift, bar, swimming pool, restaurants (eg Novotel and Mercure groups);

**** top class, very comfortable;

****L luxury class, with superbly equipped bedrooms, gracious public rooms, many facilities.

Logis de France. A grouping of small, normally family run hotels, with good regional and 'home' cooking. Head Office (which will supply their current brochure) 25 rue Jean Mermoz, 75008 Paris, France (or from French Government Tourist Offices).

Gites de France. Self-catering cottages, apartments, farms, often in rural areas. All have running water, inside loo, shower. (List available from Tourist Offices.)

Chambres D'Hôte. Bed and breakfast often in farms or cottages, sometimes in small *châteaux*. (List available from tourist offices)

Camping Sites. The area (especially along the coast and on inland farms) abounds with camping sites, from sophisticated (with showers and many other facilities) to basic. On some, caravans can be hired. Lists from national or local tourist offices.

Changing Information

Tourism is a transient industry! The reader must be aware that all tourist information is subject to frequent change.

Hotels and restaurants change management and sometimes standards, or simply close down.

Museums change their opening times, admission prices, exhibits, or they, too, in the case of private organisations, simply close down. Sometimes they do not open according to their advertised opening times. Therefore the visitor must take any tourist information as a guide and appreciate that it is as correct as possible it at the time of going to press. Phone numbers are given where available so that visitors can phone ahead to confirm details.

Veterans/Entrance Fees

D-Day or Normandy battles veterans should not be required to pay entrance fees in official museums. They may, however, be asked to sign the museum's *Livre d'Or* (VIP Visitors' Book).

2

BACKGROUND TO THE INVASION

A BRIEF HISTORICAL SUMMARY

BLITZKRIEG — WAR BEGINS — THE FIRST TWO YEARS

At dawn on Friday 1 September 1939 Operation WEISS (White) began. Almost fifty German divisions, including six Panzer divisions, supported by over fifteen hundred aircraft invaded Poland. It was the start of World War II. In Britain general mobilisation was proclaimed. The French went a stage further and instituted martial law.

The German *Blitzkrieg* (lightning war) was overwhelmingly successful. The basic tactic was a close co-operation between tanks and aircraft with a rapid movement deep into enemy territory to sever the defending army from its supplies and communications. The original concept of *Blitzkrieg* has been attributed to both General Hans von Seeckt of the Reichswehr in the 1920s and to Captain Basil Liddell Hart in the 1930s, but its formidable exponents in September 1939 were two German Army Groups: North, commanded by Colonel General Fedor von Bock, and South, commanded by Colonel General Gerd von Rundstedt.

The progress of one formation in particular stood out as a prime example of *Blitzkrieg* at its most formidable — the advance of the XIX Panzer Corps commanded by General Heinz Guderian.

It was all over by 5 October when the last Polish troops surrendered near Warsaw. The Russians too had marched into Poland on 17 September and in accord with their non-aggresion pact the Germans and Russians divided Poland between them. Then the Germans and the Russians stopped.

The Phony War

President Roosevelt sent emissaries from America to investigate the possibility of a negotiated settlement. The BEF went to France and the European nations eyed each other across the Franco-Belgian borders and prepared for war. Eight months later, after the period known as the 'Phony War', or the *Sitz-krieg*, the Germans struck again.

Dunkirk

On Friday 10 May 1940 in Operation GELB (Yellow) seventy-seven German divisions, including ten Panzer divisions and two airborne divisions, invaded Belgium, Holland and Luxembourg. Three Panzer Corps, one of which was Guderian's XIX, struck east through the Ardennes forests outflanking the French in the Maginot Line.

That same day the BEF, strung along the Belgian border, advanced into Belgium under the Dyle plan, and in England the 'Pilgrim of Peace', Neville Chamberlain, resigned and Winston Churchill became Prime Minister.

The German *Blitzkrieg* worked again. Confused by the speed of the German advance, and with no proper liaison between British and French commanders, the Allied response was ineffective. The BEF withdrew to the Channel and at Dunkirk between 26 May and 4 June a quarter of a million British soldiers were evacuated — among them the the 3rd Division's commander, Major General Bernard Law Montgomery.

Two weeks later General Erwin Rommel's 7th (Ghost) Panzer Division entered the port of Cherbourg in Normandy as British troops were being evacuated under the covering fire of the French battleship *Courbet*. His division had covered over 140 miles the previous day. At the end of the same week, the French signed an armistice in Marshal Foch's old railway carriage at Compiègne. Adolf Hitler went on a sightseeing tour of Paris. All of Europe was his — except for Britain.

Alone

One of the planks of Adolf Hitler's rise to power was his insistence that all he wanted to do was to redress the wrongs inflicted upon Germany by the Treaty of Versailles after World War I. In addition, he claimed, he did not want to go to war with Britain.

At the end of June 1940 various overtures for a negotiated peace were made by Berlin to London. Lord Halifax, the British Foreign Secretary, was 'strictly forbidden to entertain any such suggestion' by Prime Minister Churchill. Hitler had overlooked the fact that Britain's new leader was a descendant of Marlborough and not inclined to give in.

Even before the fall of France, the Prime Minister had told the nation, 'We shall defend our island whatever the cost may be'. The Germans, distrustful of their new ally Russia, planned to attack her, but first, since they would not negotiate, the British had to be dealt with. Southern England had to be invaded.

The Battle of Britain

The German plan for the invasion of Britain, Operation SEALION, could not be implemented until the Royal Air Force had been destroyed.

Hitler's directive for the invasion began, 'The Landing operation must be a surprise crossing on a broad front extending approximately from Ramsgate to a point west of the Isle of Wight ...', and as an essential preparation to the invasion the directive continued, 'The English Air Force must be eliminated....'

The task fell to the Luftwaffe under Reichsmarschall Hermann Goering and he had little doubt that it could be achieved. The Germans had over three thousand combat aircraft available while the British had less than half that number. Allowing for the fact that the British had to spread their aircraft in anticipation of attacks anywhere in the South of England and the Germans could concentrate theirs, the odds against the RAF were much greater than 2:1.

The Luftwaffe offensive against the Royal Air Force began on 'Eagle Day', 13 August 1940 and by 5 September the RAF, its bases badly damaged and losing pilots and planes faster than they could be replaced, was on the point of collapse. Then, in retaliation for air raids on Berlin, Hitler changed his plans and ordered an all-out offensive on London. The pressure on the RAF eased. Planes and airfields were repaired. Knowing too that the Germans' target was London, the RAF could now concentrate against their enemy and even-up the odds. Radar (Radio Aid to Detection and Ranging) and ULTRA helped too. German air losses increased. Daylight bombing was replaced by less costly night attacks and then when it became clear that Britain could not be defeated quickly, Operation SEALION was cancelled. It was 17 September 1940.

The Battle of Britain had been won, the Invasion had been stopped. Now came the Blitz.

The Blitz

The bombing of London and other industrial cities and ports in Britain was a night-time terror which lasted from September 1940 until May 1941. During this period 39,600 civilians were killed and 46,100 injured.

On Sunday 22 June 1941, Germany launched her invasion of Russia — operation BARBAROSSA. The Luftwaffe, needing every available aircraft — including bombers — on the Eastern Front for what was expected to be only a 6-month's campaign, turned its attention away from Britain. The Blitz was over.

Before the end of the year Winston Churchill spoke in secret to his Combined Operations Staff about another cross-channel invasion. This one however, would be going in the opposite direction to SEALION and would eventually be called OVERLORD.

COUNTDOWN TO OVERLORD
1941

March   The Lend-Lease Act was passed in America, and President Roosevelt immediately declared that the defence of Great Britain was vital to the defence of the United States. Thus, every form of support for Britain short of American intervention began.

June   Hitler invaded Russia in Operation BARBAROSSA.

October   Winston Churchill told Lord Louis Mountbatten and his Combined Operations Staff to prepare plans for 'our great counter-invasion of Europe'

December   On 7 December Japanese aircraft attacked the American naval base at Pearl Harbor in Hawaii and Japan declared war on Britain. The following day the United States declared war on Japan. Britain and America were allies now in every way. At Christmas, Prime Minister Winston Churchill and President Roosevelt met in Washington to plan allied strategy. The Americans agreed to concentrate on Europe and 1943 was chosen as the invasion year. Under the code-name BOLERO American forces were to be assembled in Britain in preparation for the assault. During 1941 Hitler ordered the construction of a fortified wall to protect the coastline of occupied Europe from invasion. Known as the Atlantic Wall, it was to stretch from Norway to Spain and incorporate 15,000 strong-points.

1942

June   Eisenhower was sent to Britain to command the build up of US Forces. He established his HQ in 20 Grosvenor Gardens and had flats in Claridges and the Dorchester Hotel. Because of appalling Russian casualties, Soviet dictator Josef Stalin insisted that Churchill and Roosevelt open a second front in order to relieve the pressure on the USSR. The British resisted an early cross-channel invasion, the Americans supported it. Two plans were considered, called ROUNDUP and SLEDGEHAMMER. The British view prevailed and a European invasion was replaced by an attack on Dieppe and a landing in North Africa.

August   A mainly Canadian force attempted a frontal assault on the Nazi-occupied and defended harbour of Dieppe. It was a disaster. But two major lessons were learned — **1**, that armoured vehicles capable of defeating pill-boxes had to land with the assault troops and **2**, that a frontal assault on a fortified harbour must not be repeated. These lessons led to the development of floating tanks and floating harbours.

October Montgomery won the 2nd Battle of El Alamein and began the advance which drove Rommel out of North Africa.

November The Allied landing in North Africa, Operation TORCH, was commanded by General Eisenhower. The landings were successful. It was almost a rehearsal for what would happen in June 1944.

1943

January The Russians completed the destruction of the German armies at Stalingrad. Coupled with El Alamein the victory marked the Nazis' high-water mark. Hereafter their fortunes declined.

At Casablanca, Churchill and Roosevelt appointed Lt Gen F.E. Morgan as Chief of Staff to the Supreme Allied Commander (COSSAC) with the task of preparing plans for the invasion of Europe that would:

1. Lead the Germans to believe that the main landing would be in the area of Calais. The general code-name adopted for these deception plans was BODYGUARD.

2. Allow a full-scale assault to be made across the Channel early in 1944.

COSSAC HQ was established in Norfolk House in St James' Square, London.

June Lord Louis Mountbatten held a conference with COSSAC, code-named RATTLE, at which Normandy was chosen as the area for the main landings, and it was decided that floating harbours, code-named MULBERRY, would be towed across the Channel for use off the beaches.

August At the QUADRANT conference in Quebec, Churchill and Roosevelt agreed upon a date for the cross-channel invasion. It was 1 May 1944 and its code-name was OVERLORD.

December On Tuesday 7 December President Roosevelt told General Eisenhower that he would be the Supreme Commander for OVERLORD.

On Sunday 12 December Hitler appointed Rommel to command his Atlantic Wall defences.

On Friday 24 December the Allied team that was to command the invasion was announced:

Supreme Commander	General Eisenhower
Deputy Supreme Commander	Air Chief Marshal Tedder
Naval C-in-C	Admiral Sir Bertram Ramsay
Ground Force Commander	General Montgomery

1944

1 January General Montgomery relinquished command of his be-loved 8th Army in Italy and flew to England to set up his invasion HQ at his old school, St Paul's in Hammersmith.

15 January General Eisenhower arrived back in London and took up quarters in Hayes Lodge just off Berkeley Square.

21 January Generals Eisenhower and Montgomery agreed changes to General Morgan's COSSAC invasion plans that set the target date as 31 May, extended the landing area west across the Cotentin Peninsula towards Cherbourg and increased the initial seaborne force from three divisions to five divisions.

5 March Supreme Headquarters Allied Expeditionary Force (SHAEF) moved from Grosvenor Gardens to an old US 8th Air Force HQ at Bushey Park near Hampton Court. Its code-name was WIDEWING. General Eisenhower lived nearby in Telegraph Cottage, Kingston-upon-Thames.

6 April All leave cancelled for troops destined for OVERLORD.

22-9 April Operation TIGER, a D-Day rehearsal for troops assaulting UTAH beach, took place at Slapton Sands between Ply-mouth and Dartmouth. Nine German E-boats stumbled upon the force at sea during the night, sinking two landing craft full of men. Some 700 men were killed, three times more than would die on UTAH on D-Day. Fortunately, however, the Germans did not connect the action with an invasion of Normandy.

1 May General Eisenhower and Admiral Sir Bertram Ramsay, aware that the energetic Rommel was thickening Hitler's Atlantic Wall and covering the beaches with below-the-water obstacles, decided that the landing would be in daylight, and at low tide, so that the obstacles would be visible. Admiral Ramsay was responsible for NEPTUNE, the sea transportation and landing phase of OVERLORD.

2-6 May Operation FABIUS, the final rehearsal for OVERLORD, took place at Slapton Sands.

8 May	SHAEF selected 5 June as D-Day — invasion day. The only other totally suitable alternatives that month were the 6th or 7th.
15 May	HM The King, General Eisenhower, Field Marshal Smuts and others attended a conference at General Montgomery's St Paul's HQ to review the final plans for OVERLORD.
18 May	German radio said 'the invasion will come any day now'.
23 May	The camps containing the soldiers who were to land on 'D-Day' were sealed with barbed wire. Many had armed guards. Senior Commanders were told that D-Day was 5 June, and detailed briefings began.
28 May	The time that the leading troops were to land, 'H-hour', was settled as, 'a few minutes before 0600 hours and after 0700 hours'. The Americans were to land first on beaches named UTAH and OMAHA. Then minutes afterwards, to allow for the difference in the time of low tide, the British and Canadians were to land on GOLD, JUNO and SWORD. Generals Eisenhower and Montgomery moved elements of their HQs to HMS *Dryad* at Southwick House near Portsmouth, in order to be near the embarkation ports.
1 June	The first regular morning and evening meetings were begun between senior commanders at Southwick House, principally to discuss the deteriorating weather conditions in the Channel. General Eisenhower began a daily shuttle between his Forward HQ at Southwick, Bushey Park, his Main HQ, and Stanmore, where SHAEF Air HQ was located. The weather forecast was not good.
4 June	At 0415 General Eisenhower decided that the weather was too bad for the landing to take place and postponed the invasion for twenty four hours. All the convoys at sea had to reverse their courses. But two British midget submarines, X20 and X23, continued on their way, and just before midnight took up their positions off the beaches to act as markers for the invasion army when it arrived.
5 June	At 0415 General Eisenhower sought the opinions of his fellow Commanders. Should he postpone again? The weather was still bad, though a brief lull was hoped for during the next 48 hours. Any more delay and the sea-sick army might not be fit to fight. What was worse, the Germans might find out what was going on. 'OK', said Eisenhower, 'we'll go'.

THE INVASION PLANS

THE ASSAULT PLAN

The plan for the allied assault on the beaches of Normandy was code named OVERLORD. The Supreme Commander was General Eisenhower and he appointed General Montgomery to command all British and American land forces.

On 3 January 1944 General Montgomery heard a presentation of the first invasion plan drawn up by COSSAC (Chief of Staff to the Supreme Allied Commander Designate) under General Morgan in July 1943. He criticized the narrow three division front of the assault and insisted that it be extended at each end — to the west across the Carentan estuary to include beaches eventually to be named UTAH and to the east across the River Orne to include the heights above the German gun battery at Merville, the D-Day target of the 6th Airborne Division. The sea landing forces were to increase to five divisions.

The COSSAC plan also included an air lift for two thirds of an airborne division with a direct assault on Caen. General Montgomery changed this to three airborne divisions — two American ones at the western end of the beaches and one British at the eastern end. He dismissed the idea of a direct assault on Caen.

These and other changes were approved by the Supreme Commander on 21 January 1944 and they formed the basis of the final assault plan shown on page 30. There was, however, a second plan.

THE DECEPTION PLAN

The deception plan, named FORTITUDE, set out to deceive the Germans as to when and where the invasion would take place.

It was clearly impossible to hide all the preparations for invasion that were going on in England and so, by using camouflage and dummy equipment, the impression was given that things were less advanced than they were, thus suggesting a later invasion date than planned.

Further, by flying twice as many air missions in the Pas de Calais area as in Normandy, by the movement of American and Canadian troops (including General George Patton, whom the Germans considered to be the Allies' best Field General) into the Dover-Folkestone area, the picture presented to the enemy was of an impending invasion across the narrowest part of the Channel.

Immediately prior to, and during the assault, tactical deceptions were employed — dummy parachutists called Ruperts (one can be seen in the Ste Mère Eglise Museum) were dropped over a wide area to confuse the

Germans as to the strength and exact location of the attack. Silver foil called WINDOW was scattered to confuse German radar and naval and air sorties to parts of the coastline other than Normandy were made.

The deception plan did not finish with D-Day. A critical period for an assault landing comes just after the assault troops are ashore when the whole apparatus of supply has to be rewound in order to maintain and reinforce the forces already in position. If the Germans could strike quickly with their armour before the Allies got their second wind, the invasion might fail. Therefore the FORTITUDE plan included misinformation designed to convince the Germans that the Normandy landings were a large scale diversion and that the main invasion was yet to come — in the Calais area — and hence they would be unwise to commit all their forces, particularly their armour, to a counter-attack in Normandy.

All three elements of the deception worked. The invasion was not expected in Normandy, but across the Pas de Calais so most of the enemy armour, defensive strength and reserves were concentrated in the north; it was not thought likely to take place in early June (the bad weather helped here) though German intelligence had forecast it for 1944, and even after 6 June enemy armoured reserves were held back in anticipation of a second and larger assault across the Straits of Dover.

THE GERMANS

THE ATLANTIC WALL

The successful French defence of Verdun against the single-minded assault of the German army during World War I, swung the French military towards defense and, in the early 1930s, led to the building of the Maginot Line fortifications along the French borders facing Germany.

In response Hitler instituted the West Wall (known as the Siegfried Line to the Allies) in 1938, opposite the Maginot Line in the Saar. Made in depths of up to 3 miles, it consisted of mutually supporting fire positions, pill boxes and dragon's-teeth anti-tank obstacles and was carried out by the Todt Organisation, which had built the autobahns.

During the preparations for Operation SEALION, conducted under Führer Directive Number 16, the German Navy was instructed to improve and construct casemated heavy gun batteries capable of firing on England and of controlling the Channel approaches in the Pas de Calais area. At the time that Operation SEALION was called off, following the failure of the Luftwaffe to master the RAF, over seventy offensive emplacements were in position.

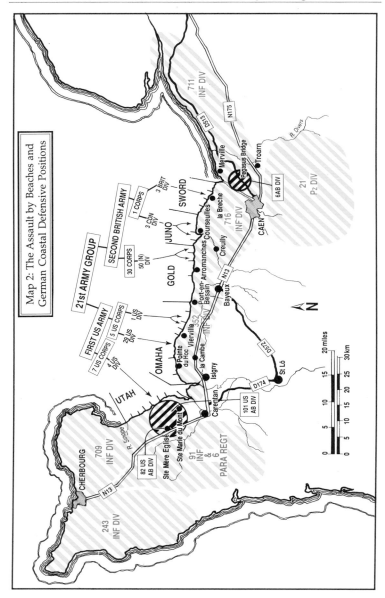

Map 2: The Assault by Beaches and German Coastal Defensive Positions

In December 1941 the Japanese attacked the US Fleet at Pearl Harbor, and America came into the war. Hitler, realising the impact that American involvement would have immediately decided to turn Europe into *Festung Europa*— Fortress Europe. The German Fifteenth Army of seventeen divisions was given the permanent task of defending Fortress Europe from the Cotentin Peninsula to the Channel.

In March 1942, following Field Marshal Von Runstedt's appointment to command Army Group West, the offensive emplacements in the Calais area were incorporated into a new defensive structure that Hitler decreed should run along the western edge of Fortress Europe, should incorporate 15,000 strong points and be built by the Todt Organisation. It was to be a new West Wall, this time to be named 'The Atlantic Wall'.

THE COMMANDERS AND THE PANZERS

Although von Runstedt, Commander in Chief West, was in command of the German Army in Normandy he did not exercise total control over it. Hitler, the German High Command (OKW), Field Marshal Rommel and General Guderian, Inspector General of Panzers, all believed that the key to the defeat of an allied invasion lay with the German armoured divisions— but they did not agree *how* the divisions were to be used and this aggravated the normally complex commander/subordinate relationship into a strained and inefficient chain of command.

Rommel had taken over Army Group B in February 1944 with responsibility for the defence of an area stretching from Holland to the Atlantic coast of France. He divided his force into two — Seventh Army West of the River Orne and Fifteenth Army East (See map 2, page 30.) In his opinion the only place to stop the invasion was on the beaches and he demanded that control of the nine armoured divisions in Panzer Group West be given to him so that an immediate counter stroke could be launched against a landing. To carry out his plan he needed to hold the armour close behind the likely landing areas and with such a long coastline to defend it would use up almost all of the German armour.

Guderian did not like the idea of committing armoured formations to the defence of a particular landing area. In his opinion, it could lead to disaster, because if they guessed wrongly about where the invasion would come it would be difficult to correct their mistake. Von Runstedt held a quite different opinion. He believed that a landing could not be prevented and that the bulk of the armour should be held well back until the true direction of any landing was clear, when a massive and decisive counterstroke could be made.

Hitler, although he favoured Rommel's belief that the first 48 hours after a landing would be the most critical, compromised, and did not give control of the Panzers to his favourite general. Instead, three of the nine Panzer divisions were placed under Rommel's direct command while the remainder, although technically under Von Rundstedt, could not be released without the Führer's authority.

The chain of command was made even more complex because the C-in-C West had no operational authority over the Luftwaffe or the Navy, and formations in Army Group B could, and did, receive orders from three different headquarters — Rommel's, von Runstedt's and Hitler's.

Ironically, in Führer Directive No 40 of 23 March 1942, which was entitled 'Command Organisation on the Coasts', Hitler had said '...the preparation and execution of defensive operations must unequivocally and unreservedly be concentrated in the hands of *one man*.' It was fortunate for the Allies that Hitler did not follow his own orders.

In all, Rommel's command had thirty-nine Infantry Divisions and three Panzer divisions at the time of the landings. 21st Panzer was just south of Caen, moved there from Rennes in April to support the 7th Army. The other two Panzer divisions, one west of Paris, the other near Amiens, were to support the 15th Army in the Pas de Calais. In May 1944 Rommel had asked OKW to move the four reserve Panzer divisions nearer to the coast. Von Runstedt protested. The request was denied.

When the Allies landed Rommel had only one Panzer division available in the area, the 21st, and that was at the extreme eastern end of the invasion area behind Caen and the British beaches.

THE INFANTRY

German divisions were classified into four categories, mainly according to their degree of mobility. These categories were: 'capable of full attack', 'limited attack', 'full defence' or 'limited defence'. But mobility, could mean a unit equipped with anything from bicycles via horses to motor transport and the mobility of Army Group West was very limited.

As an example, 243rd Division was converted to a nominal attack division from being a static division in late 1943 by issuing four of its six battalions with bicycles, but the indigenous artillery regiment and anti-tank battalion never received their planned motor transport.

709th Division alongside and to the east of 243rd Division (see map 2 page 30), and whose area included the small village of Ste Mère Eglise on the N13 Cherbourg to Carentan road, was also to be upgraded from a defence to an attack category. That had not been done by June.

More than half of Army Group West was made up from 'ear-nose-and-throat' soldiers, those who were unfit for anything other than static service, perhaps too old, perhaps recovering from wounds. Some formations were units broken on the eastern front and reformed with a mixture of unreliable conscripts — Poles, Russians and Italians.

Yet, by contrast, there were good and experienced soldiers peppered amongst the pack and one of the most highly trained formations was brought in by Rommel. That was the 6th Parachute Regiment. The average age of its soldiers was $17\frac{1}{2}$ years and each one had done at least nine jumps, several in darkness.

Rommel's energetic thickening of the Atlantic Wall defences was not confined to under-water obstacles, mines and concrete. He thickened the defenders too. Reserve infantry were brought forward, sacrificing defence in depth for manpower on the beaches, where he felt it was most needed. Every man in forward units had his own defensive position to go to. In February 1944 he brought the 352nd Division, a 'full attack' formation, from St Lô and placed it in the area from Arromanches to Carentan. It sat behind the beach the Allies called OMAHA.

Between Rommel's arrival in Normandy in 1943 and 6 June 1944, the German infantry defences, despite all the handicaps imposed by Allied bombing, poor mobility, unfit and unwilling soldiers and differences between commanders, had improved beyond measure. An invasion could not be certain to succeed.

ROMMEL

At the end of 1943 Rommel was given command of Army Group B under the C-in-C West, Von Runstedt, though he had the right of direct access to Adolf Hitler. His task was to check and progress the Atlantic Wall defences and he rapidly set out on a tour of inspection, beginning in Denmark and then going on to the Scheldt and to the Somme, working south west across Normandy towards Brest.

To his dismay he discovered that the concrete emplacements that were to form the backbone of the Wall were far from complete and he immediately ordered that other defensive works be instituted on the beaches. These included large wooden stakes with explosive mines or shells attached to them, concrete and metal structures designed to stop landing craft, Czech hedgehogs (large three-dimensional six-pointed stars made by welding or bolting three pieces of angle-iron together), concrete tetrahedrons for anti-tank defence and a variety of other underwater mined obstacles whose purpose was to delay an invading force long enough for it to come under direct fire from the defenders.

Between December 1943 and May 1944, Rommel toured furiously. At first he looked at his whole frontage and then, in February and March

1944, repeated the process, paying particular attention to the area of the Pas de Calais. In April and May he travelled extensively in Normandy, exhorting his men to utmost effort. Fields that might be used for glider landings were dotted with upright stakes placed sufficiently close together to act as anti-airlanding obstacles.

Rommel's efforts in Normandy just before the Allied invasion may have been coincidence, or related to Hitler's spring inspiration that the Allies would land on the Brittany and Cotentin Peninsulas. On 6 May Hitler insisted that the defences on the Normandy coast and in the area of Cherbourg should be strengthened. Rommel told the 7th Army, and the 91st Division was diverted from Nantes to Normandy with, under command, 6th Para Regiment and other units. Their role was plainly stated — defence against airborne landings.

Thus, barely a month before two US airborne divisions were due to drop on the Cotentin, behind the beach code-named UTAH, it was re-inforced by troops whose main role was anti-airlanding.

On 9 May Rommel noted in his daily report, 'Drive to the Cotentin Peninsula which seems to have become the focal point of the invasion'. He drove to Houlgate on the coast to the east of Merville, then to Caen for a briefing by senior officers, including the commander of 21st Panzer Division. After lunch he toured the area covered by 716th Infantry Division whose beaches the Allies called GOLD, JUNO and SWORD. Next he visited the concrete casemated naval battery at Longues and then via Grandcamp and Isigny went on to St Lô for dinner.

On 20 May at his HQ at La Roche Guyon, 30 miles west of Paris, Rommel interviewed two British Commando officers who had been captured in the 15th Army area during a raid exploring beach obstacles. They should have been turned over to the SS but Major General Speidel, Rommel's Chief of Staff, brought them to Rommel who sent them on to a prisoner-of-war camp, which probably saved their lives. What the Field Marshal did not find out was that their names were Lieutenant Roy Woodbridge and Lieutenant George Lane and that their unit was No 10 (Inter Allied) Commando. Just over 2 weeks later No 10 Commando landed on SWORD Beach near Ouistréham. Forty years later George Lane re-visited La Roche Guyon and stood on the same spot where the Field Marshal had interviewed him.

On 3 June Rommel went to see Von Runstedt to talk over his proposed visit to Germany during 5-8 June, when he intended to ask Hitler for two more armoured divisions to be transferred to Normandy.

At 0600 hours on 4 June, in rain and wind, Rommel left for Germany. He was going home for his wife's birthday.

3
PORTSMOUTH

As a prelude to a visit to the Normandy Beaches, an overnight stay in this eventful city is thoroughly recommended. Its 800 years of history are excellently recorded and presented in the city's numerous museums, preserved sites and famous ships.

The D-Day Window in Portsmouth Cathedral

The Romans, the Normans, Henry VIII, Lord Nelson, Palmerston, Dickens — all made their mark. In 1944, Portsmouth was the area from which Force 'S' and Force 'J' set sail, and in the area beyond Havant, west to Christchurch and including Winchester, was the pre-Invasion assembly area of XXX BR Corps.

The troops were confined in sealed camps and security was, in theory, very tight. Throughout the area vast dumps of supplies, vehicles and ammunitions mushroomed. Local airfields were humming with activity. More than 11,000 aircraft — Typhoons, Mosquitos and Thunderbolts — were massing to provide air cover and undertake bombing raids. Bomber Command was to drop 5,000 tons on coastal batteries in Normandy in 7,500 sorties. Parts of the mysterious caissons which were to make up the revolutionary Mulberry harbours were being assembled. It was all a secret difficult to keep from observant locals.

In 1941 Churchill's advice to Mountbatten was 'The South Coast of England is a bastion of defence against Hitler's invasion; you must turn it into a springboard to launch an attack.' On 5 June 1944 that order became reality. Portsmouth is proud of its vital role in that springboard and today preserves the memory in its many well maintained museums.

TOURIST INFORMATION

INFORMATION CENTRES

The Hard, Portsmouth.
☎ (0705) 826722
Southsea Seafront
☎ (0705) 754358
Continental Ferry Port
☎ (0705) 698111
They can book hotels, provide information and literature on entertainment, events, sports, museums, harbour trips, tours and guides to historic Portsmouth, Southsea and Gosport.

DEFENCE OF THE REALM

This project promotes historical buildings, sites and events around Hampshire and the Isle of Wight.
Heritage Project, Ferry Gardens, South Street, Gosport, PO12 1EP.
☎ (0705) 504332

MUSEUMS & MEMORIALS

Museums Information Line
☎ (0705) 296906 for information on all Portsmouth's museums

D-Day Museum

Clarence Esplanade
This is a *must* before crossing the Channel to Normandy. Housed in a modern, custom built exhibition area, its centre piece is the impressive Overlord Embroidery. It is comparable to the Bayeux Tapestry in its concept. It was commissioned by Lord Dulverton, designed by Sandra Lawrence and made by the Royal School of Needlework in 1968, taking 5 years to complete the 83m (272ft) long embroidery. It depicts the preparations for Operation OVERLORD, the 6 June Invasion and the Battle for Normandy.

There is an audio-visual theatre showing the D-Day Landings, and exhibits using modern techniques.
Open: daily 1030-1730 (except 24-26 December). Access for the disabled.

Southsea Castle (shares car park with D-Day Museum)
Open: daily 1030-1730 (except 24-26 December).

Royal Marines Museum

Eastney
Open: daily 1000-1630 (except 22 December-10 January).

Naval Heritage Area

The old Royal Dockyard area.

The Royal Naval Museum
Open: daily 1030-1700 (except Christmas week).

HMS *Victory*
Open: Monday-Saturday 1030-1630, Sunday 1300-1630.

Mary Rose
Open: daily 1030-1700 (except 25 December).

HMS *Warrior*
Open: March-October daily 1030-

D-Day Museum, Portsmouth

1730, November-February 1300-1700 (except 25 December).

Portchester Castle
Open: daily, Sunday pm only (except 24-26 December, 1 January).

Spitbank Fort
Visit by ferry from Gosport Pontoon or Clarence Pier.
Open: Easter-October 1100-1700

Old Portsmouth Fortifications
Contact the Tourist Information Centre for details of guided walks.

Royal Navy Submarine Museum
Gosport
Open: April-October 1000-1630, November-March 1000-1530.

Portsmouth Cathedral
D-Day memorial window, unveiled by the Queen Mother on 6 June 1984.
Burma Star Window.
Cathedral Book Shop, open daily 1000-1600 between services.

Southwick House: D-Day Wall Map
Now the Officers' Mess of HMS *Dryad*. The D-Day Map Room may be visited BY STRICT APPOINTMENT ONLY. ☎ (0705) 210522 Ext 4221, Monday-Friday 0900-1200, 1400-1700. The Map Room can also be seen during these times.
In 1941 Southwick House was requisi-tioned as a war-time residence and the School of Navigation moved there. The Action Information Training Centre was built in 1943 and the first control room completed in 1944.

On 26 April Admiral Sir Bertram Ramsay, Naval Commander for Operation OVERLORD, established his headquarters in Southwick House and by 1 June Montgomery parked his famous caravan in the grounds.

It was from the house at 0415 hours, 5 June, that General Eisenhower said, 'Let's go' — the signal to commence the mighty invasion. In the run up to D-Day the Supreme Commander had been making daily shuttles between here and his main headquarters at Bushey Park via his Air Headquarters at Stanmore.

The great D-Day Wall Map, on which the progress of the Invasion was to be charted, was made of plywood by the Midlands toy company, Chad Valley, in May. The two men who installed the map were held there without access to the outside world until the invasion was under way! It can still be seen, with the D-Day weather maps, in the Map Room of Southwick House, together with a painting by war artist Norman Wilkinson of the assault forces going into GOLD Beach and other action scenes.

4

CHERBOURG

Cherbourg is not included in any of the battlefield tours as it did not figure in the D-Day Landings on 6 June. However, it was a vital factor in the invasion planning and is therefore described here separately. Cherbourg is at the tip of the Cotentin Peninsula. It can be visited by continuing on the N13 from Ste Mère Eglise, passing through:

Montebourg, which was bitterly fought over from 6 June until the Germans were finally forced out on 19 June. On the night of 6 June, General Dollmann, commanding the German 7th Army, moved the 243rd Division to Montebourg to counter the American advance. For the civilians of the little town, all hell already seemed to have broken loose. See the civilian eye witness account opposite.

Rommel became increasingly aware of the threat to Cherbourg and feared that the Cotentin Peninsula was about to be cut off. On 7 June he rushed more troops to the area, including the 77th Division which was eventually sent to Montebourg. From 8 June to 1 July, General von Schlieben set up a defensive line from le Ham to the west of the N13, through Montebourg to Quineville on the coast to the east. On 10 June the 505th Parachute Infantry attacked le Ham, with the objective of taking Montebourg station. The attack bogged down after a successful start, and Montebourg was still in enemy hands by 12 June. The Germans were prepared to fight hard for what they felt was the vital key town to the defence of Cherbourg. They repelled attacks over the following days until finally, on 18 June, General Collins developed his plan for the final drive to Cherbourg with General Bradley, knowing that Schlieben was withdrawing to Cherbourg. The attacking American divisions encountered little resistance. When the 3rd Battalion of the 22nd Infantry entered Montebourg at 1800 hours on 19 June they found it deserted, but 90 per cent destroyed.

In the town a *Circuit du Débarquement* sign leads towards the Battérie de Crisbeq on the D42.

A D-DAY MEMORY

From a 12-year-old French girl living in Montebourg.

"My father was the local doctor…. But at Easter time he was taken ill and was sent to a sanatorium in the Alps. On 5 June my mother had a phone call to say he was dying. We were a large family (twelve in all, ten living still at home) and she called us together to brief us as to how we were to look after each other in her absence. Each older child was given direct responsibility for a younger, and should we have to evacuate, for looking after the practical necessities for the little one.

I was responsible for my 7-month-old brother, who had an ear infection. So I had to keep a bottle of hydrogen peroxide, as many nappies (a rare commodity at the time) as I could find and most precious of all, a tiny *burnous* [a hooded woollen cape] which we kept in a pillow case.

At five o'clock in the morning on 6 June, the doctor who was my father's replacement was called out to tend wounded soldiers — Allied soldiers — the Invasion had started.

At first we stayed on in our home, but it was terrifying. Phosphorus bombs were falling and there were fires everywhere. The Germans had recently commandeered all the town pumps and the townspeople tried to put out the fires with buckets of water. It was hopeless. Eventually a vehicle full of ammunition was hit by a bomb and exploded near our house. There was artillery fire too. We were very frightened — especially as we were without our parents. We bundled as much as we could into the baby's pram, including cans of milk — there was a large compartment under the mattress — and took refuge in a nearby abbey, then in use as a boys' school. Then the battle came to the very courtyard and there was fierce fighting. We managed to get out to a nearby farm, but it was already full of refugees. We had lost all our possessions — except the little *burnous*, still in its pillowcase.

People were very kind and generous to each other in those dangerous days. The Brothers gave us linen to use as nappies and when we were in the cowshed, a family whose farm was burnt out passed us. One of the girls was doing the washing when the house was hit. She still had the soap in her hand. It was all she had. She gave it to us for the baby.

The first Allied soldier I saw was an American. This surprised me. I had always expected to be liberated by the English. It was by the German battery in the wood on the farm and he had been taken prisoner. The Germans seemed sorry for our plight and offered us sweets. We all refused. It was our little form of 'Resistance'. The American soldier appreciated this and gave us the 'V' sign."

A D-DAY MEMORY

Lt J.J. Whitmeyer. 9th US Infantry Division. Participated in the capture of Cherbourg.

"I was at that time a lieutenant in the Infantry. We had a schedule about a week or so to go from UTAH Beach to Cherbourg. I think it was due to fall ... in about a week and actually Cherbourg was emptied on the 26th of June and I think the history records may even show that it was captured on the 27th. There was a sergeant in the 314th Infantry, who at that time was a private, who was the first man accredited for mounting the steps of the City Hall in Cherbourg, and this was like 8pm on the 26th June. As I recall his name was Finlay. We had in my own organisation only three Medal of Honour winners and two of those people were awarded the Medal of Honour, the nation's highest award as you are aware, for combat in an operation to take Fort du Roule.

Fort du Roule commanded completely Cherbourg and the success of ever utilising Cherbourg as a harbour. It took a little bit more time to do than the Regimental Commander desired. It took a day and a half, because of an underground bunker as big as a small city — railroad tracks, a number of terraced 88 guns as well as weaponry that the German used, and it required a sergeant — Hurst was his last name — from E company of my battalion to lower charges by way of a rope into the apertures to silence the gun that was firing onto the main railroad terminal area. My own particular part in that operation:-

I was on, I believe, the Avenue de Paris — it is or was the main street that leads on down to the railroad terminal and to the docks for the steam ships. This was a major harbour of course, and the Germans on the 23rd of June, as I understand it, were expecting the fort to be captured and knowing the importance to the United States or the Allied armies and navies, decided to make it impossible or to render it useless. They took all of the heavy equipment they could — box cars, locomotives, cranes — whatever heavy equipment they could find — strung it across the entrance into the main terminal, and then dynamited or exploded it in some manner. They also — the ships that were in the

Valognes. This was Schlieben's headquarters (though on 6 June he was attending the War Games at Rennes) until the retreat to Cherbourg on 20 June. On that day, the 315th Infantry cleared stragglers in the area as they advanced towards Cherbourg.

harbour — they scuttled them. I can vividly recall crawling across this tangle of steel, and on the outer edge there was a dog tank trap which, as you know, is just a large ditch, in order to get to the beaches. Truthfully, the last pill box as far as I was concerned and when I say the last, it's not the last to fall, but the furthest point on the Cherbourg Peninsula that a pill box was placed, fell to 3rd Platoon of G Company which I commanded. I was unfortunate enough to have one of the privates who was in my unit go on top side in order to lower as a remembrance the Swastika flag that the Germans had flown. It was just a short period of time. I did not have with me what we refer to as a 'walkie talkie' — they weren't any good. They weren't as good as those you can buy for $4 or $6 now in a toy store. If you got anyone on it would be some tank outfit and we really didn't have communications. I can recall sitting down to clean my rifle when some fire was directed on the pill box. I thought it was a counter attack. The gentleman who had gone top side — this soldier — he came stumbling down the steps. He was shot four times by the 4th Division who was attacking the pill box while we were in it. That is just one of the, you know, mistakes or lack of communication. We did not know and nor did they, who they were and they didn't know who we were. A sergeant by the name of Lepley, about the best soldier I've ever known. He fought in three wars. He climbed through the aperture in which a gun was placed facing the sea and tried to make his way back through that tangle of metal to say, 'Hey quit shooting. You know you're shooting at American troops.' But he didn't come back and so another fellow and myself we did the same thing and that time the fire lifted and we were able to get out this American soldier who had been wounded. And as I understand it with regard to Cherbourg, it took about two weeks for the British engineers, the American engineers — whoever were responsible — not necessarily to clear the scuttled ships but to clear the port and that shortly thereafter in landing the American troops without putting them on landing craft, and were able to dock at one time something like twenty-five vessels and numerous landing craft, and it was a tremendous job on the part of those people who had to make the clearance."

Cherbourg

That a major port should be included in the landing beaches area was always a vital factor. The beaches of Normandy were particularly suitable as they included *two* — Cherbourg and le Havre. Both were considered vital to the success of OVERLORD, as Cherbourg alone was not considered capable of supporting the twenty-nine combat divisions

V1 launching ramp, Mesnil au Val

to be put in the lodgement area. It was thought that Cherbourg should be taken by the eighth day by the Americans who had landed by sea at OMAHA and UTAH and those who were due to drop behind UTAH. The US 1st Army's main task was 'to capture Cherbourg as quickly as possible'.

When the strength of German reinforcement of the Cotentin was appreciated, the date for taking the port was revised to D+15.

That Cherbourg and le Havre were spared from heavy allied air attacks in the spring of 1944 was a clue to the Germans that the invasion might take place on the beaches between them. Hitler ordered strong defences in this area and this was enthusiastically implemented by Rommel. Troops were ordered into the Cotentin in May, but few defensive positions in the area were completed, especially the *Zweite Stellung* (second positions) due to be constructed as a further defensive line a few kilometres in from the coast, which Rommel ordered to be abandoned in May.

We have seen above how the Americans advanced as far as Valognes on 19 June. In fact Hitler had flown from Berchtesgaden to meet with Von Runstedt and Rommel on 17 June at Soissons. Sensing defeat, a furious Hitler pronounced that 'Cherbourg be held at all cost'. At first he expressly forbade Schlieben's 77th Division to withdraw to defensive positions around Cherbourg. Rommel feared they would be

German gun outside Fort du Roule Museum

senselessly sacrificed and disagreed with Hitler's edict. Eventually, however, Schlieben was forced to retreat to the 'Landfront Cherbourg' after the American advance through Valognes. The German Forces were successfully split and the 77th Division's attempt to escape south of the US 9th Division was cut off.

Between 25,000 and 40,000 Germans, including Todt Organisation and naval personnel, were locked in the peninsula as Schlieben fought a ragged retreat. General Eddy of US VII Corps was to breach the fortress of Cherbourg and block the enemy's escape route to the Cap de la Hague defences (to the west of Cherbourg). During 20 June, the Germans hastily reformed their 'Landfront' into four regimental '*Kampfgruppen*'. All were understrength and weary, their combat efficiency low.

On 21 June the US 8th and 12th Infantry Regiments fought their way into the main Cherbourg defences. One of their first missions was to flush out a suspected V1 weapon launching site near Bois de Rondou (to the right of the N13 on the D56 at le Mesnil au Val). Remnants of the installation can still be seen today.

On the evening of 21 June US VII Corps was ready for the final assault. Cherbourg's capture had become even more vital because of a heavy four-day storm in the Channel which blew up on 19 June and which seriously disrupted troop and supply landings on the captured beaches. The artificial harbour at OMAHA was completely destroyed

Remnants of the Atlantic Wall defensive bunkers and the eastern arm of the harbour wall, Cherbourg. The Fishermen's Memorial is in the background

and Admiral Hall, the naval commander at OMAHA, decided not to attempt to rebuild it. General Collins ordered a renewed attack on Cherbourg, which should be 'the major effort of the American army', with 'air pulverization'. The air attack with four squadrons of RAF Typhoons, followed by six squadrons of Mustangs plus twelve groups of US 9th Air Force fighter bombers, went in at 1240 on 22 June, their object to demoralise the enemy. The previous night General Collins issued a broadcast demanding the immediate surrender of Cherbourg. Schlieben ignored the 0900 hours 22 June ultimatum. The assault went in.

The US 9th Division with the 60th Infantry and the 47th Infantry attacked on the right. The 79th Division attacked along the axis of the N13 up to the Fort du Roule. The 4th Division was to seal off the city from the east.

General Schlieben's command post was in a vast underground command bunker in the rue Saint Sauveur. On 22 June he received a message from Hitler, 'It is your duty to defend the last bunker and leave to the enemy not a harbour but a field of ruins'. 'Reinforcement is absolutely necessary,' replied the unimpressed General to Rommel.

The fighting nevertheless continued through 23 June, when the outer ring of fortresses was penetrated. On 24 June US VII Corps entered the city itself. Losses were heavy. Lt Colonels Conrad Simmons (Commander 1st Bn 8th Infantry) and John W. Merrill (Commander 1st Bn 22nd Infantry) were killed, together with many of their men. On 25 June, General Bradley brought down a naval bombardment on the Cherbourg batteries from three battleships, four cruisers and screening destroyers.

Schlieben radioed, 'Loss of the City is unavoidable.... 2,000 wounded without a possibility of being moved.... Directive urgently requested.' Rommel replied, 'You will continue to fight until the last cartridge in accordance with the order from the Führer.'

That day Fort du Roule was attacked and there were many acts of bravery by the 314th Infantry Regiment. For instance Cpl John D. Kelly, who after three attempts took an enemy pill box, and Lt Carlos C. Ogden, who destroyed an 88mm enemy gun, were both awarded the Medal of Honour. The fort was finally reduced on 26 June. That day too, General Schlieben's underground bunker was discovered in Saint Sauveur. A German prisoner was sent in to ask for surrender. Schlieben declined, but a few rounds from a tank destroyer into the tunnel entrance brought out not only General Schlieben, but Admiral Hennecke, Naval Commander Normandy, and some 800 Germans. The next day, Schlieben's deputy, General Sattler, formally surrendered the fortress of Cherbourg to Colonel Smythe, Commander of the 47th Infantry Regiment.

PLUTO
PLUTO (the Pipeline Under The Ocean, see page 127) was laid from the Isle of Wight to Cherbourg (in four pipe lines), pumping stations were set up and vital petrol came literally pouring into Normandy.

TOURIST INFORMATION

This busy port, for naval and leisure craft, cross-channel ferries (P&O and Sealink) and transatlantic ships (the QE2, for instance calls in here after leaving Southampton), makes a good base at either end of a tour, with ferries direct to and from Portsmouth.

TOURIST OFFICE
2 Quai Alexandre, near the Avant Port.
☎ 33 53 30 11.
They will supply a list of events (there are often sailing, windsurfing and other nautical competitions in the summer) and make hotel bookings.

MUSEUM & MEMORIALS
Fort du Roule Museum 'De la Guerre et de la Libération'
Set in the marvellous panoramic viewpoint of Fort du Roule (see above) the well-intentioned museum has undergone several serious burglaries which have depleted its exhibits. Now it is regaining some stature and is well worth a visit — for its original maps, posters and photographs, its record of the Free French forces and its well documented story of the battle for Cherbourg.
Open: 1 October-1 April 0930-1200, 1400-1730. Closed Tuesday. 2 April-20 September 0900-1200, 1400-1800. Every day.
Entrance fee payable. Under 18, senior citizens and groups, half price.
A *Circuit du Débarquement* sign points to the Fort Du Roule Museum to the right on entering Cherbourg on the N13.

Memorial Plaque Hotel de Ville
On the town hall, Place de la République, Cherbourg, there is a memorial plaque to Sgt William F. Finlay 39th Regiment, US 9th Division, who was the first US soldier to enter the town hall on 26 June 1944 and who died in

Cherbourg Town Hall

Plaque to Sgt Finlay, on the wall of Cherbourg Town Hall

action in Germany on 1 April 1945, aged 20. Also in the square is a memorial to civilians who were deported or shot by the Germans, surrounded by a rose called 'Resurrection'.

Remnants of Atlantic Wall Defensive Bunkers

In the harbour area, and near the Hotel Mercure, there are many examples still to be seen of massive German bunkers. For details of the Atlantic Wall remains in and around Cherbourg, see *Cherbourg Sous l'Occupation* by André Picquenot, published by Ouest, France.

HOTELS

The *** Mercure, right next to the ferry terminus and Gare Maritime, is highly recommended.

☎ 33 44 01.

There is a variety of ** hotels, a list of which is available from the Tourist Office above.

RESTAURANTS

There are many restaurants and *crêperies* in the area behind the tourist office around the Avant Port. Specialities are fresh seafood and salt lamb from the Mont St Michel area.

SHOPPING

There is a handy hypermarket to the left of the main N13 approach road, just before the Avant Port. It has a very good-value cafeteria and restaurant if you are in a hurry.

5

UTAH BEACH AND THE AMERICAN AIRBORNE OPERATIONS

The American air and sea landings north of Carentan on the Cotentin Peninsula are so interdependent that the memorials, drop zones and beaches can be seen on one comprehensive battlefield tour. Therefore, the background information for the 4th Division landing on UTAH and the 82nd and 101st Divisions' airborne landings precedes the tour.

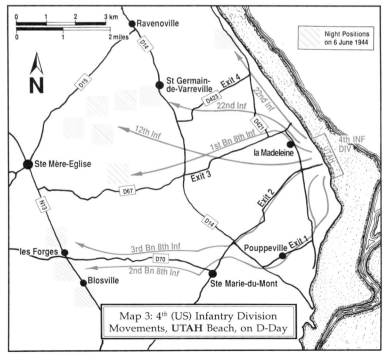

Map 3: 4th (US) Infantry Division Movements, **UTAH** Beach, on D-Day

UTAH BEACH

Assault time:	0630 hours
Leading Formations:	8th Regimental Combat Team of the US 4th Infantry Division
US 4th Division Commander:	Major General Raymond O. Barton
Bombarding Force A:	Battleship: USS *Nevada*
	Monitor: HMS *Erebus*
	Cruisers: USS *Tuscaloosa* (flagship)
	USS *Quincy*
	HMS *Hawkins*
	HMS *Enterprise*
	HMS *Black Prince*
	Gunboat: HNMS *Soemba* (Dutch)
	Eight destroyers
German Defenders:	709th Infantry Division and elements of 352nd Infantry Division
709th Division Commander:	Lieutenant General Karl W. Von Schlieben
352nd Division Commander:	Lieutenant General Dietrich Kraiss

The Plan

Before the landing, high altitude heavy bombers followed by lower altitude medium bombers were scheduled to soften up the Atlantic Wall. Then, as the troops headed for the beaches, Allied warships were to shoot them in, keeping the defenders' heads down so that the assault troops could establish a bridgehead ashore.

General Barton, commanding the 4th Division, planned to land in a column two battalions wide with a frontage of just over 2,000yd.

Leading the assault was the 8th Infantry regiment with attached to it the 3rd Battalion of the 22nd Infantry Regiment. The regiment's first task was to open the route inland by getting to the high ground in the area of Ste Marie du Mont/les Forges (the D70 road) and then to push on to make contact with the 82nd Airborne Division.

What Happened on D-Day

The weather was not good. Waves of five to six feet and winds of fifteen knots or more in mid-channel made life uncomfortable for the men on the ships. The skies were overcast and the heavy bombers, who were to bomb the Atlantic Wall, could not see their targets and had to bomb by instruments alone. This fact, coupled with the 8th Air Force decision that there should be a delay of several seconds in releasing the bombs to avoid dropping any on the assault craft, meant that most of the bombs fell too far inland. Sixty-seven of the 360 bombers of IX Bomber Command sent to UTAH failed to release their bombs at all because of poor visibility.

The medium bombers at a lower altitude fared better, but a third of their payload fell into the sea and many of their selected targets were not found. Thus the pre-landing aerial bombardment did little towards overcoming the coastal defences.

At about 0300 hours, some thirteen miles out to sea, the 4th Division began unloading from their transport ships into their LCVPs (Landing Craft, Vehicle & Personnel). It was a $3\frac{1}{2}$-hour journey to the beach and before that began many men, overloaded with heavy equipment, fell or jumped from the rigging on the sides of the transports into their assault craft, breaking their legs on impact. Others, as the boats rose and fell in the choppy sea, missed the LCVPs altogether and fell into the water.

As the craft, each with about thirty men on board, headed for the shore, many soldiers were violently sea-sick. Yet they had much to be grateful for. The sea crossing had been unopposed and as the craft neared the shore the expected hail of German fire did not materialise.

At 0550 hours, the heavy Allied naval bombardment began, concentrating upon locations where major German gun batteries were known to exist. Then closer in, the cruisers opened fire upon coastal defences such as pill boxes and machine gun posts. Finally, just before the LCVPs touched shore, the 'drenching fire' began. This was a torrent of high explosive fire by shallow draft vessels close in to shore, such as destroyers and LCVGs (Landing Craft, Gun). Then as the troops prepared to land, the fire lifted to the first vegetation line. It was the naval equivalent of the army's creeping barrage.

The LCVPs of the two assault battalions of the 8th Infantry Regiment hit the sand on time. It was 0630 hours. The ramps went down and out came the GIs, relieved to be ashore but with a hundred yards of open beach to cross before reaching the shelter of the dunes and a low concrete wall on their seaward side. There was no opposition as they crossed the sand, but Brigadier General Theodore Roosevelt, the assistant divisional commander who accompanied the first wave, quickly realised that the Division had landed in the wrong place — 2,000yd south of where they should have been.

An instant decision was needed: whether to try to correct the mistake by somehow signalling to the following waves out at sea or to accept the situation and continue the operation right there. Roosevelt chose the latter. Cane in hand he strode up and down, exhorting men to get up and off the beach and to move inland. It was a wise decision and one which won him the Medal of Honour. The intended landing place was far more heavily defended than the spot where they had actually landed and though German artillery and small arms fire did sporadically harass the

4th Division as they poured ashore, casualties were very light.

It is unwise to be dogmatic about casualty figures since they are frequently manipulated for propaganda purposes by both sides in a conflict. However, by the end of the day, best estimates suggest that some 23,250 troops had come ashore and only 210 were killed, wounded or missing.

THE AMERICAN AIRBORNE OPERATIONS

Drop Time:		0130 hours
Divisional Commanders	82nd:	Major General Mathew B. Ridgway
	101st:	Major General Maxwell Taylor
Defenders:		91st Division
		709th Division
		6th Parachute Regiment
91st Division Commander:		Lieutenant General Wilhem Falley
709th Division Commander:		Lieutenant General Karl W. Von Schlieben
6th Parachute Regiment Commander:		Major Friedrich-August Von der Heydte

The Plan

The American airborne assault on D-Day was in its own right the largest ever to have been attempted. The two divisions, the 82nd 'All American' and the 101st 'Screaming Eagles', comprised six parachute infantry regiments (PIR), a total of over 13,000 men, including attached arms and services. The parachute assault alone needed 822 transport planes.

The broad plan was that the parachute divisions would secure exits from UTAH Beach, gain control of the crossings over the rivers Merderet and Douve, prevent German movement along the N13, and gain and secure landing grounds for reinforcement by glider at dawn and dusk. Ahead of the main bodies of the parachute troops pathfinders were to jump to mark the drop zones.

Not all the Allied senior commanders liked the airborne idea. Air Chief Marshal Trafford Leigh Mallory, Commander in Chief of the Allied Expeditionary Air Forces, had opposed the plan from the time that General Montgomery first altered the COSSAC drop on Caen to a three division assault behind the beaches. Leigh Mallory maintained that flak defences were so strong, and that the terrain was so unsuitable for parachutists or gliders, that losses in men and machines could be as high as 75 per cent or more. Montgomery, supported by General Omar Bradley, persisted with his plan.

Two weeks before D-Day it was learned that Rommel had moved a fresh division into the area where the 82nd Airborne were due to drop and the plan was modified to that described here, but Leigh Mallory continued to express doubts. Barely a week before D-Day he wrote to Eisenhower setting out his fears that troop carriers and tugs flying in a straight line at 1,000ft would be easy targets for flak guns, and that the flooded and swampy ground in and around the rivers was unsuitable for landing airborne forces. Eisenhower over-ruled him.

On 5 June the Supreme Commander said to his British driver, Kay Summersby, 'I hope to God I know what I'm doing', and that evening they drove to Newbury where the General visited three airfields. There he talked to General Maxwell Taylor and men of the 101st Airborne Division. They were to be among the first American troops to land in France.

What Happened on D-Day

The thick cloud and bad weather made it difficult to navigate and some of the pathfinders missed the drop zones and set up their homing beacons in the wrong places. Although the enemy flak was not as deadly as Leigh Mallory had forecast, there was enough of it to cause the relatively inexperienced troop carrier pilots to take avoiding action. They therefore weaved and flew higher and faster than they should have done so that when the paratroopers jumped, they were not only too high and moving too quickly, but they were probably also in the wrong place.

The 82nd Airborne Division, dropping west of Ste Mère Eglise and astride the River Merderet, was more fortunate than the 101st. The 505th PIR, the first 82nd regiment to jump, landed pretty well on its drop zone, Zone 'O', and within three hours had taken Ste Mère Eglise one mile to the east, thus controlling any movement by the Germans from the north down the N13. The division's other two regiments, the 507th and 508th, were scattered west of the River Merderet which resembled less of a river and more of a broad ribbon of swamp. Thus the division was divided by the water, and the bridges at Chef du Pont and at la Fière, by which the 82nd could communicate, became of particular importance.

The 101st Airborne Division was distributed over an area of almost 400 square miles. By dawn only 1,100 men of the division's 6,600 had reached their reporting points and only a further 1,400 assembled by the end of the day. The countryside added to their confusion. Small fields bordered with strong hedges were typical. They all looked the same. It was difficult to know which way to go. Yet by 0600, $4\frac{1}{2}$ hours after the main landing, the division had secured the western ends of the cause-ways leading from UTAH. Without those exits the 4th Division could not get off the beach. Thus, before the infantry had arrived, the 'Screaming Eagles' had virtually guaranteed the success of the UTAH landing.

BATTLEFIELD TOUR A

The tour leaves from Ste Mère Eglise and looks first at the area of the 82nd Division drop zones, then the 101st Division area, next UTAH beach, its museum and memorials, and then to the Crisbec battery via the Leclerc memorial. See map 4 page 54.

Total distance: 35km (22 miles). Total time: 5 hours.
Map: IGN 1311, 1:50,000 'Ste Mère Eglise'.

Ste Mère Eglise
This small town on the N13 as it heads north to Cherbourg has become famous because of an American called John Steele.

Steele was a paratrooper of the 505th PIR of the 82nd Airborne Division and shortly after 0130 hours on the morning of 6 June he, and some thirteen thousand other airborne soldiers, jumped out of over 880 transport planes flying over Normandy. Steele fell onto the church steeple in Ste Mère Eglise, slid down it and then with his parachute caught on a flying buttress hung there for all to see. His story was told in the film, *The Longest Day*. But there is more to the story of Ste Mère Eglise than the adventures of John Steele.

The Germans arrived in the town on 18 June 1940. There was no fighting and over the next four years, despite the occupation of their houses and the huge swastika flag that flew outside the town hall, the inhabitants learned to live with their invaders. As 1943 wore on the number of soldiers billeted in the area began to decrease and there was little other than high prices to remind citizens that there was a war on. Sometimes an occasional Allied aircraft would drop leaflets.

Early in 1944 German anti-aircraft gunners — Austrian and mostly old — moved in, parking their wood-burning trucks in the square but behaving well and without any apparent enthusiasm for fighting. Lt Zitt was put in charge of the town and through the mayor, Alexandre Renaud, requisitioned stores and labour to build field defences.

On 17 April the Germans turned their attention to putting up anti-airborne landing poles and ordered that all radios be handed in to the town hall. There were to be severe penalties for listening to the BBC. Lieutenant Zitt began to demand more co-operation from Monsieur Renaud, which the mayor stoutly resisted and then on 10 May all the Germans, except the anti-aircraft gunners, left. They had been moved to the Cherbourg Peninsula.

Everywhere, though, there was activity, and there were always soldiers passing through the town, including Georgians and Mongols of very Asiatic appearance. At the end of May the town was briefly fortified and then, once again, the town was quiet. Following Rommel's inspection of the Cotentin Peninsula all the weapons and fighting soldiers had been moved forward towards the beaches. Only the Austrians remained, quite at home and causing no trouble.

On the evening of 5 June yet another of the frequent Allied air-raids began, and a large house in La Haule park, opposite the church, caught on fire. The mayor and the villagers formed a long line from the village pump, passing buckets of water from hand to hand to throw upon the flames. As they struggled to pass the buckets quickly enough, paratroopers began to fall like human confetti amongst them. At least one paratrooper fell into the burning house.

The Germans shot at the Americans as they fell and ordered the French to go back into their houses. The Austrians, having no stomach for a fight, remained for about half an hour and then departed, leaving a few active soldiers here and there with only the machine gun on top of the church still firing. Just a few yards from the gun John Steele hung from the corner of the steeple pretending to be dead so that no one would shoot at him. After two hours he was cut down and taken prisoner, probably the last prisoner taken before active resistance in the town ceased at 0430 hours. The town had been liberated, the first town in France to be so. As the paratroopers gathered in the square and the sun began to rise, silence reigned.

The task of taking the town had been that of the 3rd Battalion of the 505th PIR commanded by Lieutenant Colonel Edward C. Krause. Following a good drop on and around their planned dropping zone, DZ'O', the colonel ordered his own men to enter Ste Mère Eglise by stealth, using knives and bayonets and, where necessary, grenades. The tactic worked. The Germans were taken by surprise. At 0930 hours the enemy counter-attacked from the south with two companies of infantry and some armour. Most of the 2nd Battalion under Lieutenant Colonel Benjamin H. Vandervoort, which had established a defence line north of the town, moved back to help. The Germans then launched a simultaneous attack from the north onto the remnants of the 2nd Battalion which numbered forty-two men. When the attack and counter-attack sequence finally ended, some eight hours later, only sixteen of the forty-two men had survived. Both colonels were awarded the DSC for their conduct during the capture of Ste Mère Eglise.

Soon after mid-day German artillery fire started to fall on the centre of the town and it continued sporadically all day and into the night. It

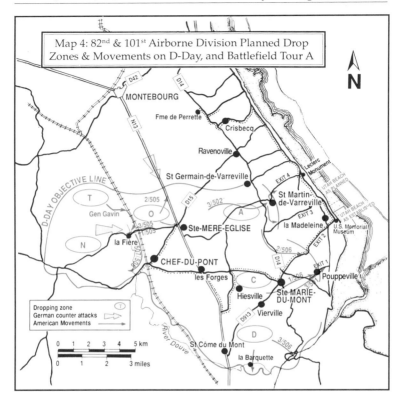

began to look as if Liberation would exact a heavy price in civilian casualties and damage to property — a higher price than Occupation.

Intense local fighting continued in the communes around Ste Mère Eglise, but on the afternoon of 7 June American tanks arrived from UTAH Beach. The beach-head was truly secure and the link-up between air and ground forces was complete.

US Airborne Museum, St Mère Eglise

Begun on 6 June 1961 when General James Gavin laid the foundation stone. The architect, François Carpentier, had designed the successful museum at Arromanches.

Since 1961 there have been many additions and improvements, including the introduction of a slide presentation of the events of 6 June 1944. Veterans are asked to sign the Book of Honour. The most

The C47 Argonia, *Ste Mère Eglise*

important single addition has been that of the C47 aircraft, *Argonia*, in its own hangar beside the museum. It is almost exactly where the burning house stood.

There is a lot to see in Ste Mère Eglise and directions may be obtained in the museum to the following sites and memorials:

Church

There are two fine stained glass windows commemorating the US paratroopers. Over the portal is the predominantly blue window, designed by Paul Renaud, son of the 1944 mayor, and made by the glassmaker Loire. It shows the Virgin Mary surrounded by paratroopers. On the 25th anniversary of the drop, in 1969, the veterans of the 82nd Airborne donated another stained glass window, which was dedicated on 4 June 1972. It shows St Michael, patron saint of the parachutists, and incorporates the Cross of Lorraine and various military insignia. Traces of machine-gun bullet marks can still be seen near the pulpit, and it was on the tower of this church that US paratrooper John Steele hung, playing dead throughout the night of 5/6 June. There is an hotel/restaurant named after Steele (who died in Kentucky in May 1969) around the corner from the Place du 6 Juin along rue du Cap-de-Laine.

Comité du Débarquement and Alexandre Renaud Memorials

These are in front of the church. Alexandre Renaud, mayor at the time

A D-DAY MEMORY

Technical Sergeant John J. Ginter Jr of the 92nd Troopcarrier Squadron. Flew paratroopers over Ste Mère Eglise in the *Argonia*.

"I was the Flight Engineer and part-time co-pilot of this aircraft, 4100825 Squadron Markings J8 Taylor E. I got this aircraft at Fort Wayne, Indiana. We left America on February 13, 1944. From there we flew to Morrison Fields in Florida. From Florida the next day we departed for Puerto Rico. From there the next day we flew to Trinidad. The next day we flew to Brazil. The next day we went to Natal, Brazil. The next day we went to Fernando Island. The next day to Dakaar, Africa, where, as I left America with a cold, the aircraft was grounded. And then weather conditions there permitted us to go over the Sahara Desert into Marrakesh, French Morocco. We were delayed for three days because of weather conditions over the Atlantic. Then we departed French Morocco and landed in Valley, Wales, England (*sic*). This flight time took 11 hours and 35 minutes. We had fuel tanks installed in this aircraft, added fuel tanks — 400 gallons. There were 804 gallons in the wing tanks, total of 1,204 gallons of gasoline.

We departed Valley, Wales and our final destination was an airfield, which is located in Newark-on-the-Trent in Nottinghamshire. Well we constantly trained in England, simulating paradrops, glider tows, and we moved our base to near Exeter.

We constantly trained there, then on 4 June in the afternoon we were alerted for the Normandy Invasion to breach Hitler's Europa — his fortress. I and my ground crew — two other people — had painted the stripes on this aircraft. Alternate white, black, white, black and the reason for that was to not shoot us down as our aircraft were shot down in Sicily. For in the Sicily invasion our own Navy had shot us down — I believe, though I'm not sure of that, and this was the reason for it. The fuselage was marked and each wing was marked, and the way I did it was I had put a piece of string around and marked with crayon and filled it in with a flat white and flat black paint. And that was the reason for the stripes.

of the Liberation, died in 1966. Monsieur Renaud was a distinguished author of books and novels about World War I (in which he was an officer), the Hundred Years' War and a futuristic account of World War III. He also wrote the most vivid and accurate contemporary account of the June 1944 drop: *Ste Mère Eglise: First American Bridgehead in France*.

Now we were taken back into interrogation (briefing). When we were ready to go we got orders from SHAPE (*sic*) High Command to postpone the Invasion for 24 hours because of the bad weather conditions across the Channel. We were then put into barracks and an MP — I mean Military Police — each set apart by 10 feet with a Thompson sub machine gun and had orders to shoot to kill if we attempted to flee from the area. And this was because of the fact it was extremely great secret information that we contained.

On the 5th we got the 'GO' and I came out at preflight of the aircraft, checking the para racks. The paratroopers were sitting, standing, constantly relieving themselves — nervous, very nervous, and as I'm under the aircraft checking the pararacks which I found later on contained mines I knew the reason. We boarded up and set up, took off — an extremely heavy load. We took every inch of the runway and we did get airborne and we formed up and we came out over the Channel. I'm up in the cockpit with the pilot and the co-pilot, checking the instruments, making sure that everything is OK and from there we found the pilot marker and made a turn going in towards the Islands — Guernsey and Jersey and, of course, the Cherbourg Cotentin Peninsula. As we were going in I see tracer bullets, but they looked just like Roman candles for sure and as we approached them they were more intensive. We seemed to have been out of range. But the second Island, as we turned, all hell started to break loose. You know .... [John Ginter felt unable to continue with this part of his recollections].

After the war we were getting new aircraft an improved version known as a C46 and I believe this aircraft (the *Argonia*) was sold by the United States Government to the French Government Naval defence. The last time I saw this aircraft was in Chateaudun."

After its chequered career, including taking part in Operation MARKET GARDEN and working as a civilian aircraft, the Douglas C47 returned to Normandy, lovingly restored, by Yves Tariel, President of the Parachutists' League of Friendship and his associates. It was unveiled in its custom-built museum in Ste Mère Eglise in June 1983.

Pump
It was from here that the line of villagers passed buckets of water to the burning house where the C47 now stands.

Plaque. Rue de la Cayenne
Erected on the house where four parachutists were killed on 6 June

25th Anniversary stained glass window, Ste Mère Eglise

The Church, Ste Mère Eglise with the dummy of paratrooper John Steele

1944. This is on the museum side of the church.

Town Hall

Outside the town hall is the pink marker stone of Kilometre Zero. The Kilometre Zero marker stones were erected by General de Gaulle's Government in 1946. They follow the path of General Leclerc's Free French 2nd Armoured Division and can be seen on roads 'from Chad to the Rhine'. One famous stretch leads to Bastogne, another traces an historic path through Reims, Verdun and Metz on the N44 towards Strasbourg. The 'Flame of Freedom' emblem, which decorates the markers, was also used on Free French postage stamps. Behind Kilometre Zero is the memorial to the twenty-two civilians of Ste Mère Eglise (including a World War I veteran) who died in the battle of June 1944, and to the left a plaque commemorating the liberation of the first town in

*The pump,
Ste Mère Eglise*

France. To the right and rear of the marker stone is a stone erected in tribute to Generals Gavin and Ridgway. Inside the town hall is the great Stars and Stripes, the first US flag to be raised in liberated France. It was also the first to fly over Naples in October 1943. In addition there is a painting by a German soldier portraying the parachute drop of 4/5 June.

US Cemetery Marker Number One

This can be found by following the signs to *Stade* (meaning Sports Field) along Rue du 505 Airborne. The commemorative stone is one of three marking the first three US cemeteries, all of which will be visited on this tour. There were some 3,000 soldiers buried here. In March 1948 they were either re-interred in the National Cemetery at St Laurent or sent home to America. The sports field was where a set was built for making the film *The Longest Day* and actor Red Buttons played the part of John Steele on a recreated steeple.

Drive out of Ste Mère Eglise to the west going under the by-pass on the D67 direction Chef du Pont. Just after the by-pass bridge there is a memorial marker on the left. *Stop.*

US Cemetery Marker Number Two

5,000 American soldiers were originally buried here, including Brigadier General Theodore Roosevelt, Junior, who led the 4th Infantry Division ashore at UTAH Beach. As with the other markers, the main formations represented in the cemetery are listed — 82nd Airborne Division, 101st Airborne Division, 4th Infantry Division, 9th Infantry Division, 79th Infantry Division, 1st Engineer Amphibious Brigade, 70th Tank Battalion, 746th Tank Battalion and the 90th Infantry Division.

Continue on the D67 through Chef du Pont to where that road crosses the River Merderet. Stop on the east bank.

508th Parachute Infantry Memorial

There is a memorial stone on the right and a memorial garden and plaque opposite on the left.

There were three drop zones for the 82nd Airborne Division all just west of Ste Mère Eglise. Zone 'O', immediately alongside and to the west of the N13 as it leaves Ste Mère Eglise towards Cherbourg, was the one where the first and most accurate drops occurred. The 505th Parachute Infantry Regiment and the 82nd's Divisional HQ came down in that area.

Zone 'N', the drop zone for 508th PIR is about 2 miles north-west across the river from here, but the sticks were scattered along a 6-mile elongated path in that direction, with extreme elements fifteen miles away due north.

Drop Zone 'T', two miles north of Zone 'N', was almost empty, though 507th PIR, who were due to land there, achieved probably the best grouping of the division, but one mile due east of where they should have been. Their extreme elements were the farthest flung of all, from fifteen miles north of here to twenty-three miles south.

As part of their defensive measures the Germans had flooded the Cotentin area. The river here looked more like a shallow lake than the small stream there now. Two of the division's three regiments, 507th and 508th, were across the other side of the water (that is away from you). Their task was to control the lateral routes into the Cotentin by establishing a defensive line three miles west of the bridges over the Merderet. This was one of the bridges and it was supposed to be taken and secured by 505th PIR, the third divisional regiment which had landed pretty well on target three miles north of here alongside Ste Mère Eglise.

Unfortunately for the 82nd Airborne Division, particularly for the men west of the Merderet, they had dropped into the area defended by the German 91st Division which had been especially trained in anti-airlanding operations. In addition many men had fallen into the swamp lands caused by the flooding and under the weight of their equipment

A D-DAY MEMORY

Trooper Howard ('Goody') Goodson. I Coy 3rd Bn 82nd Airborne Division. 505th Parachute Infantry Regiment. Dropped near Ste Mère Eglise.

"It was a very secret mission and at one time we were prepared to board the aircraft on 5 June and then they sent us back because of the weather and then on 6 June .... Sometime around midnight of 5 June, we boarded the aircraft and took off for Normandy.... It was a full moon night when we left England. You could see the fighter aircraft all around the plane until we finally hit the coast of Normandy and all of a sudden it was just black. I thought it was cloud but it was smoke from German ack ack fire and I believe our plane was hit two or three times, it was shaking all over and I was scared to death.

We were wearing the authorised American jump suit which consisted of a jacket and a pair of pants with many many large pockets ... and we had a main chute and a reserve chute and about everything else you can imagine we carried into battle. We even carried land mines in on our persons, grenades ... the only place we could find to put our gas mask was the bottom part of a leg and it was the first thing we got rid of when we hit the ground. We were so heavily loaded that the crew chief on the plane had to come around individually and pull each man up. He couldn't rise up by himself. We had twelve men on each side I believe and we had a cable going through the aircraft and we used static line. When the red light came on it meant stand up and hook up and then we would wait for the green light to go on and when that went on the first in line on the door side went out. Each person should check the man in front but on the Normandy jump I don't think anyone checked anything we were all so ... in a big hurry to get out of the plane.

After I hit the ground and got my chute off ... on this jump everyone decided that we would get a piece of our parachute and that's the first thing I did ... I entered a very quiet area, I could hear battle going on in other places but where I was it was very quiet, no-one around me, so I ripped off a piece of my camouflaged parachute, put my gun together — we carried a bren/rifle that went in three pieces and was zipped up in a cloth bag ... and eventually I heard movement and I used my little cricket and it turned out to be a friend from my company called Pat and he was also the first person I saw in Sicily after I jumped. A group of us got together and advanced into Ste Mère Eglise where there was fighting going on and we were eventually taken over by our battalion commander, Colonel Krause. He set us up in a defence of the town."

Ste Mère Eglise Town Hall with 'Kilometre 0' and behind it the memorials to civilian victims and to the Liberation

were drowned.

Opposition to the paratroopers was considerable, yet the dispersion that made it impossible for them to gather in enough strength to achieve their objectives also made it difficult for the Germans to work out what was going on and thus to concentrate in order to take effective offensive action. In addition, there was confusion within the German command because two of the divisional commanders were away playing war games at Rennes when the invasion began. What is more, Lieutenant General Wilhelm Falley, commanding the 91st Division, was killed by paratroopers as he made his way back to his headquarters.

The Americans headed for the obvious dry ground offered by the railway embankment (you crossed the line from Ste Mère Eglise and will cross it again on leaving here) and by mid morning some 500 men had gathered near the bridge at la Fière 1½ miles due north of here. Several attempts were made by elements of 505th and 507th PIR to take the la Fière bridge but these failed and when General Gavin, the Assistant Divisional Commander, arrived he took seventy-five men and set off down the road you drove along, heading for this bridge.

Unfortunately a number of enemy soldiers had dug themselves in along the causeway in front of you, and on the west bank, and Gavin's

US Cemetery Marker No 1, Ste Mère Eglise

force could not move them. Rumour had it that two enemy soldiers who had stood up intending to surrender had been shot, but it is not clear who shot them — their own side or Americans.

Meanwhile the Divisional Commander, General Ridgway, had arrived at la Fière and decided upon another attack on the bridge there. Most of the men here were withdrawn, leaving a platoon to hold the ground. By good fortune a glider containing an anti-tank gun came down nearby and Captain Creek, commanding the platoon, used the gun to hold off an enemy counter-attack but he could do no more than hold tenuously on to this eastern bank.

Over to the west, elements of the German 1057th Regiment were moving steadily towards the river and the bridges, here and at la Fière, with orders to destroy all paratroopers in the area.

To the right, in a north-easterly direction along the line of the river, there is some high ground about 1½ miles away known to the paratroopers as Hill 30. There Lieutenant Colonel Shanley commanding a group of about two companies of men of the 508th PIR took up position and broke up repeated German attacks in this direction, thus saving Captain Creek's small force and denying the Germans use of this bridge. That is why the 508th memorial is here.

Return to Chef du Pont and take the D70 east towards the N13. One hundred yards before the D70 passes under the N13 there is a memorial marker on the left beside the road. Stop.

US Cemetery Marker Number Three. les Forges

This is les Forges, the site of US Cemetery Number 3, the third of three large burial grounds established in Normandy by the Americans. It was opened in June 1944 and remained a cemetery until 1948. Then the men buried here were repatriated or re-interred in the National Cemetery at St Laurent above OMAHA Beach. There were 6,000 burials of soldiers from 9th Infantry Division, 79th Infantry Division, 1st Engineer Amphibious Brigade, 101st Airborne Division, 82nd Airborne Division, 746th Tank Battalion, 4th Infantry Division and 70th Tank Battalion. The memorial was erected on 21 January 1958.

By the evening of 6 June 1944 elements of the 8th Infantry from UTAH Beach had reached this point and established overnight positions here. The tour now effectively leaves the area of the 82nd Airborne Division assault and enters into that of the 101st Airborne Division.

Turn right on to the N13 direction Carentan and 1$\frac{1}{2}$ miles later turn left at a crossroads onto the small D129. Half a mile later stop at the junction with the D329.

Hiésville. General Pratt Memorial

Brigadier General Don F. Pratt was the first American general officer to be killed in the Liberation of France. The area to the right of the D129 down which you have driven was LZ'E' which had been secured by the 3rd Battalion of 501st PIR. The division, the 101st, was due to be reinforced here and on other LZs by two glider landings on D-Day, the first one at 0400 hours. There were fifty-three WACO gliders in all, carrying 148 men, and in the dawn light many aircraft crashed or ran into hedges. Five men were killed here, including General Pratt. He was the Assistant Divisional Commander of the 101st Airborne Division and ironically had originally been scheduled to cross to France by sea. It had pleased him greatly to hear that he would be going by glider. In the village of Hiésville is a memorial plaque to General Taylor and the headquarters of 101st Airborne Division.

Continue along the D129 to the crossroads with the D70 and turn right towards Ste Marie du Mont.

The fields to the right were DZ'C' for the 101st Airborne Division. Owing to the scattered drop there was a mixture of men from 502nd PIR, who should have been on DZ'A' three miles to the north and 501st and 506th PIR who were supposed to be on the DZ. The latter however, dropped in and around the village as well. The parachute landings in the

Detail of the General Don F. Pratt Memorial

General Don F. Pratt Memorial, Hiésville

D 129
4.7 TURQUEVILLE

D 329
HIESVILLE 1.2

fields that are passed on the right were probably the most concentrated of the whole American operation.

Stop outside the church in the village.

Ste Marie Du Mont

This small village is at the end of Exit 2 from UTAH Beach, which is about 3½ miles ahead. The church was probably the first thing that the Americans who dropped in this area recognised as the sky lightened. It enabled them to deduce where they were.

The drop had been in darkness, and very badly scattered and, as the men of the 'Screaming Eagles' landed amongst the hedgerows and small fields, or fell into the flood water, they suddenly felt alone. The noise of the aeroplanes and the crack of the flak explosions had gone. Now everything was unfamiliar and in the moonlight every shadow a threat. Each man had been given a small metal click-clack device which made a noise like a cricket and in a staccato avalanche of snapping noises men gradually came together.

The story of the two American airborne divisions on D-Day is one of countless acts of leadership at very junior levels. Private soldiers displayed initiative worthy of high commissioned rank and commanders showed dogged determination to get on with their appointed tasks no matter how few men they had or how far astray they had been dropped.

General Maxwell Taylor, commanding the 101st Division dropped just south of the village. As the divisional history puts it — the 'commander of 14,000 men found himself on a battlefield without a single one of those men within sight or hearing, any order he might have given would have been received only by a circle of curious Normandy cows.'

The General knew that it was vital to secure the causeways and to do so quickly before the sea armada arrived. As officers and men slowly gathered, he ordered Colonel Ewell, who commanded the 3rd Battalion of the 501st PIR, to take a group of about a hundred men to secure Exit 1, and on seeing that the party was very heavy on officers rather than soldiers, commented, 'Never were so few led by so many'. Moving from the area of DZ'C' and around the southern side of Ste Marie du Mont the Americans had a short-fire fight with some Germans in a dug-out, killing six. It was their first contact with the enemy. They moved on, accompanied by General Taylor, to the village of Pouppeville, 1½ miles north-east of here and at the end of Exit 1 from UTAH Beach. There the general left the securing of the causeway to Colonel Ewell who, with his men, engaged in a house-to-house struggle with grenadiers of the 1058th Regiment of 91st Division. After some hours the Germans surrendered with twenty-five dead and wounded out of a force of sixty-three.

The commune of Ste Marie du Mont has placed a dozen signs around the village which describe the actions in the area. A booklet about them can be bought in the Boutique du Holdy which also houses a small collection of historical items and souvenirs. In the church are modern commemorative stained glass windows, replacements for those destroyed during the fighting, and opposite in the Hotel Estaminet are some 1944 photographs of GIs in the village.

Continue through the village on the N13d signed to UTAH Beach. This is Exit 2.

Exit 2

Exit, or causeway, 2 is typical of the four exits that were the only routes by which the sea-borne invasion force would be able to get off the beach. The whole area had been flooded and nowadays it is not difficult to imagine how it must have looked and how vital it was to secure the causeways. The task of controlling Exit 2 was that of 506th PIR, but their

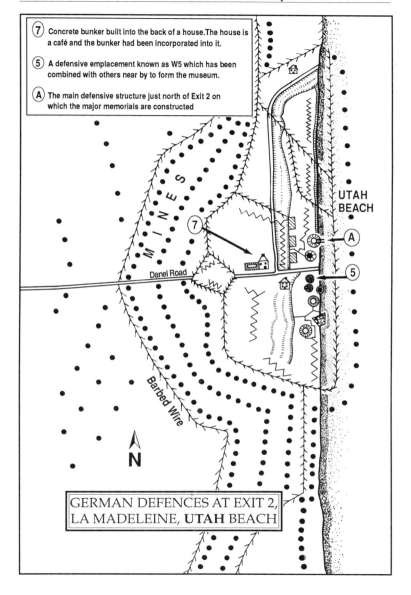

(7) Concrete bunker built into the back of a house. The house is a café and the bunker had been incorporated into it.

(5) A defensive emplacement known as W5 which has been combined with others near by to form the museum.

(A) The main defensive structure just north of Exit 2 on which the major memorials are constructed

UTAH BEACH

M I N E S

Danel Road

Barbed Wire

N

GERMAN DEFENCES AT EXIT 2, LA MADELEINE, **UTAH** BEACH

transport planes only managed to put ten loads out of eighty-four in the right place. However, Lieutenant Colonel Strayer who commanded the 2nd Battalion, and who had dropped four miles north of here, gathered elements of his battalion, plus some men of the 82nd Division who had dropped even further off target, and fought his way south. By 1330 he had Exit 2 under control.

Along the roadside are markers naming part of the road after non-commissioned American soldiers. There are forty-three of them marked by seventy-six signs. The first one here is Sonnier Road, then Jones Road, then Hinkel Road and finally down to the beach is Danel Road.

At the point where Jones Road becomes Hinkel Road, by a bridge over a small stream, is a memorial statue on the right. Stop.

UTAH Danish Memorial

This memorial, raised in 1984 and designed by Danish architect Svend Lindhardt, commemorates the 800 Danes who took part in the landings. *Continue down Exit 2 to the museum where Danel Road exits from the beach.*

UTAH Beach Museum

The museum, opened in 1962 and steadily improved since, offers a splendid account of all the events that took place here on 6 June 1944 and immediately thereafter. It is built into and around German Blockhouse W5 and on entering there is a sequence of events to be followed. A visit takes approximately one hour.

First the visitor is able to see a most detailed diorama of thousands of model soldiers and pieces of equipment which illustrates the way that UTAH Beach looked at different times on D-Day. Then there is a film show using actuality footage followed by an opportunity to examine artefacts and ephemera, many donated over the years by veterans. Finally in the observation room of W5, there is a map explanation of the fighting linked to working models of military equipment in small glass cases around the walls.

Veterans of the landings are asked to sign the Book of Honour and postcards and booklets are on sale.

It is helpful to walk down to the beach and to consider the basic story of what happened here before going into the museum.

The area had been visited by Rommel early in May in line with Hitler's premonition about Normandy being a likely invasion target. When Rommel was pleased with what he found he often gave a concertina or mouth-organ to one of the soldiers putting up obstacles, in the hope that the soldier would play and encourage his comrades to sing, thus building

The Danish Memorial,
UTAH Beach

morale. When he came here however, he was not pleased.

He inspected the beach and the obstacles, and then demanded that Lieutenant Arthur Jahnke, in charge of blockhouse W5, take off his gloves and show his palms. Jahnke did so and on seeing the weals and scratches on the young officer's hands, which had clearly come from helping to put up beach obstacles, Rommel relented and told him that the blood he had spilled in putting up obstacles was as important as any he would spill in combat.

Just a week before the invasion General Marcks, LXXIVth Corps Commander, held a small parade in front of W5 during which Jahnke was awarded the Iron Cross for service in Russia.

Early on the morning of 6 June Jahnke was in W5, woken by the noise of aeroplanes and puzzled by the sound of gun-fire coming from the direction of Ste Marie du Mont. He despatched a patrol to find out what was going on and to his surprise they returned in half an hour with seventeen American prisoners. The Americans told him nothing.

Then the air and naval bombardment began. Huge spouts of sand, pieces of concrete and clouds of dust filled the air. In little more than half

Sherman tank, landing craft, US anti-aircraft gun and 4th Division Obelisk at the Utah Beach Museum

an hour W5 was ineffective. Their weapons, 50mm, 75mm and 88mm guns, were all out of action. Those men who had not been killed were dazed and shocked by the noise and brutality of the explosions.

Jahnke was wounded. As the noise lessened and the disorientated defenders looked out to sea they saw the approaching armada and, in the leading waves, floating tanks. The lieutenant tried to activate his own tanks — small wire-controlled tractors carrying explosives, called GOLIATHS, but they would not start. The Americans, encouraged by a 57-year-old general called Roosevelt, charged up the beach, engineers blew a hole in the sea wall and then supported by their armour they rushed W5. Jahnke and his men surrendered. UTAH beach belonged to 4th Division. Roosevelt, who had once commanded the 1st Infantry Division, had been removed from active command and given a desk job. After much lobbying, he had got himself the appointment as second in command of 4th Infantry Division and, at 57, was the oldest officer to land with the assault troops. Sadly, he died of a heart attack on 12 July, in an orchard near Carentan. He never learned that he had redeemed himself and had been given command of 90th Division.

In 1987 Arthur Jahnke returned to W5 and shook hands with another veteran of that 6 June — an American of the 8th Infantry Regiment who had led the charge ashore.

Kilometre 00, UTAH Beach

Force U for UTAH had launched its thirty-two DD tanks only 2 miles from shore, instead of the planned 4 miles, because of the bad weather. It was a fortunate decision and twenty-eight tanks made it to the beaches providing direct fire support to the infantry and helping the assault engineers to deal with the obstacles. The costly lesson of Dieppe had been learned. By mid-day UTAH Beach was clear and the 4th Division was on its way inland across the causeways to link up with the airborne forces.

By the end of the day the 4th Division had achieved almost all of its objectives. Over the beach had come 23,000 men and 1,700 vehicles. The causeways were secure and the beachhead firm.

Around and about the museum the following memorials and objects may be found within walking distance:

Sherman Tank
Landing Craft
US Anti-aircraft Gun
4th Division Memorial Obelisk
Kilometre 00 — This marks the beginning of 4th Division's Liberty Highway which runs both into Holland and across France to the German border. Through Normandy, markers can be seen every kilometre showing the distance from '0' at Ste Mère Eglise.
Rowe Road Marker at exit from beach.

Rowe Road Marker,
UTAH Beach

Bunker System A (see diagram page 67) — This carries the 24ft-tall polished red Baveno granite memorial obelisk to the American forces of VII Corps, who landed here and liberated the Cotentin Peninsula between 6 June and 1 July 1944. It was erected in 1984 by an agreement between the governments of France and America which included it as part of the permanent arrangement for commemoration, which already covered Pointe du Hoc and the St Laurent Cemetery. It bears the words 'Erected by the United States of America in humble tribute to its sons who lost their lives in the liberation of these beaches. June 6, 1944'. There is also a marker to 90th Infantry Division, the first follow-up division. It commemorates their dead from 6 June 1944 to 9 May 1945, and proudly carries the division's nickname, 'The Tough Hombres', and the statistic that from UTAH Beach to Czechoslovakia the 90th Combat Team fought five campaigns in 300 days. On top of the steps is a memorial to the 1st Engineer Special Service Brigade and a light anti-aircraft gun. On the low wall to the seaward side of the Engineer Memorial are fifty-eight markers pointing the directions to ship locations, to where acts

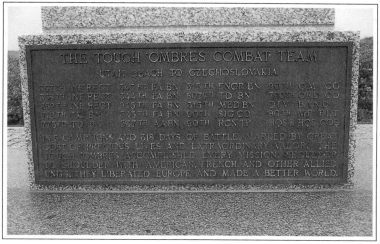

The 90th Infantry Division Memorial, the 'Tough Hombres', UTAH Beach

of heroism were performed (including Free French pilots), to ports and towns and even to Berlin. Below, and part of, the bunker is a memorial crypt with an illuminated display including a portrait of Major General Eugene Mead Caffey who was responsible for erecting the memorial in 1945. In and on the walls of the crypt are plaques from or about:

Souvenir Francais.

Major General Eugene Mead Caffey.

The Commander of the 1st US Engineer Special Brigade.

The use of the blockhouse by the US engineers.

The names of those Engineers who gave their lives.

The actions of the airborne and seaborne forces on D-Day.

Due west from here on the next and parallel road inland is the Chapelle de la Madeleine, a small chapel which has four beautiful stained glass windows. One immediately behind the altar records that in 1944 the Free French Forces took part in the Landings with the Allied troops.

Continue northwards along Route des Alliés, the beach road, following signs to the Leclerc Monument.

After just over a mile at a crossroads is Blair Road, Exit 3. The inland end of this causeway was due to be secured by the 502nd PIR. Their drop was so scattered that some came down on the wrong DZ, yet despite that, the CO of the 502nd, Colonel Cole, and a force from the 3rd

US VII Corps Memorial,
UTAHA Beach

Memorial Crypt, Major-
General Caffey Memorial,
UTAH Beach

Battalion, moved onto the village of St Martin de Varreville, 2 miles to
your left and cleared it by 0730 hours. An additional task for the 502nd
had been the elimination of a battery of Russian 122mm guns just west
of the village, but they found that the Germans had moved them. So
Colonel Cole dug in his men inland of the causeway and waited. At about

Comité du Débarqument Signal Monument to
General Leclerc and the Free French

0930 hours a number of Germans driven back from the beaches up Blair Road ran into the paratroopers who killed seventy-five of them.

The Leclerc Monument
UTAH Beach was the landing place for General Patton's 3rd Army and Frenchman General Leclerc's 2nd Armoured Division. This was where Leclerc's force came ashore and there is a Comité du Débarquement memorial to commemorate the fact. There may well also be an armoured car and a half track vehicle, but they seem surprisingly mobile and may not always be there. There are also formidable blockhouses and bunkers hidden in the sands and the defenders here held out for some hours. This was where the 4th Division had been scheduled to come ashore and things might have been quite different for them if they had.

A stroll past the Leclerc memorial through the dunes to the beach leads to the centre of what was once a typical infantry strongpoint of the Atlantic Wall.

A large blockhouse is visible 250yd away to the left, and other remains are obvious in the sand around. The position originally stretched for some 150yd both to left and right and also inland. Sea approaches were covered by 50mm and 4.7cm guns, plus a 3.7cm Renault turret mounting. Flank defence was provided by a 75mm and two 4.7cm anti-tank guns, while facing inland was a 50mm weapon. The whole position was surrounded by barbed wire and minefields, with remotely controlled flamethrowers. Individual posts were connected by trenches and the artillery weapons were supported by infantry firepower, such as 81mm mortars.

Out to sea at low tide, blockship debris can be seen.

Continue north following signs to Battérie de Crisbecq.

Just on leaving, a junction with Begel Road is passed. This is Exit 4. Like Exit 3, it had been allotted to the 502nd PIR. Two miles inland from here the village of St Germain de Varreville sits just above the inland end of the causeway. In the village on 6 June was a German artillery battery which put up a stubborn fight and delayed Colonel Strayer and the men of the 506th who were on their way to clear Exit 2. They by-passed the enemy position, though part of Colonel Strayer's force joined up with a group of tanks from the 70th Tank Battalion, which they brought up from the beach, and destroyed the guns. Lieutenant Colonel Cassidy, CO of the 1st Battalion of the 502nd, gathered as many of his own men as he could find plus a few of the 506th and established roadblocks to cover Exit 4 and Exit 3. By mid-morning he reported that Exit 4 was open.

Battérie de Crisbecq

There are formidable concrete remains here of control bunkers and gun emplacements. The central bunker has been converted into a small museum and information centre with signs in English, French and German, and it is possible to climb on top of it to get a good view towards UTAH Beach. Opening times are very erratic.

The works were begun in 1941 by the Todt Organisation and on 6 June the main armament in position was two 155mm guns. In addition there were three 21mm Skodas, six 75mm anti-aircraft weapons and three 20mm guns. An all-round defensive position was established with minefields, barbed wire and seventeen machine-gun posts. As part of the coastal defence organisation the battery came under the German Navy and the position was commanded by 1st Class Ensign Walter Ohmsen with a force of some 300 men. In the early morning of 6 June, following a raid in which some 600 tons of bombs were dropped around the battery without damaging it, some paratroopers of the 501st and 502nd PIRs, miles off course, landed nearby and twenty were taken prisoner. As daylight came the 155mm guns opened up on the invasion fleet off UTAH Beach, hitting a cruiser and sinking a destroyer as well as damaging others. In the return fire many guns were destroyed though the casemates remained intact, and despite continued counter battery

Battérie de Crisbecq

work from the sea, and local attacks by troops from UTAH Beach, the position held out until 12 June when men of the 39th Infantry Regiment entered the silent battery.

All the officers and NCOs had been killed or wounded. Ensign Ohmsen and seventy-eight men had withdrawn during the night. The damage that can now be seen is the work of US engineers who attempted to destroy the battery after its capture.

Take the D69 west to the junction with the D14 and turn north towards Fontenay-sur-Mer. Barely half a mile after the turning is a small farmhouse called 'de Perrette' and just beyond it a memorial marker on the left. Stop.

The Perrette Air Force Memorial

The US 9th Air Force Association in concert with friends in France plans to erect over a dozen memorials to commemorate its actions during the battle of Normandy. This one, marking the landing strip used by the 365th Fighter Group, who were here from 28 June to 15 August, was dedicated on 21 September 1987 by a group of veterans who came over from America for the occasion.

The end of the tour.

The Perrette US 9th Airforce Memorial

KILOMETRE 0/KILOMETRE 00/'FIRST TO BE LIBERATED'
The visitor may be somewhat confused by rival claims along the Landing Beaches.

For instance, which is the historical beginning of Liberty Highway — Kilometre 0 outside the town hall at Ste Mère Eglise, or Kilometre 00 at Utah Beach? Both communes proudly claim that *their* marker is the rightful monument, and countless discussions and newspaper articles have argued their respective cases for many years.

Both have a case. Chronologically Ste Mère Eglise was the first town to be liberated — by the Americans — when Lt Col Krause, commanding 3rd Battalion of the 505th PIR 82nd US Airborne Division, hoisted the Stars and Stripes there (see page 59) at 0430 hours.

Geographically UTAH Beach, between Exits 2 and 3, was the first section of French soil to be occupied by the Americans landing from the English Channel.

Bayeux (14 June) claims to be the first city to be liberated (see page 123), Courseulles (6 June) the first port. The café at Pegasus Bridge (see page 198) makes the earliest claim of all — to have been liberated on 5 June, before midnight. However, John Howard's watch, broken on landing in his glider, firmly fixes the time as 0016 hours on 6 June.

As visitors drive into the small sea-side resorts along GOLD, JUNO and SWORD beaches, they will be greeted many times by a 'Welcome' sign that proudly claims 'First town/village to be liberated, 6 June 1944'. You will often be driving along 'Avénue de la Libération' or a street named after the individual Allied commander who led the invasion force in that area.

The rivalry indicates the pride and joy of the occupied French people on being liberated, plus a certain amount of Gallic exuberance, and should be accepted as such by the somewhat puzzled visitor.

TOURIST INFORMATION

MUSEUMS

Ste Mère Eglise
US Airborne Museum/C47 Museum (See page 54 for a detailed description)
Open: 1 April-31 May, 15-30 September: 0900-1200, 1400-1900; 1 June-14 Sept: 0900-1900; 15 December-15 January: closed; rest of year 1000-1200/1400.

☎ 33 41 4135
WC in grounds.
Entrance fee payable. Reductions for children, senior citizens and groups.

UTAH Beach (See page 68 for a detailed description)
Open: Easter to All Saints: 0900-1200, 1400-1900; All Saints to

Easter: 1000-1200, 1400-1600
Sundays and public holidays only.
☎ 33 71 5335
Entrance fee payable. Reductions
for children and groups.

HOTELS
See Cherbourg or Carentan pages
46 and 114.

RESTAURANTS

Ste Mère Eglise
John Steele Hotel/Restaurant
Main Road, on right beyond square
(Rue Cap du Laine).

Crêperie — with superb *gallettes*.
On main road just before square.

Ste Marie du Mont
'Estaminet'
Opposite church in main square. A
range of meals is available. Photographs of June 1944 on wall.

UTAH Beach
Bar Le Danois
Run by the Ledanois family, serves
simple meals as well as drinks. An
excellent spot for a 'café-Calva'
when UTAH Beach is particularly
bleak.
There is usually a hot-dog stall in the

parking area in the season.

Grandcamp Maisy
Near Pointe du Hoc.
A selection of sea food restaurants
round the harbour/pleasure port
area. A pleasant lunch break in fine
weather.

SOUVENIRS
Books, slides and other souvenirs
are on sale at both museums above.

Ste Marie du Mont
Boutique du Holdy in square sells a
booklet describing the marked and
numbered 6 June 1944 points of
interest in the village, as well as
maps, books, souvenirs, postcards.

Ste Mère Eglise
Maison de la Presse. Bookshop with
an excellent selection of maps, etc
about the landings (near Hotel John
Steele).

OTHER ATTRACTIONS

Ste Mère Eglise
Musée de la Ferme du Cotentin.
Open: 1 April-30th September 1000-
1200, 1400-1900. Closed Tues.
Entrance Fee payable.

6

OMAHA
AND POINTE DU HOC

'**B** loody OMAHA' is how most Americans who know refer to the more easterly of the American landing beaches. OMAHA was the critical beach and on the 4 miles of sands below its 100ft high frowning cliffs the Allied invasion came perilously close to failure. Once again, as with the paratroopers, it was the spirit and determination of small groups of GIs that won through.

During World War I, groups of men from British villages, football teams and local clubs had volunteered together to fight. They had joined up together and in the mass casualties on the Western Front, died together. Villages lost almost all their men at one stroke. Battalions that had been formed from such groups of friends were known as 'Pals Battalions'. On OMAHA the Americans were to have their own Pals Battalions and it is a story that has been overlooked in the popular history of the landings.

OMAHA BEACH

Assault Time:	0630 hours
Leading Formations:	116th Infantry Regiment (attached from 29th Division) and 16th Infantry Regiment of the 1st Infantry Division
US 1st Division Commander:	Major General Clarence R. Huebner.
Bombarding Force C:	Battleships: USS *Texas* (flagship)
	USS *Arkansas*
	Cruisers: HMS *Glasgow*
	FFS *Montcalm* (French)
	FFS *Georges Leygues* (French)
	Eleven destroyers
German Defenders:	352nd Infantry Division and elements of 716th Coastal Defence Division
352nd Division Commander:	Lieutenant General Dietrich Kraiss

The Plan (Map 5 page 83)

General Huebner's plan was to attack on a two-regiment front with the 16th Regiment on the left and the 116th Regiment on the right. In turn each regiment was to land two battalion teams on its own section of front with the task of clearing the beach obstacles and moving some two miles inland to secure the beachhead for follow-on landings. Almost 300 special assault engineers were to follow the leading waves of infantry in order to blow up the obstacles.

The set-piece plan had been prepared in great detail and perhaps reminded General Huebner of the way plans had been prepared for the American offensive at St Mihiel in 1918 in which he had taken part. The beach had been divided into eight sectors of different lengths beginning with DOG in the west and ending with FOX in the east. The infantry landings were to follow the air and naval bombardment at 0631 hours. The beach approaches were to be cleared by 0700 hours when for the next two hours another wave of infantry was scheduled to come ashore every thirty minutes. The plan continued in its detail — enemy strongholds to be neutralised by 0830 hours — artillery to begin landing at 0830. It was a plan that had similarities to the one in September 1944 for Operation Market Garden which prompted the Pole, General Sosabowski, to complain, 'But what about the Germans?' Here, as in Holland, the enemy was not prepared to co-operate.

What Happened on D-Day

The effect of the weather on Force O for OMAHA was far worse than on Force U for UTAH because the 1st Division did not have the benefit of shelter at sea from the Cotentin Peninsula. The troops were loaded into their assault craft some eleven miles offshore, about twice the distance out that the British would use and against the latter's advice. Being so far out, the operation had to be done well before 0630 hours and it was, therefore, dark. Many craft got out of position including those carrying the engineers, whose task it was to clear the beach obstacles.

Six thousand yards offshore, twenty-nine DD (duplex drive) floating tanks were launched. Only two of these reached the beach. Many did not float at all but went straight to the bottom taking their crews with them.

There were losses too amongst the LCVPs carrying the infantry. Ten were swamped by the heavy seas and sank. The men, loaded with almost 70lb of equipment each, had little chance of survival. Much of the intrinsic artillery to provide close-support for the infantry combat teams had been loaded on to amphibious DUKWs, but they proved to be top heavy and as a result they capsized losing more than twenty guns.

As the leading waves of landing craft approached the beach they were off target, without their beach-clearing engineers, without supporting armour and short on artillery. The men, crouched down in the bellies of the LCVPs, had been there for three hours. They were cramped, cold

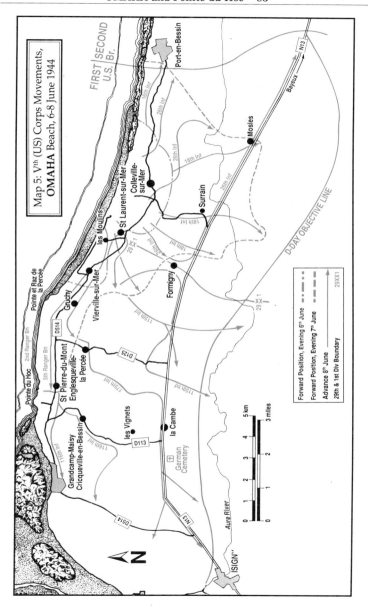

Map 5: Vth (US) Corps Movements, OMAHA Beach, 6-8 June 1944

and sea-sick and then before they reached the shore the enemy opened fire on them.

What happened on the beach is told in the battlefield tour. Despite all difficulties, despite a situation that looked so desperate to General Bradley that he considered evacuating OMAHA, by the end of D-Day the Americans were on the cliffs above the beach and around the villages of Vierville and Colleville. They owed a great deal to the on-the-spot leadership of Brigadier General Cota, the Assistant Divisional Commander of the 29th Division. That evening the first follow-up force, the 26th Infantry Regiment, came ashore to defend the bridgehead. However, the landing was behind schedule and only two of the five exits from the beach were secure. If the Germans were to counter-attack with armour within 48 hours, the beach might yet be lost.

BATTLEFIELD TOUR B

The tour starts at St Côme du Mont, three miles north of Carentan at the extreme southern edge of the 101st Airborne Division landing area and works eastwards to include the German cemetery at la Cambe, the US Rangers' action at Pointe du Hoc, OMAHA Beach and its memorials and the American National Cemetery at St Laurent. See map 6 page 86.

Total distance: 50km (31 miles). Total time: $4\frac{1}{2}$ hours.
Map: IGN 1411, 1:50,000 'Grandcamp-Maisy'

St Côme du Mont
At the end of D-Day the 101st Airborne Division had achieved most of its objectives, but around the locks on the outskirts of Carentan, which controlled the flood waters of the Douve River, the paratroopers were struggling against fierce resistance.

The High Command of the German 7th Army, responsible for the defence of the area, was still not certain that the main invasion had arrived. Reports coming in were confusing. The use of WINDOW had upset German radar and the Rupert dummy parachutists had fooled the Germans into believing that air drops had been made very far afield from the true DZs. The scattered drop also made life difficult for the defenders. Although some German forces, such as elements of von der Heydte's 6th Parachute Regiment, were fighting well, there was little co-ordinated resistance. It was small unit against small unit, often in contest over the possession of a village strongpoint or a road or railway bridge.

The N13 leading south from St Côme du Mont had been turned into a causeway by opening the locks on the Douve and flooding the fields. It was the obvious route to Carentan from the 101st Airborne landing areas and German resistance in St Côme was stubborn.

At 0430 hours on 7 June the 506th PIR with half-a-dozen Sherman tanks of 746th Tank Battalion advanced on the village from the direction of Vierville in the north east. Attack and counter-attack followed, but by nightfall the Germans had not been moved. Over at the locks, after a day's fighting and following the initiative of Colonel Johnson, CO of the 501st PIR, who walked towards the enemy carrying a flag and suggested that they might capitulate, remnants of the 1st Battalion of the 6th Parachute Regiment surrendered — though not before some had been shot by their own officers for wanting to give up. However, enemy fire from Carentan prevented any exploration south.

At 0445 hours on 8 June, behind a rolling barrage, a mixed force of the 101st Airborne Division under Colonel Sink attacked St Côme from the north-east. Some eight fierce actions followed, but when the Americans established a defensive line south of the village across the N13 at about 1600 hours, the Germans withdrew to the west. Equipment abandoned in St Côme suggested that the defenders had been the young paratroopers of the 6th Parachute Regiment.

In concert with the attack from the east there had been an assault from the north in the area of Houesville by the 502nd PIR and it was there that General McAuliffe (the same General that would say 'Nuts' to the Germans in Bastogne) found Colonel George Van Horn, the Commanding Officer of the 502nd, sitting in a wheelbarrow with his ankle in plaster directing the assault. It is a story described in the film, *The Longest Day*. John Wayne played the part of Colonel Horn.

Steadily over the next two days, the Americans linked up along the Douve and re-organised for a drive upon Carentan.

Between St Côme and Carentan were four bridges over the four main waterways — the Jourdan, the Douve, the Groult and the Madeleine. Before Carentan could be taken the bridges had to be crossed.

On 7 June, Lt General Omar N. Bradley, Commanding the American First Army, had decided to alter the priority task given to Major General J. Lawton Collins' VII Corps which had landed on UTAH (4th Infantry Division was part of VII Corps). The corps' objective was changed from the capture of Cherbourg to the linking up with V Corps on OMAHA. The heavy resistance encountered, particularly on OMAHA, made it advisable to concentrate and co-ordinate the two American forces before the Germans could exploit the gap between them.

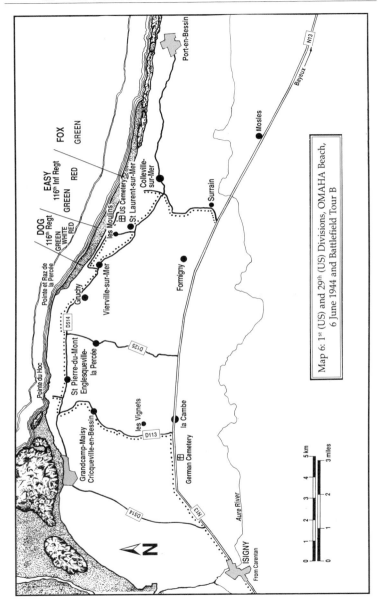

Map 6: 1st (US) and 29th (US) Divisions, OMAHA Beach, 6 June 1944 and Battlefield Tour B

The key to the joining of the forces was Carentan, set squarely on the N13 and at the base of the Douve, and its canal system running to the sea. The Germans were aware of the town's importance and 7th Army Headquarters ordered 6th Parachute Regiment to 'defend Carentan to the last man'.

On 10 June glider and paratroop forces of the 101st Division began their move towards Carentan, scrambling over and under the bridges and paddling in rubber dinghies. The Germans countered with 88mm and machine-gun fire, supported by a brief air attack by two German planes, but the Americans pressed steadily on towards Bridge Number 4, the last one before the town.

Drive along the N13 towards Carentan, crossing the rivers Jourdan, Douve, Groult and Madeleine. The bridge over La Madeleine was Bridge Number 4. *250yd after crossing it stop on the right by a memorial and flagpoles in front of a warehouse building.*

502nd PIR Memorial, Carentan

The American attack petered out in the early hours after the leading company lost fifty-seven men out of the eighty that had begun the assault, and both sides, exhausted by their efforts, rested during the remainder of the night. Taking advantage of the lull, Lt Colonel Robert G. Cole, commanding the 3rd Battalion 502nd PIR, led his men over Bridge Number 4 and then came under fire from a house in a field behind the warehouse (which was not built at the time). Calling down a smoke screen from the artillery, the Colonel told his men to fix bayonets and at 0615 hours on 11 June he and Major John Stopka led a charge upon the house from across the road and past where the memorial now stands which was then a cabbage patch. It was probably the first bayonet charge in France since the one led by Major Pat Porteous at Dieppe in 1942. Major Porteous won the VC for his leadership. Colonel Cole won the Medal of Honour, the first man in the 101st to do so, and Major Stopka won the DSC — sadly the colonel was killed in Holland and the major at Bastogne. Major Porteous survived the war. The memorial reads:

11 June 1944. Here, in a cabbage patch, the decisive attack of the 502nd Parachute Infantry Regiment of the 101st Airborne drove out the Germans and liberated Carentan.

Continue into Carentan and stop at the town hall opposite the railway station.

Carentan

The first contact between troops from UTAH and OMAHA, that is between the Vth and VIIth Corps, had been made at Brevands, east of

Carentan Town Hall and Comité du Débarquement Signal Monument

Carentan, when men of 327th Glider Infantry Regiment met soldiers from the 29th (Blue and Gray) Division on the afternoon of 10 June. That contact was sealed when Carentan was cleared by an attack from the east by the 327th on 12 June. The German 7th Army's appreciation of the importance of Carentan led to a counter attack on the town on 13 June along the railway from Baupte, by the 17th SS Panzer Grenadier Division supported by thirty-seven assault guns and what was left of the 6th Parachute Regiment. The 101st Airborne Division was badly mauled but, with support from the 2nd Infantry Division from OMAHA and a P47 strike by the American 9th Air Force, the town was held.

The paratroopers then pushed out defensive lines to the south and south-west of Carentan and stayed there until they were relieved by the 83rd Infantry Division on 29 June. It was not quiet all the time though. On 20 June the representatives of units within the 101st Division had assembled on the square behind the town hall for a ceremony in which the Silver Star was to be presented to officers and men when German artillery fire hit the square. The ceremony ended quickly. There was another one though on 7 July in Cherbourg. Then General Maxwell Taylor, the division's commander, was awarded the DSO by General Montgomery in recognition of the division's achievements. On 13 July the division arrived back in England.

In front of the town hall are three memorials:

Comité du Débarquement Memorial.

Plaque commemorating the Screaming Eagles, presented by the 101st Airborne Association on their 'Heritage Tour' in 1973.

An eagle's head floral tribute (in summer time).

In Carentan church there is a 101st Airborne Division memorial stained-glass window.

Continue to Isigny on the N13 and stop in the centre of the town beside the Comité du Débarquement memorial.

Isigny

The towns of Isigny, Bayeux and Caen, all on the N13 road behind the landing beaches, were D-Day objectives. None was taken on D-Day. Isigny was scheduled to be taken by 29th Division who were due to land in strength once a foothold had been established at OMAHA by the 1st Division. Major General Gehrhardt commanding the 29th Division was to take back under command the units attached to 1st Division for the landings and head for Isigny while the 1st Division under Major General Huebner was to drive east to link up with the British at Port en Bessin.

When the Americans landed at OMAHA they had expected formidable fortifications, but less than formidable defenders of the 'ear-nose-and-throat' 716th Static Division. What they found were good quality troops of the 352nd First Attack Division. Instead of there being just four battalions of indifferent troops to overcome between Bayeux and Isigny, there were those plus four from the 352nd Infantry Division.

Because of the difficulties on OMAHA, Major General Gehrhardt did not assume formal command of the 29th Division until 1700 hours on 7 June and that evening the task of taking Isigny was given to the 175th Infantry Regiment supported by the 747th Tank Battalion. In a remarkable night-time offensive the 29th Division cleared la Cambe before dawn on 8 June and that night, following a naval bombardment that destroyed 60 per cent of the town, moved unopposed into Isigny.

Continue to the German cemetery on the right just before the village of la Cambe on the N13. Stop.

The German Cemetery at La Cambe

This was originally an American cemetery, with burials of both American and German dead.

In 1947 the Americans were repatriated or re-buried at St Laurent. The following year the British and French War Graves organisations began bringing in German dead and in 1956 work began on concentrating all German burials in the area into six cemeteries. The German People's Organisation for the care of War Graves (*Deutsche Kriegs-*

Comité du Débarquement Signal Monument, Isigny

gräberfürsorge) established, and continues to care for, this and similar cemeteries. (See Memorials and War Graves Organisations, p233). The work here was completed on 21 September, 1961, most of the re-internments and landscaping having been done by students of many nations at an International Youth Camp in 1958. Groups of German school children and students regularly come and camp nearby and spend time in tidying the area. The Allied nations would do well to follow this example in order to bring home the terrible cost of war to their young.

To the left and right of the arched entrance are rooms which house

---

A D-DAY MEMORY

A memory of 1944 by a soldier of VII Corps

"I was present when this cemetery was inaugurated. We were picked ... three people were picked from each company of the 175th Regimental Combat Team. We were trucked down to la Cambe and dedicated this cemetery, which was for the dead of 29th Division. I happened to be one of the people chosen. It was a very touching ceremony with the dead not yet buried piled up on either side of the honour guard. We were dressed in the cleanest battle uniforms we could find and three people from each Regiment carried guidons."

Symbolic crosses in the German Cemetery, la Cambe

AUGUST 14 1944 THE
367 TH FIGHTER
GROUP WAS
OPERATIONAL
FROM ADVANCED
LANDING GROUND A 2
BUILT BY THE
820 TH BATTALION
AAF ENGRS OF
9 TH AIRFORCE

LA CAMBE 13091988

367th Fighter Group, 9th US Air Force Memorial, les Vignets

the visitor's book, the cemetery registers and war graves literature. Generally, there are postcards freely available beside a collecting box. On the walls are the names of the missing and there are frequently wreaths of dried ferns and flowers on the floor left by visiting relatives.

Inside the cemetery are small groups of black stone crosses. These are symbolic and do not mark graves. The graves are marked by flat stones engraved with the names of those below — often four or more together. The Germans call this 'comradeship in death', though a more practical reason is that the French were unwilling to give up land for the invader to use and the Germans have had to bury all their Normandy dead in six cemeteries. Here there are 21,160 dead, including 296 in a mass grave under the grassed mound in the centre of the cemetery.

The mound, or ossuary, is ringed at the bottom by stones carrying the names of the dead and surmounted by a huge black cross and two figures representing mourning parents. There are steps to the top of the mound from the rear and it is quite proper to climb up and to look over the graves. In winter the steps can be extremely slippery, as can be the stone path leading from the entrance to the mound.

The impression here is one of solemnity and of sadness, a typical reaction in German cemeteries. Whether this is due to the Teutonic inheritance showing through in the cemetery architecture, or to the wide use of dark oak trees (symbols of strength) or to a deliberate intent to express remorse is impossible to say. It is, however, worthwhile making an effort to contrast the style of the three national cemeteries that are visited on the recommended tours — German, American and British — and asking the rhetorical question, 'What is their purpose?'

Do not forget to sign the register.

Continue along the N13 to la Cambe and turn left onto the D113. In les Vignets, to the right of Savigny is a memorial to the 367th Fighter Group of 9th U.S. Airforce. *Pass through Cricqueville en Bessin, which has a memorial in the church to the American Rangers, to the junction with the D514 coast road. Turn right and follow signs to Pointe du Hoc.*

Pointe du Hoc

The small road down which you have driven from the D514 is Rangers Road. In June 1944 it was much narrower and the entrance to the coastal area was controlled halfway down by a manned guardpost. The area between the guardpost and the sea, which is today the memorial area, was completely sealed off by barbed wire and sentries. The only way in was past the guardpost.

Allied intelligence had taken great pains to locate all coastal gun batteries that could menace the invasion, and a total of seventy-three in

Ruined German gun bunker, Pointe du Hoc

fixed emplacements had been identified. The most formidable along the American beaches was the six-gun battery at Pointe du Hoc, which was capable of engaging targets at sea and of firing directly onto UTAH and OMAHA Beaches.

The guns were thought to be 155mm, with a range of 25,000yd and, in preparing their bombardment plans, the Americans placed Pointe du Hoc on top priority. It was decided that the gun positions would be steadily bombed during May, with a heavier than average attack by both day and night three days before D-Day, and then again during the night of 5 June. The potential threat of the Pointe du Hoc battery was seen to be so great that the 2nd Ranger Battalion was given the task of capturing the position directly after H-Hour.

The battery position is set upon cliffs that drop vertically some 100ft to a very small rocky beach. In addition to the main concrete emplacements, many of which were connected by tunnels or protected walkways, there were trenches and machine-gun posts constructed around the perimeter fences and the cliff's edge. The German garrison numbered about two hundred — men of the static 716th Coastal Defence Division, mostly non-Germans.

The responsibility for the assault on Pointe du Hoc lay with General Gerow's V Corps and hence with the 1st Infantry Division and thence with the right-hand assault formation, the 116th Infantry Regiment attached from 29th Division. They were given two Ranger battalions under command to do the job. The position was out on a limb, separated from DOG Green, the nearest edge of the main OMAHA beach at Vierville, by four miles of close country. Between them was another prominent feature, Pointe de la Percée, which like Pointe du Hoc jutted out into the sea.

The plan called for three companies of 2nd Ranger Battalion to land below the cliffs, climb them and then make a direct assault on the battery. Meanwhile, a fourth company was scheduled to land on DOG Green with the 116th Infantry and to move west to tackle fortifications at Pointe de la Percée in order to cover the flank of the main Ranger force here.

On D-Day the Rangers were late. The strong easterly tide had pulled them too far east, and in the morning light and confusion of the air and sea bombardment Lieutenant Colonel James E. Rudder, commanding the 2nd Battalion, mistook Pointe de la Percée for Pointe du Hoc.

Walk along the James E. Rudder footpath to the Ranger Memorial at the edge of the cliff.

Over to the right the prominent feature jutting into the sea is Pointe de la Percée. Realising his mistake, the Colonel turned his small flotilla of seven British-crewed LCAs (three had already sunk in the heavy seas and the men were baling out with their steel helmets in the ones which remained afloat), and moved in this direction, parallel to the shore and some 100yd out. They came under the direct fire of those manning the trenches, and the Rangers turned inshore and landed some 500yd away to your right. There, Colonel Rudder established his HQ, featured in a well known photograph showing the spread-out American flag. The Rangers headed for the cliffs. In a novel approach they had fitted DUKWs with fireman's ladders, but the small beach had been so cratered by the earlier fire support by the battleship *Texas* and others, that the vehicles could not reach the cliff. Rocket-fired grapples were tried, but the ropes, heavy with sea water, held many down, and so with ladders and daggers the Americans began to climb.

The responsibility for the defence of the area had been taken over by the 352nd Division, a full attack formation, following its move forward to the coast by Rommel in February 1944, but fortunately the troops here were those of the Coastal Defence Force. In anticipation of commando landings, the Germans had placed 240mm shells attached to trip wires at 100yd intervals along the cliff, and the forward troops were amply supplied with hand grenades which they rolled down as the Americans climbed up. The area was in a state of great confusion. Minutes before the Rangers arrived eighteen medium bombers raided the German

German lookout bunker and Ranger Memorial, Pointe du Hoc

positions, driving the defenders underground and, as the attacking troops struggled to gain the top of the cliffs, they had direct and very effective fire support from the US destroyer *Satterlee* and the British destroyer *Talybont*. Only very stubborn or foolhardy defenders remained at the cliff's edge to take a personal part in the proceedings and, once on top, the Rangers, scattering small arms fire around them, worked quickly across the torn and smoking ground to the gun emplacements. When they got there they found that the guns had been removed.

Colonel Rudder then split his small command into two. One stayed where it was and prepared a defensive position while the other set off up the road, now called Rangers Road, to find the guns, which fortunately they did. They were hidden in an orchard at the back of the field where Rangers Road meets the D514. They were well camouflaged but unguarded and, using thermite grenades, the Rangers destroyed them.

To this point, despite the difficulty of assault and because of the air and naval fire support, the Americans' casualties had been relatively light, probably thirty to forty, but later that day the 1st Battalion of the 914th Regiment began a series of counter-attacks that nearly wiped out the small bridgehead and caused most casualties. Aware of the isolation of the men at Pointe du Hoc, the 116th Infantry Regiment, with the 5th Ranger Battalion which had landed with them at OMAHA four miles to your right, attempted to link up with the 2nd Ranger Battalion but were stopped 1,000yd short. That night the 914th Regiment drove the Americans into a small enclave along the cliff, barely 200yd wide, but the Rangers held on, helped by fire from destroyers. On the night of 7 June General Kraiss ordered the 352nd Division to withdraw during the following day to a defensive position along the river Aure, just south of the N13, but it was not until just before noon on 8 June that the Rangers were relieved by a tank and infantry force of 116th Infantry Regiment, supported by the 5th Ranger Battalion. Before that, however, they had been bombed by Allied planes and fired on by their own side. Such is the fog of war. Their final casualties were 135 killed, wounded and missing out of a total of 225 that landed at Pointe du Hoc. This is a casualty rate of 60 per cent.

Perhaps the most difficult question to answer about the struggle at Pointe du Hoc is, 'Why was the assault made from the sea when the cliffs alone were so formidable?' It seems in retrospect, and appears reasonable to assume, that the same conclusion could have been drawn at the time, that an airborne assault would have been the best way of carrying out the task — and with less likelihood of such a high casualty rate. It may be that the Rangers existed and had to be used, perhaps all available airborne forces were committed elsewhere, or maybe the position was too near the cliff's edge to plan operations like Merville (page 213) or Pegasus Bridge (page 193). In the light of what happened to the drops of the 82nd and 101st Airborne Divisions, it was fortunate that the planners had opted for an assault from the sea.

The memorial area is 30½ acres and the site was preserved by the French Comité de la Pointe du Hoc. In 1960 a dramatic granite 'dagger' memorial was raised on top of a German concrete bunker, with inscriptions in English and French that commemorate the Rangers' action. On 6 June 1979, in a ceremony attended by General Omar Bradley, the American Battle Monuments Commission took over responsibility for maintenance of the area and just prior to, and since, the visit of President Reagan in 1984, a great deal of tidying-up has taken place. There is a widened Rangers Road, a substantial car park, modern toilets, gravel paths and easy access to many of the bunkers and gun positions. The ground is still scarred with huge craters from the bombing or from the 14in guns of the *Texas*. On 6 June 1944 it must have been the nearest earthly equivalent to Hades.

It is interesting to note that most accounts refer to 'Pointe du Hoc' as 'Pointe du Hoe'. The latter is incorrect, and probably has been carried onward from a spelling mistake in early secret planning documents. The puzzle over the name leads on to the puzzle about the guns. Why did Allied intelligence not know that they had been moved? The answer probably rests with the strict security that the Germans maintained in the area. The only access was via the guard post and no Frenchmen were allowed in under any circumstances, so that the French Resistance, who sent back details about most other gun positions before D-Day, were unable to help. The largest question of all in regard to Allied intelligence, however, lies with their total failure to notice Rommel's movement of the 352nd Division onto the beach called OMAHA. That slip might have cost the Allies the war. As it was, it was a close run thing.

Return to the D514 and follow the signs to Vierville, but before deciding where to stop, read the next paragraph.

It is invidious to single out particular actions for special mention since every soldier who took part in the events of 6 June 1944 did the best he could measured by his own standards.Some did a great deal more. However, there are perhaps three events of the day that attract the greatest comment — the Rangers assault on Point du Hoc, the 6th Airborne Coup de Main on Pegasus Bridge and the landings on OMAHA Beach. It was on OMAHA that the Americans suffered grievous losses — almost one-third as many again as the combined totals of the 82nd

5th Engineer Special Brigade Memorial, OMAHA Beach. (Diag 2, Point 2)

2nd Infantry Division and Provisional Engineers Special Brigade Memorials, OMAHA Beach. (Diag 2, Point 4)

Airborne Division, the 101st Airborne Division and UTAH Beach, and more than the entire total of all British casualties. As a result, OMAHA

First US Cemetery Marker
OMAHA Beach.
(Diag 2 Point 7)

Beach has become a particular place of pilgrimage and there are a number of memorials and features to be seen.

The diagram on page 100 shows the location of fifteen points of interest and the traveller is left to decide how many to visit and for how long. The tour begins with a visit to the Vierville private museum and then goes on to the National Guard Memorial and, using that as a viewpoint, the events on the beach are described. The 'Point' numbers referred to are those shown in the diagram.

Vierville 'Exposition OMAHA' Private Museum Point 15.
See Tourist Information on page 114 for details.
Continue past Point 13 (Vierville Château) and turn left down the D517 to the National Guard Memorial, Point 8, by the Hotel du Casino and stop. OMAHA Beach is ahead of you.

OMAHA and the 'Pals Battalion' (Map 6, page 86)
To the left along the beach can be seen Pointe de la Percée. Where you are, however, is effectively the western end of OMAHA Beach and it stretches away to the right in a concave arc for almost four miles. It is very

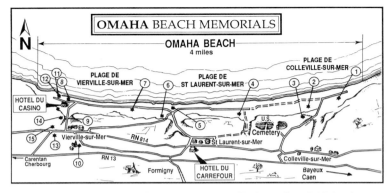

1. 2nd Armoured Division (Hell on Wheels) and 749th Tank Battalion Memorial wall and plaques in the Village Vacances Familiales.

2. 5th Engineer Special Brigade memorial accessible from the American Cemetery.

3. 1st Infantry Division (Big Red One) memorial obelisk and seat. Accessible from the American cemetery. The first three points overlook EASY Red.

4. 2nd Infantry Division memorial on German bunker with Provisional Engineers Special Brigade plaque. Accessible from the beach road.

5. Comité du Débarquement memorial with side panels to 1st Infantry Division and 116th Infantry Regimental Combat Team of the 29th Infantry Division. This is junction between DOG and EASY sectors.

6. 6th Engineer Special Brigade memorial.

7. First American cemetery in Europe memorial marker.

8. National Guard Memorial. This overlooks DOG Green.

9. 29th Infantry Division (The Blue & The Gray) memorial.

10. 81st Chemical Mortar Battalion plaque on churchyard wall.

11. 58th Armoured Field Artillery Battalion pillar and plaque.

12. Mulberry harbour section incorporated into a fishing jetty.

13. HQ 11th Port US Army plaque on Château gate pillar.

14. 5th Ranger Battalion plaque on wall.

15. Vierville private OMAHA beach museum.

obviously a place to defend rather than to attack. The cliffs, nowhere less than 100ft high, stand guard over the seashore and there are only five exit gullies (the Americans called them 'draws') through to the heights above. You are standing at the entrance to the Vierville draw.

Below the cliffs is a mixture of dunes, scrub and waterpools leading down to the beach road on the sea-side of which is a wall marking the edge of the beach some six feet below. The beach is broad and flat and

'Exposition OMAHA' private museum, Vierville. (Diag 2, point 14)

at low tide a good 100yd separate the beach wall from the water's edge. That 100yd is clearly visible to anyone on the cliffs.

On 6 June 1944 there were many people on the cliffs and they were not, as had been thought, just the conscript mixture of the 716th Static Division, but a force hardened by the addition of trained combat soldiers of the 352nd Division. To compound the situation further, one of the battalions of the 352nd Division was just completing an anti-invasion exercise in the area and was therefore deployed correctly to counter a landing — a situation similar to that at Salerno when von Kesselring's Panzers seemed to be waiting for Mark Clark's 5th Army to come ashore. The defensive positions were formidable too, though they tended to be bunched around the five draws. Estimates indicate that along the beach were eight big guns in concrete bunkers, thirty-five anti-tank guns in pillboxes and more than eighty machine-gun posts. Then there were the beach obstacles.

The thickening of the Atlantic Wall that Rommel had inspired was very evident at OMAHA. On the sand were log obstacles in three jumbled lines each about 20ft apart, carrying mines and shells, whose function was to prevent landing craft reaching the shore. Amongst and inland of them were metal hedgehogs producing a combined obstacle belt of some 50yd thick which was totally submerged at high tide. From the beach wall to the bottom of the cliffs were mines and wire, particularly

Honour Guard at the inauguration of the 29th Infantry Division Memorial

29th Infantry Division Memorial

Vierville Château

Plaque detail, HQ 11 Port, Vierville Château

concentrated in the five draws and, sprinkled along the slopes as if from some ghastly pepper-pot, were anti-personnel mines.

The 1st Division's landing plan was simple. The beach was to be divided into two main sectors, DOG where you are now, and EASY to the east (to the right). On DOG would land the 116th Infantry Regiment under command from the 29th Division. Once a foothold had been established the 116th would revert back to its division and clear the area to the River Aure beyond the N13 as far west as, and inclusive of, Isigny. On EASY the 16th Infantry Regiment were to land and then head east to link up with the British at Port-en-Bessin. Each regiment had attached to it supporting forces to help it in its task — two battalions of floating DD tanks to provide direct fire support against enemy fortified positions and two special brigades of engineers to clear beach obstacles ahead of the bulk of the landing craft carrying the infantry. The combined forces were known as RCTs (Regimental Combat Teams) ie the 116th RCT and 16th RCT, a confusing nomenclature for the British today, to whom 'RCT' means 'Royal Corps of Transport'. It was planned that by the end of D-Day the 1st Division force would have a bridgehead 16 miles wide and 5 miles deep. In reality by nightfall on the day the bridgehead was barely the length of the beach and averaged less than 1 mile wide with most units still below the cliffs.

At first, despite the swamping of the DD tanks almost as soon as they were launched, the loss of supporting artillery in the top-heavy DUKWs and the absence of the main force of the special engineers who had got out of position in the heavy seas, things seemed to be going well. The landing craft were not being fired upon. It was when the ramps were dropped for the men to go ashore that the enemy made his presence felt. The leading company of the 116th Regiment was Company 'A'. It came ashore below where the National Guard Memorial stands and a regimental account of what happened was prepared by survivors and approved by the Commanding General. This is an extract:

> The first ramps were dropped at 0636 in water that was waist deep to cover a man's head. As if this had been the signal for which the enemy waited, the ramps were instantly enveloped in a crossing of automatic fire which was accurate and in great volume. It came at the boats from both ends of the beach. Company 'A' had planned to move in three files from each boat, center file going first, then flank files peeling off to the right and left. The first men tried it. They crumpled as they sprang from the ship, forward into the water. Then order was lost. It seemed to the men that the only way to get ashore with a chance for safety was to dive head-first into the water. (Pvt Howard L. Gresser)

> A few had jumped off, trying to follow the SOP, and had gone down into water over their heads. They were around the boat now, struggling with their equipment and trying to keep afloat. In one of the boats, a third of the men had become engaged in this struggle to save themselves from a quick drowning. (Pfc Gilbert G. Murdock)

> That many were lost before they had a chance to face the enemy. Some of them were hit in the water and wounded. Some drowned then. Others, wounded, dragged themselves ashore and upon finding the sand, lay quiet and gave themselves shots, only to be caught and drowned within a few minutes by the on-racing tide. (Murdock)

> But some men moved safely through the bullet fire to the sands, then found that they could not hold there; they went back into the water and used it as cover, only their heads sticking out above it. Others sought the cover of the underwater obstacles. Many were shot while doing so. Those who survived kept moving shoreward with the tide and in this way finally made their landing. (Murdock and Pfc Leo J. Nash)

> They were in this tide-borne movement when Company 'B' came in behind them. (Pvt Crosser).

Others who had gotten into the sands and had burrowed in, remained in their holes until the tide caught up to them, then they, too, joined the men in the water.

Within 7 to 10 minutes after the ramps had dropped, Company A had become inert, leaderless and almost incapable of action. The Company was almost entirely bereft of Officers. Lt Edward N. Gearing was back where the first boat had foundered. All the officers were dead except Lt Elijah Nance who had been hit in the head as he left the boat, and then again in the body as he reached the sands. Lt Edward Tidrick was hit in the throat as he jumped from the ramp into the water. He went on to the sands and flopped down 15ft from Pvt Leo J. Nash. He raised up to give Nash an order. Him bleeding from the throat and heard his words: 'ADVANCE WITH THE WIRE CUTTERS!' It was futile, Nash had no wire cutters. In giving the order, Tidrick himself a target for just an instant, Nash saw machine-gun bullets cleave him from head to pelvis.

German machine-gunners along the cliff directly ahead were now firing straight down into the party. Captain Taylor N. Fellers and Lt Benjamin R. Kearfoot had come in with 30 men of Company 'A' aboard L.C.A. No. 1015, but what happened to that boat team in detail will never be known. Every man was killed; most of them being found along the beach.

In those first 5 to 10 minutes when the men were fighting in the water, they dropped their weapons and even their helmets to save themselves from drowning, and learning by what they saw that their landing had deteriorated into a struggle for personal survival, every sergeant was either killed or wounded. It seemed to the others that enemy snipers had spotted their leaders and had directed their fire so as to exterminate them. A medical boat came in on the right of Tadrick's boat. The Germans machine-gunned every man in the section. (Nash)

Their bodies floated with the tide. By this time the leaderless infantrymen had foregone any attempt to get forward against the enemy and where men moved at all, their efforts were directed toward trying to save any of their comrades they could reach. The men in the water pushed wounded men ahead of them so as to get them ashore. (Grosser and Murdock).

Those who reached the sands crawled back and further into the water, pulling men to land to save them from drowning, in many cases, only to have them shot out of their hands or to be hit themselves while in these exertions. The weight of the infantry equipment handicapped all of this rescue work. It left many unhelped and the wounded drowned because of it. The able-bodied who pulled them in stripped themselves of their equipment so as to move more freely in the water, then cut away the assault jackets and the equipment of the wounded and dropped them in the water. (Grosser, Murdock and Cpl. M. Gurry)

Within 20 minutes of striking of the beach, Company 'A' ceased to be an assault company and had become a forlorn little rescue party bent on survival and the saving of the lives of the other men.

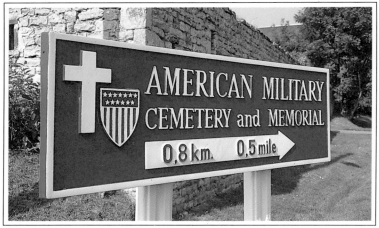

Road sign to the Normandy American Cemetery

The 29th Division was a National Guard Division. The nearest British equivalent would be a Territorial Division, but the British geographical recruitment net was much wider than the American one. The Americans were pals and many had been since childhood. The leading companies of the 1st Battalion were A, B and D, recruited and based respectively around the Virginian towns of Bedford, Lynchburg and Roanoke. Sergeant John R. Slaughter who landed with D Company and who returned to OMAHA in 1988 to share in the unveiling of the 29th Division Memorial, recalled the landing:

> We landed in column of companies. 'A' Company about 0630, B Company some ten to fifteen minutes later and D Company about 0710, though we probably all were late. We hit the eye of the storm. The battalion was decimated. Hell, after that we didn't have enough to whip a cat with.

The tactical story of OMAHA beach, the casualties and the bravery are usually associated with the 1st Division, because their General commanded the landing. In a sense they get the glory, yet the heaviest casualties on this bloody beach, indeed anywhere along the whole invasion coastline, were taken here on DOG Green, just below where you stand, by A Company of the 1st Battalion of the 116th Infantry Regiment of 29th Division, a Pals battalion from Bedford Virginia. John Slaughter tells the story:

> The small town of Bedford lost twenty-three men on D-Day. It's a town of

Bronze statue Spirit of American Youth, *Normandy American Cemetery*

A D-DAY MEMORY

Pte Lee Ratel. 18-years old. 16th Infantry Regiment, 2nd wave. Never in action before. A replacement. Landed on OMAHA beach.

"It was waist deep when we went in and we lost, I'd say, probably one third between getting off the boats and to the edge of the water and then probably another third between there to the base where you get any protection at all, because it was straight down and they were zeroed in there. They're very, very good defensive soldiers, but they're not trained the same ... they're trained to think how they're told to think and Americans are more independent, they can think on their own resources and this makes a lot of difference in a battle. Most, except myself, were seasoned men, they knew what to do ... there were landing craft blown up in the water, lying in the water, they never got in ... direct hits ... bodies of men who didn't even get into the sand and there were a lot of them lying on the sand ... there was crossfire from pillboxes ... the beach here cost an awful price in men, good men ... it was a job that had to be done and we were allotted to it. That's it. You do what you have to do."

3,000 people. Twenty-two of those men were from A Company of the 116th Regiment. There were three sets of brothers in A Company. Raymond and Bedford Hoback were killed. Raymond was wounded and lay on the beach. Then when the tide came in he was washed out to sea and drowned. They never found his body. He was carrying a Bible and it washed up upon the sand. The day after D-Day a GI found it. It had Raymond's name and address in Bedford inside and the soldier mailed it to the family. On the Saturday (D-Day was a Tuesday) the family got a telegram that Bedford was killed and then on Sunday they got another one saying that Raymond was too. There were two Parkers killed. Then Roy and Ray Stevens who were twins, Roy was wounded and Ray was killed.

Further east, at the les Moulins draw where DOG sector became EASY, the two other battalions of the 116th landed on either side of the exit. There was less opposition on the beach, and smoke, from grass and buildings set on fire by the naval bombardment, produced a screen that saved many lives. On EASY Red though, the 2nd Battalion of the 16th Infantry Regiment of the 1st Division were suffering the same fate as the 1st Battalion of the 116th on DOG Green, having landed opposite the Colleville draw. The minefields claimed many victims and the Americans, without the specialised armoured vehicles developed by the British for clearing beach obstacles, were confined to single-file movement through the mined areas. This led to slowness in getting off the beaches and a log-jam of men and material, excellent targets for enemy fire from strong points, unaffected by the pre-assault bombing which had been dropped too far inland.

The Americans come in for much criticism over the planning for the OMAHA assault. In particular the following are singled out:

1. The decision not to use the British-developed specialised armour was foolhardy in view of the lessons of Dieppe.

2. The assault plan was too 'clockwork' and in particular ignored British advice about when and where to launch assault craft.

3. The frontal assault went against British advice, with rumours that a bloody victory in a Presidential election year would not only re-elect the President but also reaffirm the nation's pledge to deal with Germany before Japan.

Later the British, in particular Montgomery, were to have their share of criticism for being too slow in breaking out from the Normandy beach-heads. Much of the criticism would come from the Deputy Supreme Commander, the same officer that had said that it would be too dangerous to use the 82nd and 101st Airborne Divisions on the Cotentin Peninsula. We have the benefit of hindsight to aid our assessments.

A tour of the monuments and features associated with OMAHA Beach may be made using the diagram on page 100. After that, use the les Moulins draw to return to the D514 and follow signs to the American National Cemetery at St Laurent.

The Normandy American National Cemetery and Memorial at St Laurent

This cemetery was built and is maintained by the American Battle Monuments Commission (see page 233). The site was chosen for its historical importance — overlooking the OMAHA landing beaches. It covers 172 acres, all beautifully landscaped and tended, which were donated by the French people.

It contains 9,286 burials, 307 of whom are unknown and whose white marble crosses or Stars of David bear the inscription, 'Here rests in honoured glory a comrade in arms known but to God'. On the known graves is inscribed the rank, unit, name, date of death and home state of the serviceman or woman commemorated. The headstones are set out in straight lines, perpendicular, horizontal and diagonal, which form a dramatic geometric pattern on the immaculate emerald green grass, whichever way the eye looks.

Medal of Honour winners' headstones are lettered in gold. The most famous is that of Brigadier General Theodore Roosevelt (Plot D, Row

The Reflective Pool, Normandy American Cemetery

28, Grave 45), 12 July 1944. Beside him lies his youngest brother, Lt Quentin Roosevelt, a World War I aviator who died in France on 14 July 1918, and who was reinterred here when the cemetery was made. The cemetery was completed in 1956, and the landscape architect was Markley Stevenson of Philadelphia.

There are thirty-two other pairs of brothers who lie side-by-side and a father and son, Col Ollie Reed (Plot E, Row 20, Grave 19) and Ollie Reed, junior. There are also some women Red Cross nurses and WACs (Mary Bankston Pfc, D-20-19; Mary Barlow Pfc, A-19-30; Dolores Brown, Sgt, F-13-19; Elizabeth Richardson, Red Cross, A-21-5).

The servicemen and women resting here were re-interred from temporary cemeteries (eg at Ste Mère Eglise, la Cambe and OMAHA Beach — now marked by memorials). 14,000 others of their comrades were repatriated at government expense. This impressive cemetery receives more than $1\frac{1}{2}$ million visitors each year — not only veterans or their families, but local French people.

Approach Avenue/Car Parks. A tree-bordered avenue, $1\frac{1}{2}$ miles long leads from the N814 to the main entrance. To the right are ample, well-signed car parks.

Visitor's Building. To the left of the main entrance, this well-appointed room houses the superintendent's office, the cemetery registers, and the visitor's book, as well as literature about this and other American Battle Monuments cemeteries.

Time Capsule. Embedded in the ground on the right-hand side just inside the entrance, the time capsule, dedicated to General Eisenhower, contains sealed reports of the 6 June 1944 landings. It is to be opened 6 June 2044.

Memorial. This area, to the right as one progresses into the cemetery, consists of a semi-circular colonnade, with stone loggias at each side which are engraved with vivid battle maps, picked out in coloured enamel and designed by Robert Foster of New York. Ornamental urns at each side flank a 22ft-high bronze statue of *The Spirit of American Youth Rising from the Waves*, sculpted by Donald de Lue of New York.

In 1987 the American Veterans' Association donated a memorial bell which tolls every hour and at noon and at 1700 hours plays a tuneful sequence. It is reminiscent of the memorial bell in the church of Belloy on the Somme, donated as a memorial by the parents of the American poet Alan Seeger, who fell in July 1916. They both toll for Americans who gave their lives in France.

Garden of the Missing. Behind the memorial, the garden's semi-circular wall bears the names of 1,557 missing with no known graves. It is planted with ornamental shrubs and roses.

Reflective Pool/Stars and Stripes. To the left of the memorial is the rectangular pool with water lilies and beyond it, two enormous flagstaffs. The American flag flies proudly from them, raised each morning, lowered each evening.

Orientation Tables. Continuing past the memorial, one reaches the first orientation table, overlooking OMAHA Beach, with a map pointing to features on the nearby landing beaches. From here one can descend a deceptively gentle-looking path down to the beach itself. (It seems very long and steep on the way up.) It is well worth the effort as from the bottom one can look up at the formidable cliffs and the sites of the heavily defended German positions which faced the Americans as they landed.

On the way down, a second orientation table shows the Mulberry Harbour designed for OMAHA, washed away in the storm of 19 June.

Graves Area. This is laid out in ten lettered plots (A-J), with numbered rows and graves to help visitors to find the graves of friends and relatives. Plans and registers are kept in the visitors' building.

Chapel. Along the central pathway is the non-denominational chapel with a fine mosaic designed by Leon Kroll of New York depicting 'America' blessing her sons as they leave to fight for freedom in France and 'France' bestowing a laurel wreath on a dead American.

Statues of United States and France. At the end of the main axis beyond the chapel are two granite figures sculpted by Donald de Lue representing the two countries.

Return to the Cemetery entrance, and continue south on the D208 to the les Barrières junction with the N13, west of Surrain. Stop and visit the private museum at Surrain (see Tourist Information below for details) to end the tour.

TOURIST INFORMATION

TOURIST OFFICES

Carentan
Place du Grand Valnoble.
In 12 years of visiting, the authors have never found it open! So try the Départemental Office in:

St Lô ☎ 33 57 5280 or
Isigny ☎ 31 21 4600.
Known by the Americans as 'Easy Knee', it claims to be the birthplace of Walt Disney's forebears.

OMAHA Beach and the path from the Normandy American Cemetery

MUSEUMS & CEMETERY

Vierville-sur-Mer
'Exposition OMAHA'
Private museum housed in a 1944
Nissen hut (used for Allied troop entertainment). Good collection of
American and German arms,
uniforms and insignia.
Open: 1 April-1 October 1000-1200,
1400-1800. No lunch-closing in July
and August or on 6 June.
Entrance fee payable. Reductions
for groups and students.
☎ 31 22 4366.

Surrain
Privately owned museum.
On the main N13 between Formigny
and Mosles. Contains uniformed
Allied and German models, weapons, insignia, World War II ration
kits. Outside a variety of vehicles.
Sale of World War II souvenirs and
collectables.

Open: every day 0900-1930
Entrance fee payable. Groups half
price.
☎ 31 22 5756

Normandy American National Cemetery and Memorial
St Laurent
Open: Summer, weekdays 0900-
1800, weekends, holidays 1000-
1800; winter, weekdays 0900-1700,
weekends and holidays 1000-1700.
☎ 31 22 40 62

HOTELS AND OTHER ACCOMMODATION

Carentan
* Hotel du Commerce.
On corner of main road and road
leading to square, near Town Hall.
☎ 33 42 00. Typical tourist hotel, as
is the
* Hotel du Marché, in Market
Square. ☎ 33 42 0688.

The museum at Surrain

Les Veys
** Aire de la Baie.
Motel type 'Logis et Auberge de France', between Isigny and Carentan on N13.
☎ 33 42 0099

Isigny
** Hotel de France. In main street.
☎ 31 20 0033

Colleville
Village de Vacances Famille.
Near Com Deb Mem VVF.
Basic hostel type accommodation.
Superb setting on OMAHA beach.
Open April-November.
☎ 31 22 4181

RESTAURANTS

Carentan
Both the hotels listed above have excellent restaurants (The 'Commerce' closes on Fridays). Also in the main square is the Restaurant Les Marroniers — small, family run. Monday is market day, so restaurants tend to be very busy.

Isigny
Hotel de France (see Hotels above).

Vierville
* Hotel du Casino.
Opposite National Guard Memorial.
Superb position overlooking OMAHA DOG Red. Slow service in authors' experience.
☎ 31 22 4102

SOUVENIRS

Surrain Museum above.

7

BAYEUX, ARROMANCHES AND GOLD BEACH

The background information given first covers the whole 2nd (British) Army plan. The actions on GOLD, the beach adjacent to Arromanches, are then described, in conjunction with a battlefield tour.

The 2nd Army (Map 2 page 30)

The Supreme Commander had three subordinate Commanders in Chief — for the sea, the air and the land. Although General Montgomery was never formally appointed C-in-C Land Forces, that was in effect his position. Under his command were four armies, known collectively as 21st Army Group. They were divided as follows:

Assault armies	First (US) Army	General Bradley
	Second (British) Army	General Dempsey
Follow-up armies	Third (US) Army	General Patton
	First (Canadian) Army	General Crerar

General Montgomery stated that:

In the initial stages of this campaign [OVERLORD] the object [is] to secure a lodgement on the Continent from which further offensive operations [can] be developed ....

This basic aim was later expanded and in the expansion developed a point of controversy which was to lead to some senior Allied officers petitioning the Supreme Commander to have General Montgomery removed as C-in-C Land Forces. In a speech to the Royal United Services Institution in October 1945 the then Field Marshal said:

Once ashore and firmly established, my plan was to threaten to breakout on the eastern front, that is in the Caen sector, by this threat to draw the main enemy reserves into that sector, to fight them there and keep them there using the British and Canadian armies for the purpose. Having got the main enemy reserves committed on the eastern flank my plan was to make the break-out on the western flank, using for this task the American armies under General Bradley and pivoting on Caen.

To many observers this explanation sounded like being wise after the event. True, the British *had* stuck at Caen and there *had* been bloody battles there attracting the main force of German armoured reserves, and the Americans on the western flank *had* benefited and broken out, but not everyone believed that it had been planned that way in advance. The Americans and the Deputy Supreme Commander believed that in the days following D-Day General Montgomery was too cautious, too bound by the lessons he had learned as a junior officer in the trenches of the Western Front during World War I. They petitioned for his removal. He was slow to follow-up Rommel after El Alamein, the argument persisted, and everyone knew what had happened at Anzio when General John P. Lucas was too cautious and sat on the beach after landing instead of immediately heading inland for the Alban hills.

The Supreme Commander was not moved by the arguments. He kept his team intact, manipulating the senior prima-donnas to give of their best, using their rivalries to spur each to greater effort. If one man can be said to have ensured the success of the D-Day Landings it has to be General Eisenhower. Yet Monty was to claim that the Americans, including Eisenhower, did not ever really understand his plan, even though he had spelled it out well in advance of the invasion. In his October 1945 speech he had continued:

> This general plan was given out by me to the General Officers of the field armies in London in March 1944, that is to say, three months before D-Day. The operations developed in June, July and August exactly as planned.

The British Second Army's part in the plan was 'to make straight for Caen to establish the pivot while 6th Airborne Division was given the task of seizing the crossings over the Caen canal and of operating on our extreme left.'

The Second Army's sea-borne element was made up from two Corps: XXX Corps right under General G.C. Bucknall, landing on GOLD Beach, and 1st Corps under General Dempsey landing on JUNO and SWORD Beaches.

The preparatory fire-plan of bomber strikes, naval bombardment and tactical fighter support was common along all beaches, though timings varied slightly to allow for the different H-Hours occasioned by the variation in tide from west to east. However, there was one major difference in assault tactics between the American and British beaches, and that was in the use of specialised armour to provide close support to the assaulting infantry. The British had it, and the Americans did not, which has since resulted in a lot of criticism of the Americans.

The specialised armour used on GOLD, JUNO and SWORD Beaches had been developed by Major General Sir Percy Hobart's 79th Armoured Division. General Hobart had commanded the first tank brigade created in 1934, but his innovative ideas were strongly resisted by an Army high command which was still wedded to the horse. In 1938, while in Egypt, he built up the 7th Armoured Division, later to be known as 'The Desert Rats', but, still frustrated by a blinkered military hierarchy, he retired in 1940 to become a corporal in the Home Guard. In 1942 the débacle of the Dieppe raid made it clear that assaulting infantry needed close armoured support if they were to get ashore against determined opposition — that is, if they were to get ashore without suffering horrendous casualties.

The Chief of Staff to the Supreme Allied Commander (COSSAC), prompted by Winston Churchill, recalled Generãl Hobart to command 79th Armoured Division which from 1943 was given the task of developing armour to accompany a sea-borne assault. The range of equipment produced was extraordinary and with a colourful vocabulary to match:

DD Tanks: floating ('Donald Duck') Duplex Drive M4 Sherman tanks. Engine power could be transferred from the tracks to twin propellers and by erecting high canvas screens all around, it could float. Once on shore power was returned to the tracks and the screen jettisoned.

Crocodiles: mainly Churchill tanks modified to be flame throwers.

Crabs: generally a standard M4 Sherman tank fitted with an extended pair of arms carrying a flail. Its purpose was to clear minefields by beating the mines into explosion — a sort of military Hoover, beating, sweeping and cleaning at 1 $\frac{1}{2}$mph.

BARV: Beach Armoured Recovery Vehicle, usually, but not invariably, a Sherman. The gun turret was replaced by a superstructure allowing the tank to drive into deep water and through fitted winches or small dozer blades it was able to clear beaches of stranded vehicles.

Petard: an AVRE (Armoured Vehicle Royal Engineers, see below) based on a Churchill chassis with its normal main armament replaced by a 290mm short-barrelled mortar which fired a 40lb 'flying dustbin' explosive charge. Its function was to destroy enemy pillboxes and fixed obstructions.

Bobbin: a normal Churchill tank adapted to carry a 110yd-long spool of flexible coir coconut matting that could be laid in front of the vehicle to form a road over soft or slippery ground for itself and following vehicles.

ARK: 'Armoured Ramp Carrier', a turretless Churchill tank carrying two runways across its flat top. It could be used to provide a ramped road up and over a beach wall or could be dropped into ditches or streams to form a bridge.

AVRE: 'Armoured Vehicle Royal Engineers'. This is a generic title for a whole range of specialised armoured vehicles. They include those above plus others carrying huge 2-ton bundles of wood called fàscines used to fill holes in roadways, bridge-layers, craned recovery vehicles, etc.

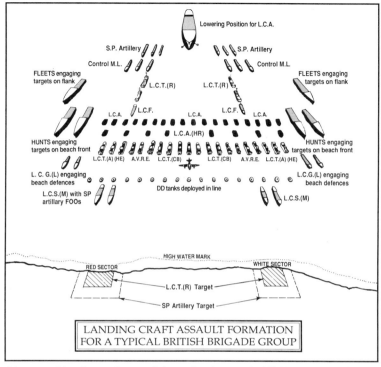

Diagram of landing craft assault formation for a typical British Brigade Group

Key:
LCA	Landing craft, Assault
ML	Motor Launch
LCT(R)	Landing Craft, Tank (Rocket)
LCF	Ladfing Craft, Flak
LCA(HR)	Landing Craft, Assault (Hedgerow). Used to explode enemy mine-fields
LCT(A)(HE)	Landing Craft, Tank (Armoured) (High Explosive)
AVRE	Assault Vehicle, Royal Engineers
LCT(CB)	Landing Craft, Tank (Concrete Buster)
DD Tanks	Duplex Drive Tanks, fitted with flotation device
LCS(M)	Landing Craft, Support (Medium)
LCGL	Landing Craft, Gun (Large)
FOO	Forward Observation Officer to direct artillery fire

The specialised armoured vehicles were known to most soldiers as 'Hobart's Funnies'. Despite the complexity of types, the Funnies divide

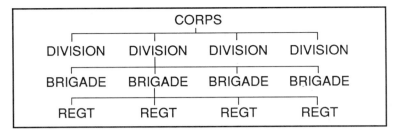

Diagram of a simplistic 'square' command structure. In this example there are sixty-four regiments in the Corps

into just two main varieties defined by their purpose. One is the DD tank, designed to float ashore with the infantry in order to provide immediate fire support, the other is the rest. The second collective type came from General Hobart's recognition that the destruction of the few Churchill tanks that were landed at Dieppe was due to the failure of the assault engineers to clear the mines and obstacles, or to prepare exits from the beach. The Americans, offered the opportunity to have their pick of the Funnies, opted for a few DD tanks but decided against having any specialised armour to help them to get off the beaches. There is no doubt that the men of the 1st and 29th Divisions could have done with some Funnies on D-Day. British casualties were comparatively low, thanks in part to the specialised armoured support. Casualties on OMAHA Beach might have been dramatically fewer if armoured obstacle clearance had been possible. However, it must be remembered that the landings on UTAH Beach went almost perfectly without the specialised armoured support and that OMAHA Beach was backed by very high cliffs where armoured manoeuvrability was limited. Therefore while *any* additional obstacle clearance capability would have been effective on OMAHA Beach on D-Day, the presence of the 79th Division equipment might not have made a major difference. The question remains however, 'Why didn't the Americans take the Funnies?'

General Montgomery had no doubts about the value of the DD tank or the Funnies of 79th Armoured Division and divided the division's force between the three British beaches, putting its components under command of the assaulting division. Thus, in the planned approach of the sea armada to the French shore along GOLD, JUNO and SWORD Beaches, the DD tanks and AVREs were prominent. See diagram on page 119.

GOLD BEACH

Assault Time:	0725 hours
Leading Formations:	8th Armoured Brigade DD tanks
	6th Battalion, The Green Howards.
	5th Battalion East Yorkshire Regiment
	1st Battalion Dorset Regiment
	1st Battalion Royal Hampshire Regiment
50th Division Commander:	Major General D.A.H. Graham
Bombarding Force K:	Cruisers : HMS *Orion*
	HMS *Ajax*
	HMS *Argonaut*
	HMS *Emerald*
	Gunboat : HNMS *Flores* (Dutch)
	13 destroyers including ORP *Krakowiak* (Polish)
German Defenders:	716th Division
	352nd Division
352nd Div Commander:	Lieutenant General Dietrich Kraiss
716th Div Commander:	Lieutenant General Wilhelm Richter

The Plan (Map 7, page 123)

The D-Day mission of the 50th Northumbrian Division was complicated. It was to capture Bayeux, to establish a bridgehead across the N13 Bayeux to Caen road, to take the German gun battery at Longues and to establish contact with flanking formations. This latter involved the capture of Port en Bessin to link up with Americans from OMAHA Beach.

The beach was subdivided into JIG and KING sectors, west and east respectively, and each sector given to a brigade formation to attack. Thus there were two leading brigades, 231st Brigade on JIG and 69th Brigade on KING. The non-military reader can be easily misled by statements such as 'the attack was made on a brigade front'. A simplistic and apparently correct interpretation would be that a whole brigade's complement of men attacked simultaneously. Nothing could be further from the truth. The art of delegation from higher to lower formation steadily reduces the size of force. On KING, for example, the formation which attacked at H-Hour was not of brigade size but the size of two battalions — the Green Howards and the East Yorkshires. An elemental view of the structure of the British Corps is shown in the diagram on page 120, but this ignores the complications of forces being attached for special purposes such as Royal Engineers and DD tanks. It does, however, help to keep the relative sizes of formations in perspective.

The divisional plan was that the 231st Brigade would land east of le Hamel (Asnelles), clear the village and then drive along the coast towards the Americans at Port en Bessin, the latter having been taken by commandos from the rear. The 69th Brigade was to land west of la

Rivière (Ver sur Mer) and to head inland towards the N13 Bayeux to Caen road. The leading brigades were thus moving apart. Into the gap between them at 1000 hours were to come two follow-up brigades, the 56th and the 151st. Their task was to take Bayeux.

What Happened on D-Day

The weather was bad, probably at its worst, opposite GOLD Beach. When the troops clambered down into their LCA's some 10,000yd offshore, the Force 5 wind was whipping up waves of over 4ft. Those who had survived sea sickness in the relative calm of their transport ship now fell prey to the pitching and rolling of their small craft. Despite their hyoscine hydrobromide anti-sea sickness tablets few men failed to fill their 'Bags, Vomit'. So rough was the sea that it was decided that the DD tanks, scheduled to land ahead of the infantry, would not be launched but would be landed directly onto the beach.

The air and naval bombardment followed the pattern established on the American beaches, although the British opted for a longer naval bombardment. Anticipating that the German armoured threat would come against the British beaches, General Montgomery had over 130 warships in the British Task Force begin firing twenty minutes before the Americans at 0530 hours and continue until H-Hour. His idea was to give the assaulting troops the maximum opportunity to break through the crust of defenders and to move inland at speed in preparation for an armoured counter-attack.

The leading formations touched down within a minute or two of their allotted time and at the right place. At le Hamel a German strongpoint held out until noon causing considerable casualties by raking the beach with machine-gun fire. At la Rivière the preliminary bombardment had been very effective and there was relatively little opposition, although German resistance was stiffer than had been anticipated because of the presence of troops of the 352nd Division. The reserve and follow-up formations were landed successfully and while not all of the D-Day objectives had been achieved, by the end of the day the 50th Division beachhead measured six miles by six, the N13 was in sight, reconnaissance patrols had entered the outskirts of Bayeux and 47th Royal Marine Commando were on the heights above Port en Bessin. Although there had not been any contact with the Americans from OMAHA Beach in the west, contact had been established with the Canadians from JUNO Beach in the east.

BATTLEFIELD TOUR C

The tour starts at Bayeux and then covers the GOLD sector coastline from Port en Bessin in the west, to Longues and then Arromanches. After Arromanches come le Hamel and la Rivière, followed by General Montgomery's châteaux at Creully. The tour ends at Tierceville.

Total distance 40km (25 miles). Total time 6¹/₂ hours.
Map IGN 6, 1:100,000 'Caen/Cherbourg'.

Bayeux
This historical city was one of the D-Day objectives of 50th Northumbrian Division landing on GOLD Beach, and reconnaissance patrols of the 151st Brigade entered its outskirts at about 2030 hours on the

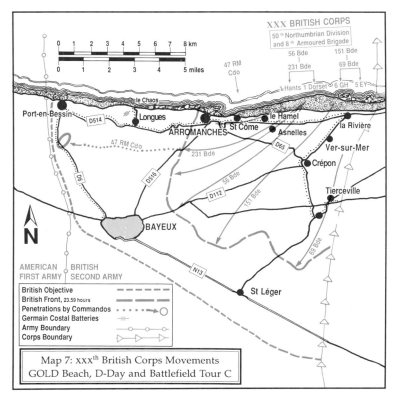

Map 7: xxxth British Corps Movements
GOLD Beach, D-Day and Battlefield Tour C

evening of 6 June. They spent the night in the Saint Sulpice suburb.

There is no disputing Bayeux's claim to be the first major town to be liberated. German resistance was weak. German General Kraiss had vacillated, moving troops of his 915th Division towards the Cotentin Peninsula where he had heard of the American drops, then pulling back towards Bayeux as the British approached, and finally withdrawing.

By midday on 7 June members of 56th Brigade and tanks were entering the city. Miraculously its historic treasures — the cathedral, the ancient and picturesque buildings — were all spared the fearful damage that many Norman towns endured. The precious Bayeux Tapestry had long since been removed and was hidden in the Château de Sources near Le Mans. The citizens celebrated their liberation by flying their Tricolores, but their greatest joy was to be shown a week later.

At 1530 hours on 14 June a car with a loudspeaker raced through the narrow streets blazoning the marvellous news that General de Gaulle was in France and would address the citizens at the Place du Château (now renamed Place Gen de Gaulle) in half an hour. De Gaulle was the focus of Free French determination, the symbol of resistance, the hope for a return to freedom. His single-minded crusade often made him unpopular with Allied leaders, but his broadcasts on the forbidden BBC rallied the spirit of France, the morale of the resistance workers: 'My aim, my only aim, is to act in such a way that ... the French forces shall not cease to fight, that the French forces shall be present at the Victory ....'

De Gaulle's aim was fulfilled. French forces landed with the Commandos at Ouistreham, with Leclerc at UTAH Beach. French pilots flew with the RAF, and they made a meaningful contribution to the Invasion.

In Bayeux de Gaulle was greeted with rapture. His long, lonely struggle had been rewarded fruit. The citizens, at first almost too overwhelmed with emotion to react, eventually broke into joyous cheers. De Gaulle marched through the main street. The people fell in behind him in a spontaneous victory procession, singing the *Marseillaise*. The moment is crystallised for posterity on a striking bas relief (see page 127) in Bayeux, and by an oft-published photograph which shows him towering above the surrounding townsfolk.

As there was no French government recognised by the Allies, they were urged to accept General de Gaulle's 'Comité Français de la Libération Nationale' as the provisional government of France. His reception in Normandy on this historic visit — unanimously acclaimed by all political shades — convinced them that they should recognise it.

De Gaulle then created Monsieur Raymond Triboulet (see page 246) Sous-Prefet of the newly liberated *arrondissement* — the first political appointment to be made in Free France.

The intervening week had been very active for the British. Their engineers constructed a wide road round the city, its ancient streets being too narrow for modern military transport. That road was the prototype of today's ring road. Hospitals were set up, as were supply dumps, and Bayeux was to remain as a major supply base for the Allies on the route of the American 'Red Ball Express' all the way to Brussels.

Musée de la Bataille de Normandie

Boulevard Fabian Ware (over the road from CWGC Cemetery).

This superb museum is, as its name explains, about the battle for Normandy, *not* the landings, which are covered in the museums at Arromanches, Bénouville, Ste Mère Eglise and UTAH Beach.

It is the story of the 'battle of the hedgerows', of 'the break out', of operations EPSOM, GOODWOOD, TOTALISE and TRIDENT, and the 'Falaise Pocket'. They are vividly portrayed in this modern, custom-built, museum, with a cinema (35 minute film with French or English sound showing the battle for Normandy), diorama of the Falaise Pocket battle and separate galleries for the Americans, British, Canadians and Germans and some impressive new set-piece, life-sized scenes, with models and original 1944 vehicles.

Allow plenty of time (at least $1\frac{1}{2}$ hours) if you wish not only to see the film, but to peruse thoroughly the fascinating documents, photographs, posters and newspapers. There are also uniforms and weapons, rations and maps.

The book stall is temptingly well equipped (even with books in English) about World War II and Normandy; there is a snack/drinks dispensing machine, clean WCs and ample free parking.

Outside are a number of well-restored vehicles, guns, and tanks (including a Hetzer SP anti-tank gun, a Sherman tank, a Churchill AVRE, and a 40mm Bofors gun).

The basis for the original museum, now extended, was the personal collection of local dentist, collector, historian, researcher and author of many books on the Normandy Campaigns, Dr Jean Pierre Benamou. Local buffs quibble about the over-emphasis on German exhibits to the detriment of the recognition of Resistance and Free French participation, and an embarrassment of riches where documents are concerned. It is, indisputably, a magnificent museum.

Bayeux Commonwealth War Graves Commission Cemetery and Memorial

Boulevard Gen Fabian Ware (founder of the CWGC), near museum.

Sherman tank outside the Bayeux Museum

This beautifully maintained cemetery is the largest British World War II cemetery in France. It contains 4,648 graves — 3,935 from the United Kingdom, 181 from Canada, 17 from Australia, 8 from New Zealand, 1 from South Africa, 25 from Poland, 3 from France, 2 from Czechoslovakia, 2 from Italy, 7 from Russia, 466 from Germany and 1 unidentified. The internationality of the invasion, and the support given by the Commonwealth and other Allies, is well illustrated here. All lie under standard CWGC headstones, but the visitor will note that each nationality has a differently shaped top to its stones. In the shelter to the left of the stone of remembrance, the visitors' book and cemetery register are housed in a bronze box.

Over the road is the Bayeux Memorial to the Missing with no known graves, designed by Philip Hepworth. It bears the names of 1,805 Commonwealth service men and women (1,537 from Britain, 270 from Canada and 1 from South Africa) who fell in the Battle of Normandy.

The Latin inscription above reads '*NOS A GUILIELMO VICTI VICTORIS PATRIAM LIBERAVIMUS*'. (See page 10.)

Bayeux Cathedral
Inside is a plaque to commemorate the 56th Brigade, who liberated the city. By the south gate is a plaque to the 50th Inf Div Rue de Bouchers. The Badge of 50th Infantry Division is on the exterior wall.

British Memorial to the Missing, Bayeux

Place Général de Gaulle
Column to commemorate De Gaulle's speech on 14 June 1944. Plaque on wall of Sous-Prefecture, erected on 14 December 1946.

Bayeux Liberation Memorial
Ring road (boulevard d'Eindhoven), opposite Hotel Novotel.
This striking bas relief, sculptured by M. Lamourdedieu commemorates the D-Day Landings and General de Gaulle's historic visit to Bayeux on 14 June. In its grassed centre is the holder for the Flame of Liberty, rekindled each year. (See page 128.)

Take the D6 road north-west out of Bayeux following signs to Port en Bessin. After crossing the D514 follow signs to 'le Port', drive over the lock road to the hard standing below the cliffs and stop.

In order to supply the estimated one million gallons of petrol that the Liberation Army would need, pipe lines were laid under the sea from England. The PLUTO (Pipe Line Under The Ocean) system in its various forms supplied most of the needs of the Allies from August 1944 onwards. At Escures, a village on the D6 en route to Port en Bessin, there was a junction in the PLUTO line that started in Port en Bessin. The main line ran some 200yd to the east of the D6 to Bayeux and around behind the British War Cemetery and the other leg ran to the N13 to the west and thence to Cherbourg. The idea for PLUTO was said to have

The Ceremony of the Flame

In September each year young people come from Eindhoven in Holland (the first Dutch city to be liberated) to Bayeux, (the first French city to be liberated,) to rekindle the Flame of Liberty and Friendship at the Bayeux Liberation Memorial. This event started in 1945.

Sporting and social events take place between young Dutch boys and girls and local Bayeux youngsters. Then at 2100 hours on 16 September the local band accompanies the procession from the town centre to the memorial. There local World War II veterans, resistance workers and others bring their standards as the children, the Mayor of Bayeux and members of the Bayeux Council, members of the twinning committee and representatives from Eindhoven Council congregate. Messages of remembrance, friendship and peace are exchanged, the flame is rekindled and the young light their torches from the flame, around which stand young people bearing the national flags of France, Holland, Great Britain, America and Canada. During this moving ceremony the national anthems of the countries are also played.

The following morning the flame starts its journey to Holland (630 kilometres) transported by young Dutch cyclists. At 2100 hours on 18 September the young people with their torches arrive in Eindhoven and the flame is rekindled there at a similar ceremony, which is always extremely well attended by veterans' organisations and local people.

come from Lord Louis Mountbatten and development began in 1942. There were two different types of pipe. The main one, laid at sea, was flexible and called HAMEL. The name derived from the first letters of the names of the men who invented it: Mr H.A. Hammick of the Iraq Petroleum Company and Mr B.J. Ellis of the Burmah Oil Company. The pipe was towed across the Channel from Southampton in 70-mile lengths on enormous 'cotton reels' called CONUNDRUMS, each with a wound weight of 1,600 tons, which is roughly the weight of a destroyer. The whole operation, known as 'Force PLUTO', was run by about a thousand men from a main base at Southampton and pipe laying began as soon as the routes across the Channel had been cleared of mines.

Port en Bessin

This busy, picturesque town, with its fishing harbour and pleasure port, boasts a tower built by Vauban in 1694 which, though damaged, survived the invasion. Below it on the beaches, beside the hard, is a Todt bunker, facing out to sea, with a memorial plaque to the 47th (RM) Commando. On the jetty of the outer harbour is a Com du Deb Mon Sig,

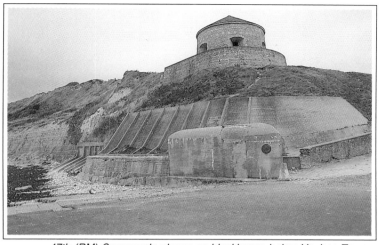

47th (RM) Commando plaque on blockhouse below Vauban Tower,
Port en Bessin

commemorating the landings. On the cliffs overlooking the port there are gun emplacements and bunkers. These formidable positions were attacked by the 47th (RM) Commando on the afternoon of D+1, having worked their way, some ten miles, along the coast from Le Hamel carrying almost 90lb per man of weapons and supplies. Two of the strongpoints were taken with the help of a naval bombardment from HMS *Emerald's* 6in guns, rocket-firing Typhoons and artillery smoke. A German counter-attack, supported by flak-ships in the harbour, retook one of the hills, but at dusk the German commander and 100 men surrendered, though sadly the commandos' troop leader, Captain T.F. Cousins, was killed by a sniper. The commandos had captured a port which was to play an important role in maintaining the flow of vital supplies, and they had secured the junction between the British 50th Division on GOLD Beach and the US 1st Division on OMAHA Beach. By 14 June the port was handling more than 1,000 tons of supplies a day, much more than it had ever done in peacetime.

Return to the D514 coast road and turn east following signs to Longues or Arromanches. At the crossroads after the church in Longues turn left towards the sea following signs to 'Battéries de Longues'.

Longues (le Chaos) Battery
Construction began in September 1943. There were four gun positions,

German gun battery at Longues

a two-storey observation bunker, anti-aircraft guns, defence works and search lights.

The battery has been well preserved and progressively restored in recent years, although rock falls at the cliff's edge have put the observation bunker out of bounds. Each of the four casemates contained a 155mm rapid-firing naval gun and, although 1,500 tons of bombs had been dropped around the weapons, they were totally protected by the thick concrete. When the Allied naval bombardment began, just before sunrise, the Longues battery replied. Its first salvo straddled HMS *Bulolo* carrying the HQ of the British XXX Corps. HMS *Ajax* immediately brought her own 6in guns into action and, at a range of some $7\frac{1}{2}$ miles, despatched 114 rounds at Longues. Within 20 minutes the battery was silenced. Three guns were destroyed, and it was claimed that shells from *Ajax* entered the slits of two of the casemates. The fourth gun recommenced firing in the afternoon and, following a duel with the French cruiser *George Leygues*, fell silent shortly after 1800 hours. The total number of shells fired at the battery was estimated to exceed 175. The garrison surrendered to British troops from Arromanches on D+1.

Return to the D514 and continue east following signs to Arromanches and then to 'Musée'. On entering Arromanches, the area around the coach park and the Syndicat d'Initiative has been renamed 'Place du Groupe de Lorraine'. There is a memorial there to 'Groupe Lorraine

Forces Aériennes Françaises Memorial, Place du Groupe Lorraine, Arromanches

Forces Aériennes Françaises Libres'.

Continue down and park in the car park on the sea front by the museum. There is a 'buy your own ticket' parking meter and a uniformed attendant to make sure that you use it.

Arromanches

Arromanches was made ready to resist an invasion, houses were blown up to improve fields of fire and machine-gun positions prepared, but the invaders did not come from the sea. The town was liberated on the afternoon of D-Day by the 1st Battalion Royal Hampshire Regiment who had landed on GOLD Beach and descended upon the German defenders from the heights of St Côme to the east, where they had spent the whole morning dislodging elements of the 352nd Division. There was very little damage to buildings in the town and only six civilian deaths, despite the naval fire support that preceded the Hampshires' arrival.

Arromanches is remembered for the harbour that was towed across the English Channel — the Mulberry. The name has no special meaning. When a code word was needed for the project the list of available words was consulted and the next one was 'Mulberry'. The idea of the floating harbour is said to have originated in a memo from Sir Winston Churchill to Vice-Admiral Mountbatten Chief of Combined Operations on 30 May 1942. It ran:

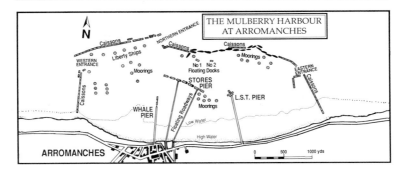

PIERS FOR USE ON BEACHES

CCO or deputy
They must float up and down with the tide. The anchor problem must be mastered. Let me have the best solution worked out. Don't argue the matter. The difficulties will argue for themselves.

In August 1942 the frontal attack on the harbour at Dieppe proved that such a thing should not be done again, and that since an army invading France would need harbours for re-supply, they would either have to be captured from behind or built in England and taken across the Channel. In June 1943 the Normandy coastline was chosen as the site for the invasion and in August, at the Quebec Conference, the Combined Chiefs of Staff approved the construction of artificial harbours code named Mulberry. The Directorate of Ports and Inland War Transport under Sir Bruce White, and a special staff known as 'X Staff' in Norfolk House, St James's Square, London under Commodore Hughes-Hallett set to work. They had less than ten months to design and construct two harbours each roughly the size of that at Dover. One was to be for the Americans at OMAHA Beach, the other for the British at Arromanches.

The basic concept was simple. First a line of sixty old ships would be sunk off all five beaches. It would provide an elemental breakwater on the landward side of which the seas would be calmed. These ships were called 'Gooseberries'. Inside the Gooseberries, off OMAHA Beach and Arromanches, a huge semi-circle of hollow concrete boxes, called caissons and codenamed Phoenixes, would be sunk to form a harbour wall. In all 146 Phoenixes would be needed, the sixty largest displacing over 6,000 tons of water each. Work on the caissons went on around the country, but the greatest number in a single location were built in pits dug along the banks of the River Thames. The movement of men and material from the Mulberry caissons to the shore was to be along flexible

The Mulberry Harbour at Arromanches

roadways, named Whales or Beetles, running over floating pontoons. Seven miles of floating roadway was constructed for the two harbours. Even so it was felt that in order for the ships within the Mulberry Harbour to be unloaded quickly enough a ferry service of small craft would be needed and over 2,000 vessels with some 15,000 staff were earmarked for the purpose. The whole complex Mulberry structure involved over four hundred towed components weighing $1\frac{1}{2}$ million tons.

The Mulberry force began to sail to France on the afternoon of D-Day. The aim was to have both harbours in place within fourteen days. The British naval officer in charge of the Arromanches harbour had as his HQ ship the old light cruiser *Despatch*, bristling with anti-aircraft weapons and manned by soldiers with a major as the gunnery officer. It was the first time in over 280 years that the main armament of one of the ships of the king's navy had been manned by soldiers. Then it had been the Queen's Regiment and in 1944 it was again the Queen's.

The first Phoenix arrived at Arromanches at dawn on 9 June and by 18 June 115 had been sunk in a huge 5-mile-long arc around the town, from Tracy in the west to Asnelles in the east. The area was festooned with barrage balloons and anti-aircraft weapons, but the Luftwaffe was

Aerial view of Arromanches and the museum

very little in evidence. It was the weather that was to prove the enemy. Thirteen days after D-Day a north-east storm broke that shattered the OMAHA Mulberry and even settled the Gooseberry ships there in the mud so that they became ineffective. After the storm, which lasted three days, there was no harbour left at OMAHA and a special camp had to be established on the beach to accommodate some 1,100 crew from the small vessels destroyed or blown onto the beach. The Arromanches harbour fared better and survived, battered but serviceable, a thankful matter since there were over 150 craft in the harbour at the time. Nevertheless over 800 vessels were stranded and almost 50 per cent of the 650 LCTs (Landing Craft Tank) available for the assault and build up were incapacitated. The gale caused more damage in three days than the Germans did in two weeks, yet by the end of the year 39,000 vehicles and 220,000 soldiers had made dry landings at Arromanches.

The town calls itself 'Arromanches Port Winston' and has adopted a coat of arms showing the British Lion, and the American Eagle, breaking the chains of occupation. The parking area, once tennis courts, faces the museum, the 'Exposition Permanente du Débarquement', designed by François Carpentier, sometime Mayor of Arromanches. Financed by the Comité du Débarquement, it was opened by President René Coty in 1954. It has a working model of the Landing Beaches, a model of the Mulberry Harbour, a diorama of the landings with a commentary by

View of Arromanches and the Napoleonic Memorial, St Côme

Monsieur Triboulet, the first Sous-Prefet appointed by General de Gaulle in June 1944, a variety of documentary exhibits and a 1944 British Admiralty film of the construction of Port Winston. Commentaries are given in French, English and German.

The museum is very popular and it is wise to avoid it immediately after lunch when the scrum can make a visit uncomfortable. Outside are a number of artillery pieces and on the hill behind a Sherman tank.

Leave Arromanches eastwards on the D514 coast road, a difficult thing to do because of the one-way streets and the curious road signs. The target is St Côme de Fresne where the tall column carrying the Virgin Mary stands on the cliffs above Arromanches.

St Côme de Fresne

There are the remains of German bunkers which contained field guns which menaced GOLD Beach and were silenced by HMS *Belfast*. In the sea, the remains of the Arromanches Mulberry Harbour can be seen, and to the left below is Arromanches itself. There is an orientation table here with an information kiosk below, and a footpath which leads down to the Arromanches museum.This position, and Arromanches itself, were taken by the Hampshires before 2100 hours on D-Day, by which time the 50th Division bridgehead measured 5 miles by 5 miles.

47th (RM) Commando landed on your right on GOLD Beach, just

A D-DAY MEMORY

Lieutenant L.E. Anderson. The Border Regiment. Beach Signals officer, No 1 Beach Group. Landed on GOLD beach.

"D-Day 7.30am. An assault craft heading for GOLD Beach with some of my signallers and myself, together with a Naval boatswain. The rule was that, as long as we were at sea, the boatswain was in charge, but that I was in command as soon as we touched shore. We ended up on an underwater obstacle sticking up through the bottom of the boat, which made it spin round like a roulette wheel in the rough sea. There then ensued what seemed to be a lengthy discussion between the boatswain and myself as to whether we were at sea or ashore. Ultimately I won and he let down the ramp. With the famous cry of 'Follow me chaps', I ran off the ramp to find myself up to my neck in water."

below these heights, and swung around behind you to your left, heading for Port-en-Bessin, a 10-mile march away, due west.

On the downward slope of the hill along the footpath towards Arromanches is a memorial marker — an obelisk with two cannon balls in a plinth. It commemorates a Napoleonic naval battle off Arromanches 133 years earlier in 1811 and was erected on the 100th anniversary.

Continue on the D514 downhill to the crossroads with the D205 just east of le Hamel (Asnelles). Stop and walk 100yds down the small road to the sea.

D514/D205 Crossroads

At low tide this is the best view of the remaining Phoenixes of the Arromanches Mulberry, built to last a hundred days and still around after almost fifty years. There is also a typical German beach bunker with deadly fields of fire across the open beaches, yet many of the German guns had limited traverse and this was to save countless British lives.

The Germans had assumed that any landing would be made close to high tide so that landing craft could float over the beach obstacles. Therefore they had arranged their arcs of fire to cover an area of the beach between the high water level and the sea wall. The landings, however, were made before half tide and thus not into the teeth of small arms opposition at the moment of landing.

The 1st Battalion Royal Hampshires landed on the beach here and to the east, accompanied by DD tanks and Hobart's Funnies. With the armour ahead of them as they jumped from their landing craft the soldiers of the Hampshires had the firepower to cover their movement

British troops coming ashore at GOLD Beach King Sector on D-Day

across the sands. The German fire from le Hamel was heavy and the first three CRABS which flailed their way up the beach were bogged down or stopped by an anti-tank gun. A fourth CRAB beat its way into le Hamel giving cover for two companies of the Hampshires to bypass the village and to take Asnelles behind it. Even so it was not until after mid-day that the area was cleared. The enemy was able to hold out longer here because both the CO and the 2nd in Command of the Hampshires became casualties early on and, therefore, due to lack of central control, no requests were made for naval fire support against the strongpoints.

It was about one mile to the east along this stretch of beach that 47th (RM) Commando landed at 0825 hours having boarded their LCAs some seven miles offshore. The fourteen LCAs headed in towards Arromanches and had to turn east towards their correct beach at le Hamel, losing four craft in the process. There was considerable confusion at the water's edge with burning vehicles, mined beach obstacles and a strong running tide, not to mention the intense German machine-gun and mortar fire, and the commandos got mixed up with the Hampshires and the Dorsets who had landed further east at la Rivière

German bunker at Asnelles with Mulberry in the background

and were working their way west. All of this delayed their departure for Port en Bessin until 1945, otherwise it might have been taken on D-Day.

Continue to the crossroads in the centre of Asnelles where the D514 meets the Rue de Southampton. Stop.

Asnelles

The crossroads area is known as 'Place Alexander Stanier' after the commander of the 231st Infantry Brigade of the 50th Northumbrian Division, Sir Alexander Stanier Bart, DSO MC. At the small road 'Rue The Devonshire Regiment', there is a memorial to the division, the leading brigade the 231st, and three battalions — the 2nd Battalion Devonshire Regiment, the 1st Battalion Hampshire Regiment and the 1st Battalion the Dorset Regiment. The two assault battalions, the Hampshires and the Dorsets, received 'Normandy' as a battle honour. The Dorsets, landing off the beach here, were out of range of the German guns at le Hamel and, covered by the CRABS and working in conjunction with a variety of AVREs, were off the beach within the hour, having cleared three exits. It was as they moved south-west towards the high ground behind Arromanches, their main objective, that they met members of 47th (RM) Commando and encountered opposition from entrenched elements of the 352nd Division. However, by nightfall they had reached Ryes, three miles inland.

50th Northumbrian Division Memorial, Asnelles

Continue along the D514 making particular note of the wet and marshy land between the road and the beach. At the small crossroads just after the sign indicating that you are entering Ver sur Mer, stop.

KING Sector, GOLD Beach and Stan Hollis VC

The German defences here were mainly sighted along the line of the road or just south of it on the high ground. Thus they overlooked the wet and marshy land below, which was mined and traversed by an anti-tank ditch. It was here that Hobart's Funnies really paid off. Without them the infantry might have been stuck, floundering in the soft ground under the eyes of the defenders and without a scrap of cover. The weather was so bad that the DD tanks were not launched, and they and the Funnies were landed directly onto the beach. This assault, scheduled for 0725 hours, was the earliest of the British landings. The small road leading to the sea was an exit from KING Beach where the 6th Battalion Green Howards landed on 6 June 1944. On page 137 is a view down it in June 1944.

The main enemy position here was known as the Fleury battery and consisted of four 150mm guns in concrete casemates on Mont Fleury. It was situated in what is now a new housing estate half a mile uphill from where you are and to the west of the exit. The casemates are still there today though steadily being masked by new houses.

The assault of the 69th Brigade was led by the 6th Battalion Green

Howards under Lieutenant Colonel Robin Hastings. In his force for the landing he had a squadron of the 4th/7th Dragoon Guards with DD tanks, two teams of AVRE and flail tanks (CRABS), one platoon of medium machine-guns of the 2nd Cheshire Regiment and a detachment of Royal Engineers. The front on which the force landed was some 900yd long and in addition to the Mont Fleury position the Germans had half a dozen pillboxes with machine-guns and at least one 105mm cannon. Colonel Hastings allocated different tasks to different companies within his battalion, though all had the general purpose of reaching the high ground of the Meauvaines Ridge on the skyline to the south of your present position. D Company was given the task of capturing Mont Fleury.

The Green Howards had boarded their transport ship, the *Empire Lance*, on 1 June and spent their time in physical exercise, cleaning their weapons, attending religious services on deck (General Montgomery's message to them, indeed to his whole force before the invasion, had said, 'Let us pray that "The Lord Mighty in Battle" will go forth with our armies ....') eating and sleeping. They also studied aerial photographs updated daily showing the beach obstacles. Their ship assembled with others of Force G for GOLD off the Solent and after the 24-hours delay everyone was relieved to hear the Navy announce over the Tannoy system at 1700 hours on 5 June, 'At 1745 hours this ship will weigh anchor and in passage with the remainder of the armada, sail for the coast of France'. At 0315 hours on 6 June reveille was sounded and at 0500 hours seven miles offshore the battalion began climbing into the assault craft that the *Empire Lance* had carried under her davits. As everywhere else along the invasion coast the sea was rough. Very soon everyone was wet and almost everyone was sick. At 0730 hours the leading companies began their final approach to the beach. Overhead thundered the express train shells from HMS *Warspite* accompanied by the smaller calibre fire of cruisers and destroyers. 25-pounders of the Royal Artillery, firing from landing craft, added their enthusiasm to the affair and in the last few yards came the dragon's roar of the rocket ships, 100yd out, firing four salvos a minute of ninety rockets each.

The Green Howards had most of their casualties at sea on the run in, including some who drowned, unable to wade the last stretch to the shore after having been dropped too far out. But despite heavy mortar and machine-gun fire Captain F.H. Honeyman led 'A' Company across the beach to the sea wall, and there, in a grenade and sten-gun battle, aided by Lance Sergeant H. Prenty and Lance Corporal A. Joyce, cleared the beach of small arms opposition. All three were killed five days later and were posthumously awarded the Military Cross and

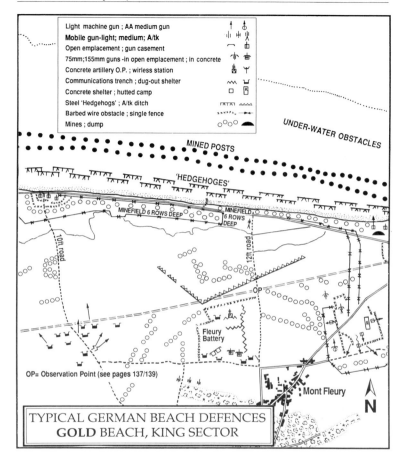

Light machine gun ; AA medium gun
Mobile gun-light; medium; A/tk
Open emplacement ; gun casement
75mm;155mm guns -in open emplacement ; in concrete
Concrete artillery O.P. ; wirless station
Communications trench ; dug-out shelter
Concrete shelter ; hutted camp
Steel 'Hedgehogs' ; A/tk ditch
Barbed wire obstacle ; single fence
Mines ; dump

UNDER-WATER OBSTACLES

MINED POSTS

'HEDGEHOGES'

MINEFIELD 6 ROWS DEEP

MINEFIELD 6 ROWS DEEP

10th road

12th road

OP

Fleury Battery

OP= Observation Point (see pages 137/139)

Mont Fleury

N

TYPICAL GERMAN BEACH DEFENCES
GOLD BEACH, KING SECTOR

Military Medals respectively for their action on the beach. Captain Honeyman is buried in the Commonwealth War Graves Commission cemetery at Bayeux.

'D' Company meanwhile, had come up against mines and deep water and suffered casualties. The company commander, Major R. Lofthouse, rallied his men in conjunction with his CSM, Stan Hollis, and personally led them off the beach and up the road you can see, on route to their objective at Mount Fleury. He too was awarded the Military Cross. CSM Hollis, however, won the VC, the only man to do so on D-

Admiral Ramsay's HQ, Ver-Sur-Mer

Day. His citation reads:

In Normandy, on June 6th, 1944, during the assault on the beaches and the Mont Fleury battery, CSM Hollis's Company Commander noticed that two of the pill-boxes had been by-passed, and went with CSM Hollis to see that they were clear. When they were twenty yards from the pill-box a machine-gun opened fire from the slit, and CSM Hollis instantly rushed straight at the pill-box, recharged his magazine, threw a grenade in through the door, and fired his Sten gun into it, killing two Germans and making the remainder prisoner. He then cleared several Germans from a neighbouring trench. By his action he undoubtedly saved his Company from being fired on heavily from the rear, and enabled them to open the main beach exit. Later the same day, in the village of Crépon, the Company encountered a field gun and crew, armed with Spandaus, at a hundred yards range. CSM Hollis was put in command of a party to cover an attack on the gun, but the movement was held up. Seeing this, CSM Hollis pushed right forward to engage the gun with a PIAT [Projector Infantry Anti-tank] from a house at fifty yards range. He was observed by a sniper who fired and grazed his right cheek, and at the same moment the gun swung round and fired at point blank range into the house. To avoid the falling masonry CSM Hollis moved his party to an alternative position. Two of the enemy gun crew had by this time been killed, and the gun was destroyed shortly afterwards. He later found that two of his men had stayed behind in the house, and immediately volunteered to get them out. In full view of the enemy, who were continually firing at him, he went forward alone using a Bren gun to distract their attention from the other men. Under cover of his diversion the two men were able to get back.

Memorial to the Liberators of Ver-sur-Mer

Wherever fighting was heaviest CSM Hollis appeared, and in the course of a magnificent day's work he displayed the utmost gallantry, and on two separate occasions his courage and initiative prevented the enemy from holding up the advance at critical stages. It was largely through his heroism and resource that the Company's objectives were gained and casualties were not heavier, and by his own bravery he saved the lives of many of his men.

One of the authors, while at the Army Staff College at Camberley, was fortunate enough to accompany CSM Stan Hollis back to Normandy on a battlefield tour, and to hear at first hand what happened on the beach below you, on the road that passes you and on the ridge above. The citation gives the facts, but the following anecdote gives the man. We make no apologies for the language. This short gem is from Stan's own commentary and illustrates the indomitable spirit of the British soldier and his use of humour as a means of easing tension. We tell it like it was.

As 'D' Company made its way towards France the soldiers were busily arranging ammunition and other supplies into their landing craft.

CSM Hollis described the activities and then said — 'The Company Commander came to me — Major Lofthouse. He was a very good friend of mine. We had been through a lot of war together and had a good working relationship. He gave me a square box and he said, "Give one of these to each of the men Sergeant Major". So I opened it and it was a box of French letters, and I said, "What's to do? Are we going to fight 'em or fuck 'em?" '

A D-DAY MEMORY

Fitter/Gunner (R.A.) Harry Cooper. 514th Battery, 150th Regiment (South Notts Hussars) R.H.A. Landed on GOLD beach.

"Perhaps the most vivid memory for a good many, was when the advance party of the SNH led by the CO Colonel Mitchell, the 2I/C and the adjutant were driven ashore by Gunner Armitage. Having left the landing craft to descend the ramp, the vehicle went straight into the water almost completely disappearing from sight and had to be abandoned. It was recovered at low tide the next day, a great relief to members of 434th Battery whose NAAFI packs it contained."

CSM Stan Hollis died of a heart attack in the early 1970s and his VC was sold in 1983. It fetched £32,000.

Continue on the D517 to the crossroads with the D112 in the centre of Ver-sur-Mer (la Rivière). Stop.

The East Yorkshire Regiment had landed alongside the Green Howards and after them the Hertfordshires.

Ver-sur-Mer (la Rivière)

This is KING sector. the extreme eastern end of GOLD beach. The D514 continues into JUNO, LOVE sector. The road leading to the beach is Avénue Colonel J.R. Harper and on the corner is a memorial to the battalion he commanded, the 2nd Battalion Hertfordshire Regiment. Almost opposite, a few yards along the D514 towards JUNO, is a substantial house used by Admiral Sir Bertram Ramsay, Allied Naval Commander in Chief, as a headquarters and there is a memorial plaque on the gate post. On the corner diagonally opposite to the headquarters is a memorial anchor and plaque in honour of 'Our Liberators'. It was given by Julien Costy, 'A fisherman of Ver-sur-Mer'. On the beach road overlooking the beach there is a huge German bunker now used as a sailing equipment store.

Take the Avénue du 6 juin, the D112, via Crépon and the D65 to the crossroads with the D12. Continue straight over, down the narrow road, and stop just before the bridge over the stream which is the River Seulles. Look back to your right. This is Creullet.

The Château at Creullet

It was here on 9 June that General Montgomery parked his caravan and set up his Tactical HQ. He met Winston Churchill and Field-Marshal Smuts in the grand salon of the château on 12 June, and King George

VI on 16 June, when they came here after landing at Graye on JUNO Beach. However, shortly after arriving from Portsmouth, General Montgomery found that his caravan lacked one essential item — a chamber pot. An embarrassed ADC was sent to the château to borrow one. Madame de Druval who lived in the château, provided a small white pot, decorated with pink flowers.

On 22 June he moved to Blay, six miles west of Bayeux, to be nearer the Americans. Presumably the ADC gave the '*vase de nuit*', as Monty called it, back to Madame de Druval.

The road that you have followed from Crépon, the D65, is the one taken by the 4th/7th Dragoon Guards on D-Day after landing on GOLD Beach KING sector with the Green Howards. 1st and 3rd troops carrying infantry on their tanks arrived here, just before the bridge over the River Seulles, and found a German Tiger blocking the way. However, the Tiger disappeared and the 4th/7th were able to drive on in cautious single file through the village of Creully without opposition.

Continue over the river and up the hill turning left by the French 'Poilu' World War I Memorial into the square in Creully. Stop.

Creully Square

Inside the Mairie is part of a Royal Engineers commemorative stone and a bronze plaque with the following inscription, 'During the critical days of June and July 1944, the world listened to news of the Battle of Normandy, broadcast by radio correspondents of many nations from the BBC studio in the tower of this castle.' The tower may be climbed. You will probably have to ask at the Mairie office to be shown these memorials, so visit during normal office hours and also not at weekends.

Continue straight through Creully on the D93 towards Tierceville. On meeting the D12 turn right and drive about one hundred yards to the Y junction where there is a memorial.

Tierceville Eros

This copy of Eros, made in cement, was constructed by 179 Special Field Company RE, on 23 August 1944. Owing to a heavy frost it lost a leg, but in 1971 members of the French Resistance restored it with the help of the Comité du Débarquement.

This area became an RE enclave from early in the invasion, as the engineers sought to clear roads, mend bridges, demolish obstacles and build airstrips. Some three miles south-east from here is the small village of le Fresne Camilly where it was planned to have a 5,000yd strip by last light on D+6 (six days after D-Day). The work was the responsibility of 23rd Airfield Construction Group RE which began landing just east of

Monty's HQ, The Château at Creullet

Ver-sur-Mer on JUNO MIKE on 7 June. Two officers then set off on bicycles to reconnoitre le Fresne Camilly in anticipation of the arrival of the remainder of the group over the next few days. On 8 June the 88th Road Construction Company staged here. On 9 June 250th Pioneer Company moved in and that evening Group HQ was established here and was immediately attacked by the Luftwaffe. Work on the airstrip had begun on 9 June and the site was completed on 17 June.

Eros probably commemorates the Royal Engineers presence in general and HQ 23rd Airfield Construction Group in particular. If any reader knows more, please let us know.

TOURIST INFORMATION

TOURIST OFFICES

Bayeaux
1 rue des Cuisiniers.
Helpful and can provide hotel bookings, restaurant lists, books, maps, tourist information and guided tours.

Arromanches
By coach park, Place Groupe Lorraine. Basic information only.

MUSEUMS

Bayeux
Memorial Museum of the Battle of Normandy.
Has British, Canadian, American and German sections, with a cinema, diorama, large book stall, and clean WCs.
Open: June, July, August, 0900-

Creully Château, used for BBC broadcasts

1900; 1 November-28 February, 1030-1230, 1400-1830 weekends only; rest of year 1000-1230, 1400-1830.
Entrance fee payable. Reduction for children, groups. No charge for D-Day veterans.
☎ 31 92 9341

Arromanches
Landings Museum.
Comité du Débarquement maintained. On sea front. Large car parking area in front (parking charge payable), cinema, diorama, models, book stall and WCs. *Very* crowded in season.
Open: 13 May-3 September, 0900-1830; rest of year, 0900-1130, 1400-1730 or 1830 (open 1000 Mondays).
Entrance fee payable. Reduction for children, senior citizens, groups. Combined ticket with Bénouville Museum (see below).
☎ 31 22 3431.

Musée de l'Aviation Militaire
Rue du Maréchal Joffre.
Private museum with more than 500 authentic models of planes, seaplanes, helicopters from 1930 onwards, expecially of 1944.
Open: every day in the season 0900-1900.
Entrance fee payable. Reduction for children.
☎ 31 21 4075.

HOTELS

Arromanches
**Grand Hotel.
On outskirts on road from Bayeux.
Newly refurbished.
**Hotel de la Marine.
Promenade, super sea view.
* Hotel de Normandie.
Near museum.

Bayeux
Several new hotels have sprung up in Bayeux since 1984. It is now ex-

tremely well served for hotels and makes an excellent and highly recommended base.

***Hotel Novotel.
(The old Pacary) Rond Pont de Vaucelles (on ring road).
Smartly refurbished. Heated outdoor pool.Highly recommended.
☎ 31 92 1611

***Lion d'Or. Rue Saint Jean.
The traditional hotel in the heart of the town. Highly recommended.
☎ 31 92 06 90

**Hotel de Luxembourg/Hotel de Brunville.
Family owned, well run. Good value.
☎ 31 92 0004.

**Hotel d'Argouges.
Pleasant. No restaurant.
☎ 31 92 8886.

CAMPING

Sites throughout the sector. Apply to Bayeux Tourist Office above.

RESTAURANTS

Arromanches
Hotels de la Marine and de Normandie above.
Sea food specialities. Numerous *crêperies* — sit down or take away.

Bayeux
Hotel Novotel. Surprisingly good food for a modern hotel chain.
Lion d'Or. Superb cuisine. Crab omelettes, famous since June 1944 when Allied War Correspondents ate them here 48 hours after landings.
La Rapière, rue Saint Jean. Great cooking, friendly service.
Le Drakkar. Pleasant, reasonable, near Lion d'Or.
Hotel Notre Dame, opposite the cathedral. Attractive dining room.
The town abounds, too, with mouthwatering cake shops.

Creully
There are a couple of restaurants in this interesting town and a useful supermarket.

Port en Bessin
Numerous speciality fish restaurants and *crêperies* near the busy fishing port area and the Vauban tower. A good place for lunch.

OTHER ATTRACTIONS

Bayeux
The famous Tapestry de la Reine Mathilde, now in a splendid new setting. Cinema with English language commentary. Book and souvenir shop. Entrance fee payable. ☎ 31 92 0548.

Musée Baron Gérard. Paintings, lace, porcelain etc. Tapestry ticket gives you entry here too.
☎ 31 92 1421.

The Cathedral. Splendid Gothic/Norman building with a variety of later additions, especially to the main steeple. Guided visits (and of historic Bayeux) from Tourist Office

Port en Bessin
Many sporting activities — especially on the water — also new 18-hole golf course and club.
☎ 21 21 7294.

Creully
The château originated in 1035, taken by the English in 1356, reconstructed by Louis XI in 1471, had a chequered history until bought by the council in 1946, was used by the BBC in June 1944 (see page 145). Equally historic church.
Old Mill (on River Seulles).

8

JUNO AND SWORD BEACHES

The area covered by these two beaches falls neatly into a one-day tour and so they are both included in the same battlefield tour. However, the background to each beach is first dealt with separately.

JUNO BEACH

Assault Time:	0745 hours
Leading Formations:	6th Armoured Regiment (1st Hussars) DD tanks
	The Royal Winnipeg Rifles
	The Regina Rifle Regiment
	10th Armoured Regiment (Fort Garry Horse) DD Tanks
	The Queens Own Rifles of Canada
	The North Shore (New Brunswick) Regiment
3rd Canadian Division Commander:	Major General R.F.L. Keller
Bombarding Force E:	Cruisers : HMS *Belfast* (flagship)
	HMS *Diadem*
	Eleven destroyers including the FFS *Combattante* (French)
German Defenders:	716th Infantry Division
716th Division Commander:	Lieutenant General Wilhelm Richter

The Canadian 3rd Division had been selected to take part in the invasion in July 1943 and trained in assault landings in Scotland and in interservice co-operation, particularly with the Royal Navy, in the Portsmouth area.Throughout training the 3rd Division worked closely with the 2nd Armoured Brigade which was equipped with DD tanks. On 26 May the Division was sealed into its concentration area and on 1 June 15,000 Canadians and 9,000 British, who together made up the Division, began to board at Southampton. Four days later they set sail for France.

The Plan (Map 8 page 154)
JUNO Beach was divided into two sectors which, looking inland from the sea to the land, were right to left MIKE and NAN. The assault was on a

two-brigade front with the 7th Brigade Group landing at Courseulles on MIKE sector and 8th Brigade Group landing at Bernières on NAN sector. Each brigade had DD floating tank support from the 6th Armoured and 10th Armoured Regiments respectively, plus fire support from the 107mm mortars of the Cameron Highlanders of Ottawa. 8th Brigade was to be closely followed by elements of the 4th Special Service Brigade charged with mopping up, making contact with 3rd British Division Commandos and taking the German radar station at Douvres la Délivrande. The 9th Brigade, the follow-up brigade, was scheduled to land in either the 7th or the 8th Brigade areas according to the progress made.

The Canadians' objectives were the capture and clearance of the coastal villages and towns along JUNO Beach, particularly Courseulles, St Aubin and Bernières, and of specific villages inland. The Division had three objective lines, 'Yew', 'Elm' and 'Oak', which corresponded to three phases in their D-Day plan. The third phase was intended to be on 'Oak' which ran along the railway line just south of the N13 road from Caen to Bayeux. There the 3rd Division was to 're-organise in preparation for further advance and to repel enemy counter-attacks'.

What Happened on D-Day

During the night of 5 June, and early morning of 6 June, RAF Bomber Command hammered likely German defence positions along the Normandy coastline. At dawn the US Army Air Force took over and continued the attack until, as everywhere along the invasion front, the Royal Navy joined in. Off JUNO Beach were eleven destroyers and support craft adding their weight to the bombardment including two Canadian destroyers, the *Algonquin* and the *Sioux*.

The crossing for the troops at sea was rough and the time for the assault was put back by ten minutes because the heavy seas had delayed some of the landing craft, but despite considerable opposition from entrenched German positions relatively unaffected by the air and sea bombardments, the Canadians got ashore.

By the end of the day they were practically everywhere beyond 'Elm', their intermediate objective line, and some tanks had crossed 'Oak' but, without infantry support, had withdrawn. General Keller's men had made the greatest gains of all on D-Day, in some places seven miles inland. On their right they had made contact with the 50th Northumbrian Division at Creully, but on their left was a dangerous gap between themselves and the British 3rd Division. Into that gap General Eric Marcks, Commanding the German VXXXIV Corps, ordered Major General Edgar Feuchtinger's 21st Panzer Division. South of Caen, that evening, the leading elements of 12th SS Panzer Division began to arrive.

SWORD BEACH

Assault Time:	0725 hours	
Leading Formations:	8th Infantry Brigade Group	
	13th/18th Hussars DD Tanks	
	1st South Lancashire Regiment	
	2nd East Yorkshire Regiment	
3rd British Division		
Commander:	Major General T.G. Rennie	
Bombarding Force D:	Battleships:	HMS *Warspite*
		HMS *Ramillies*
	Monitor:	HMS *Roberts*
	Cruisers:	HMS *Mauritius* (flagship)
		HMS *Arethusa*
		HMS *Frobisher*
		HMS *Danal*
		ORP *Dragon* (Polish)
		13 destroyers including HNMS *Svenner* (Norwegian)
German Defenders:	716th Infantry Division	

The 3rd British Division had last been in action at Dunkirk, and most of its soldiers had since then only served on the Home Front. In a way it was similar in its battle experience to the 4th US Division that landed at UTAH Beach. In its training the Division had concentrated upon D-Day, and on the breaking of the Atlantic Wall which it identified with the moment of landing. That moment, because of the variation in the time of the tides between UTAH and SWORD, came one hour after the Americans and ninety minutes after dawn. Therefore the Germans would be both alert to a seaborne assault and able to see the landing craft coming in.

The Plan (Map 9 page 178)
In formulating his plan for 1st British Corps Lt General Crocker was acutely aware that the 21st Panzer Division was in or around Caen. His eastern flank was well defined by the Orne river and canal and they were to be secured by the Special Service Brigade and 6th Airborne Division, but if the 21st Panzer Division reacted quickly and 12th SS Panzer joined them, he would be much inferior in armoured strength and likely to be thrown back into the sea. Thus it was important that the extreme eastern division, the 3rd British Division, should break through the defence crust and move rapidly inland in anticipation of an armoured counter attack.

The plan of the Divisional Commander, Major General T.G. Rennie, was to attack on a single brigade front on White and Red sectors of QUEEN Beach. The 8th Infantry Brigade Group, the first to land, had a number of tasks: to secure the landing areas; to relieve 6th Airborne Division at Pegasus Bridge; 4th Commando to clear east to Ouistréham;

41st Royal Marine Commando to clear west to the Canadians at Langrune; and 1st Special Service Brigade to move east across Pegasus Bridge. Following up was the 185th Infantry Brigade Group. Their task was to pass through 8th Brigade and to 'seize Caen' — the most ambitious aim of all.

What Happened on D-Day

Naval Force S for SWORD gathered off the beach in the early hours of 6 June. Just before daylight a smoke screen was laid by aircraft between the ships and the coastal batteries at le Havre. In the morning gloom, thickened with smoke, four German E-Boats appeared, fired torpedoes, and vanished. The *Warspite* and the *Ramilles* had narrow misses but the Norwegian destroyer *Svenner* was hit in the boiler room and sank. That was all that Admiral Ramsay's invasion fleet saw of the German Navy on D-Day.

The bombardment followed the pattern employed everywhere else, though SWORD probably had the most intensive attention of all of the beaches, and was concentrated on a strip 3 miles long and $\frac{1}{2}$ mile deep.

Despite the rough seas, the DD tanks of the 13th/18th Hussars and the LCT-borne Funnies of the Engineer Assault Teams hit the beaches ahead of the LCAs of the infantry. Of the twenty-five tanks launched, twenty-one made the shore and these, together with the flail tanks of 22nd Royal Dragoons, gave immediate fire support to the infantry battalions.

Although the landing craft suffered considerable casualties from Teller mines on the beach obstacles, for almost five hours the landing sequence went pretty well to plan. The rising tide however reduced the beach to a width of 30yd and this caused congestion and confusion so that follow-up landings had to be delayed.

The South Lancashire and East Yorkshire Regiments were off the beaches within an hour, though stubborn German resistance continued in la Brêche, the centre of the landing beach, until around 1030 hours. The 185th Infantry Brigade began coming ashore mid-morning and passed through the 8th Brigade, but enemy resistance on the Periers Ridge, between Douvres and Bénouville, prevented rapid movement inland.

By the end of the day the 2nd Battalion Kings Shropshire Light Infantry, part of 185th Brigade, whose task it had been to ride on the tanks of the Staffordshire Yeomanry into Caen on 6 June, were still four miles short. Another forty-three days would pass before Caen fell.

BATTLEFIELD TOUR D

The tour begins in Caen, goes to JUNO Beach via the German radar station at Douvres, then east along SWORD Beach to Ouistreham.

Total distance: 55km (34 miles). Total time: 5½ hours.
Map: IGN 6, 1:100,000 'Caen/Cherbourg'.

Follow signs out of Caen pointing to the 'Mémorial' (museum) and la Folie Couvrechef in order to join the D22 leading to Buron in the north-west. At the crossroads in the centre of Buron turn left onto the D220 and stop in the Mairie square 200yd later.

Buron Memorials

The D220 road was a main axis for the Canadian forces moving inland from JUNO. It leads directly to the high ground at Carpiquet Airport three miles away to the south just beyond the N13. This was the object of the follow-up 9th Brigade Group. At the end of D-Day the Canadians had reached Villons les Buissons, 3½ miles north of here, and by around 0700 hours on 7 June the 9th Brigade, led by the North Nova Scotia Highlanders and the 27th Armoured Regiment (Sherbrooke Fusiliers), was advancing towards Buron. Just north of the village they came under fire from machine guns and anti-tank weapons, and a set-piece battle followed in which Canadians and Germans fought from house to house. It was not until midday that the village was secured. Meanwhile troops

Highland Light Infantry Memorial, Buron

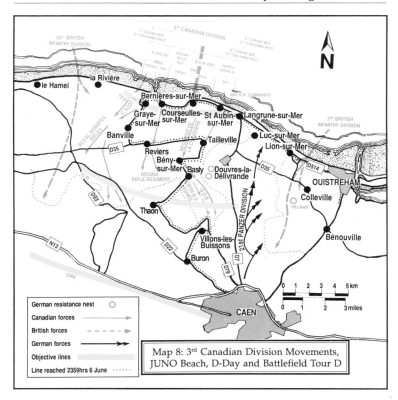

Map 8: 3rd Canadian Division Movements, JUNO Beach, D-Day and Battlefield Tour D

of the Highlanders and Sherbrookes not involved at Buron had pushed on to the edge of Carpiquet. The 9th Brigade was dangerously extended and, unknown to them, they were being watched by the enemy.

In a tower in the Abbey d'Ardenne on the north-western edge of Caen was Standarten Führer Kurt Meyer, the Commander of the 25th SS Panzer Grenadier Regiment of the 12th SS (Hitler Youth) Panzer Division, which had just arrived on the battlefield. At 1500 hours he launched a counter attack on Buron, hoping to drive to the sea in conjunction with 21st Panzer Division. Late in the afternoon the Canadians lost Buron and fell back to Villons les Buissons where they had begun the day. It had been a bloody struggle. The Highlanders had some 250 casualties and the Sherbrookes lost 21 cruiser tanks. The severity of the losses was compounded by reports that Canadian prisoners had been shot by SS troops. These and other murders formed the basis for

Sherbrooke Fusiliers Memorial, Buron

charges made against Meyer by a Canadian Military Court in December 1945. He was found guilty on three of five charges (on a charge of responsibility for twenty-three murders in the Buron area on 7 June 1944 he was acquitted) and sentenced to be shot. However, the sentence was commuted to life imprisonment and he was released in 1954.

The battle for the high ground of Carpiquet was to be a long and hard one against fanatical troops of the 12th SS Panzer Division. It had been created in 1943 from elements of the 1st SS (Leibstandarte Adolf Hitler) Division and though it had not been in battle before it had a high proportion of experienced officers and NCOs from the Russian Front. The bulk of the soldiers were youngsters under 18 years old straight out of military fitness camps and full of Nazi ideology. In all, the division, which was commanded by Brigadeführer Fritz Witt, had about 20,000 men and 150 tanks. It was a formidable fighting force and it held on to Buron and Carpiquet for another month.

At 0420 hours on 8 July a combined five-phase British and Canadian assault was launched towards Carpiquet, and once again the 9th Brigade advanced on Buron. As the second phase began the Highland Light Infantry of Canada and the Sherbrookes led off at 0730 hours and by 0830 hours were in the village. The 12th SS Panzer Division, now commanded by Kurt Meyer following Fritz Witt's death on 14 June, fought with the determination expected of them and it was not until early the following morning that the last SS man had been found and silenced. The Highland Light Infantry lost half of its attacking force in what had been its first real battle and it was to prove its bloodiest of the campaign with 262 casualties. The CO, Lieutenant Colonel F.M. Griffiths, was wounded and later received the DSO for his actions on that day.

There are memorials to the Highland Light Infantry and to the Sherbrooke Fusiliers here. The area is known as the Place des Canadians, and the Highland memorial was dedicated on 21 July 1969. The Sherbrooke memorial explains the origin of the name: ' ... recruited from the city of Sherbrooke Quebec Canada'. At Authie there is a memorial to the North Nova Scotia Highlanders.

Return to the D22 crossroads and carry straight across heading north towards Villons les Buissons. At the first road junction left, just short of the village, stop.

Hell's Corner
Here is the memorial to the 9th Canadian Infantry (Highland) Brigade that fought so determinedly between here and Buron from 6 June to 8 July. It was dedicated on 8 June 1984. The small road leading to the left is the Rue des Glengarrians.

Continue into the village and take the first turning right on Rue des Cambes along the château wall to the junction with the D79. Stop.

Norwegian Memorial
The Norwegian memorial has splendid bas relief panels representing the invasion and is dedicated to the memory of the Norwegian fighters from 1940 to 1945. The only Allied naval casualty from attacks by German naval forces on D-Day was the Norwegian destroyer *Svenner.*

Turn left onto the D79 and take the next turning left back into Villons. This is the 'Rue des Sherbrooke Fusiliers 7-11 June '44'. In the village fork right signed to Cairon and Thaon. Stop by the Mairie in Thaon.

Thaon Memorials
The street opposite is named 'Rue Régiment de la Chaudière' and a plaque on a small stone commemorates the liberation of the village by the 10th Armoured Regiment (Fort Garry Horse) on 6th June 1944. In the same way that it is unwise to be dogmatic about battle casualty figures, whether of men or equipment, it is unwise to assert that a particular place, house or person was 'liberated' at a specific time. The French remain enthusiastically grateful for their Liberation in 1944-5 and a vigorous internal contest has developed between claimants to being the 'first'. Failing the possibility of being a contender for a 'first' the next best thing is to have been liberated on D-Day, 6 June. Thaon says 'thank you

for Liberation on 6 June', while official Canadian records suggest that it was not occupied until 7 June.

The village is just south of 'Elm' the intermediate objective, and in the general line of advance of the 9th Infantry Brigade Group on 7 June. The Regiment de la Chaudière, part of 8th Infantry Brigade Group, came ashore at Bernières on NAN White just before 0830 hours on 6 June, supported by two DD squadrons of the 10th Armoured Regiment (Fort Garry Horse). By midnight the Chaudières had reached Bény four miles north of here and there can be little doubt that elements of their brigade had entered Thaon, but the main body of the force spent the night north of the village. The 9th Brigade had followed the 8th onto the beach at Bernières and pushed on early on 7 June into the actions at Buron.

Continue north on the D83 to Basly and there take the D79 to Bény sur Mer. Stop in the Place de l'Eglise.

Bény Memorial

Bény thanks the Canadians for Liberation on 6 June: *'Reconnaissance aux soldats Canadiens du Régiment de la Chaudière qui Liberèrent ce village 6 Juin 1944. Bény s/Mer. Aleppo.'* Canadians and French agree about Bény and HQ 8th Brigade actually signalled the Chaudières at 1535 hours on D-Day: 'Understand you are in Aleppo'. 'Aleppo' was the codename for Bény.

Take the small road below the church that goes due east towards Douvres la Délivrande. Go straight over the crossroads with the D219 onto the V3 signed Douvres. 500yd later as the road begins to fall, stop by a track on the left.

Douvres Radar Station

You are in the centre of what was the German radar station. It was mainly manned by the Luftwaffe with about 200 men and 5 officers. The site covered a large area some 300yd to your left and right. According to the time of year and state of the crops it is possible to see the remains of the northern blockhouses in the field to the left. There were two steel towers supporting the radar antennae, power coming from underground diesel generators. All-round defence was effected by minefields and barbed wire and the strong points were connected by tunnels. As can probably be seen, the position is on high ground and allows good observation over routes from the sea to the left and to Caen $7\frac{1}{2}$ miles away to the right.

The task of taking the radar station was one allocated to the North Shore (New Brunswick) Regiment. It had reached the village of Tailleville, barely a mile north of here, on the night of 6 June but when it moved off at 0700 hours on 7 June it met heavy opposition in the woods

9th Canadian Brigade Memorial

Hell's Corner

on the far side of the field to the left (north). Late in the afternoon the attack was abandoned and responsibility passed to the 51st Highland Division. That evening the 5th Battalion Black Watch attacked the station but made no impression, but unfortunately it seems that the Black Watch and the New Brunswicks may have briefly fought each other.

The station position, stretched along the 50 metre contour line, is plumb in the middle of the gap that existed between the British and Canadian armies, the gap that the 21st Panzer Division had its eyes on. At 1500 hours on 6 June, Major General Edgar Feuchtinger's 21st Panzer Division, led by its panzers, was advancing in two columns towards the beaches east of Douvres. Attentions from the British 3rd Division stayed the bulk of 21st Panzer but a small force of infantry and tanks reached Luc-sur-Mer to find their defences there still intact. The Canadians steeled themselves for a major assault as the Germans attempted to exploit the corridor separating the two divisions, but the follow-up armada of 250 gliders for 6AB Division arrived at 2100 hours and by the time that Feuchtinger had figured out where they had landed it was too dark to attack.

The radar station overlooked the corridor and General Dempsey, commanding the 2nd British Army, considered it essential that it should

Fort Garry Horse Memorial, Thaon

Régiment de la Chaudière Memorial, Bény

be taken so that his forces were not being watched and reported upon. On 7 June the 51st Highland Division tried again, supported by 80th Assault Squadron RE, but failed. On 11 June 48th RM Commando had

Remains of the bunker complex, Douvres Radar Station

a look at it but moved on without making a full assault.

Eventually a combat group of one squadron of 22nd Dragoons, 41st RM Commando and 26th Assault Squadron RE attacked uphill towards you from the village of Douvres ahead (with its twin church spires). Diversionary attacks were also made from the three other points of the compass. Four flail tanks led the way through the minefield, each followed by three AVREs. Heavy artillery gave covering fire. High explosive charges were laid against the blockhouses and the Commandos went in under cover of smoke. It was a short, furious battle, and the Germans raised the white flag. Eight tanks were damaged, but repairable, four AVREs were written off. Casualties were less than a dozen. Yet it was 17 June, almost 2 weeks after D-Day.

By walking up the path the northern block houses may be visited. Waterproof footwear is advisable in wet weather.

Return to the junction with the D219, turn right towards Tailleville. There turn left onto the D176.

Tailleville

This small village is at the end of the main exit road from NAN White at Bernières. When the 9th Brigade landing beach was chosen to be in the 8th Brigade area the only suitable spot was NAN White and the whole of the follow-up force had to come ashore there. The task of clearing

Tailleville had been given to C Company of the North Shore Regiment but stubborn resistance by the 736th Grenadier Regiment, whose HQ was in the village, prevented its capture until 2010 hours on 6 June, thus delaying the deployment of the 9th Brigade.

Continue westwards on the D35 towards Reviers and stop at the Canadian cemetery on the right.

Canadian War Cemetery, Bény-sur-Mer

This is the highest point for some miles around and there are two watch-towers from which excellent views may be obtained towards Courseul-les and JUNO Beach. At the bottom of the left-hand tower is a memorial tablet to the Cameron Highlanders of Ottawa. There are 2,049 graves in the cemetery, 2,044 of which are Canadian, including 335 officers and men of the 3rd Canadian Division who were killed on D-Day.

Continue towards the village of Reviers and as the road enters the village there is a road junction to the left with a small memorial.

Reviers Memorial

The small plaque and stone are to the Regina Rifle Regiment who liberated Reviers on D-Day. They and their fellow regiment of the 7th Brigade, the Royal Winnipeg Rifles, moved rapidly off the beach at Courseulles and by mid-morning were two miles inland. The Reginas had the specific task of seizing the crossings over the River Seulles which lie at the bottom of this hill. By 7 June they were astride the N13 at Bretteville-l'Orgueilleuse, west of Carpiquet. The following morning they had a head-on battle with Meyer's 12th SS Division at Bretteville when one of the German Panthers got to battalion HQ, where it was knocked out by a PIAT (Projector, Infantry, Anti-tank). Although they were over-run they held their ground and the Germans withdrew.

Continue down the hill and immediately after crossing the River Seulles turn right towards Banville. In the village turn right onto the D12 following the road through Graye sur Mer. Do not take the road to Courseulles. At the junction with the D514 coast road go straight across towards the beach and a tank in the dunes.

The Graye Churchill Tank

The Churchill tank is an AVRE with a petard and behind it is a Comité du Débarquement Memorial. Both are at the junction of the Green (left) and Red (right) sectors of MIKE Beach where the Royal Winnipeg Rifles came ashore together with elements of the 6th Canadian Armoured Regiment. They were to suffer 128 casualties the second heaviest Canadian regimental casualties of the day. Accompanying the Canadi-ans were the 1st and 2nd Troops of the 26th Assault Squadron Royal

CWGC Canadian Cemetery, Bény-sur-Mer

(inset) Typical CWGC register box and visitor's book

Engineers charged with clearing exits off the beach through the obstacles and the dunes. The leading AVRE touched down about 0755 hours, somewhat behind the DD tanks and assault infantry. Using flails and bridge-layers the squadron began to work its way through the wire and the mines and between the bunkers whose remains can still be seen. At this exit there was an anti-tank ditch and just south of it a flooded culvert connected to the River Seulles which barred the way inland. 2nd Troop's fascine tank dropped its bundle into the tank trap and 1st Troop went over it to the culvert where OC 1st Troop, Captain E.J. Hewitt, ordered his fascine tank to drop its bundle. The edges of the culvert had been cratered and instead of stopping, the tank slid slowly into the water until only its fascine was showing. The six members of the crew scrambled out but three, including the commander Lance Sergeant Ashton, were killed. The others, including the driver Bill Dunn, were severely wounded by mortar fire. That afternoon the three survivors were evacuated to England.

The sunken tank was incorporated into the exit road and there it stayed until 1976 when it was recovered by the citizens of Graye with help from British REs and REMEs and the 70-ton crane of Monsieur Desmezière, a local contractor. The ceremony inaugurating the tank as a memorial was attended by Bill Dunn.

There is an ephemeral signboard on the D514 junction commemorating the visit of Winston Churchill on 12 June and HM King George VI on 16 June. 1½ miles west, by the remains of a large German bunker, is the boundary between JUNO (where you are now) and GOLD Beaches.

Return to the D514 and turn left towards Courseulles. Cross the narrow swing bridge and immediately turn left along the harbour. Three hundred yards later stop near a Sherman tank.

Courseulles

This seaside town where the River Seulles reaches the sea was the aiming point for the 7th Canadian Infantry Brigade Group. Its task was to clear Courseulles and move rapidly inland to gain the crossings over the River Seulles. In a leap-frogging operation, including the possible use of the 9th Brigade the follow up force, the Canadians' target was the high ground around Carpiquet just south of the N13. The landing at Courseulles was complicated by the fact that there were reefs offshore and that in order to carry the landing craft over these a higher tide than desirable was needed if the obstacles were to be seen. The bad weather delayed the assault for some thirty minutes and most of the infantry landed ahead of the tanks although the latter were launched only 800yd out. The delay in the arrival of the tanks might have been greater but for

A D-DAY MEMORY

Captain John W. Winckworth, Adjutant 7th GHQ Troop RE. Landed on JUNO beach.

"As I had no opportunity to sleep from day break on D-Day until 0800 on D+3, my memories are vague and confused.

I do clearly remember that sometime on D-Day I paused to wash my hands free of oil and sand in a small stream just inland from NAN Beach. A few hours later I found that I had lost the signet ring my wife gave me on our wedding day, and which I regarded as something of a mascot. This was a serious loss to me. On mentioning it to one of my Sappers he said he'd go and have a look for it. Half an hour or so later he returned triumphant having found it with the aid of a mine detector. I still wear it today."

the initiative of some of the DD tank commanders, like Sergeant Leo Gariepy of B Squadron, who launched on their own initiative. Gariepy was probably the first to land.

The assault battalion here, east of the Seulles, was the Regina Rifles and A and B Companies hit the shore about 0800 hours. They were immediately fired upon from concrete strongpoints apparently unaffected by the pre-invasion bombardments. The following companies lost many men as their assault craft hit mined obstacles some 200yd out to sea and the Canadians had a hard struggle to get ashore. Operating to a detailed plan in which Courseulles had been divided up into twelve zones of responsibility, the Reginas, helped by the tanks of the 1st Hussars, (6th Canadian Armoured Regiment), forced their way through and around the town. Sergeant Gariepy's tank had passed a German coastal gun firing from a concrete bunker. Gariepy stopped, opened and shared a bottle of rum with the crew, then reversed and put seven rounds into the bunker. It stopped firing. At about 1200 hours the troops reached the area of Reviers and the Canadian War Cemetery visited earlier on this itinerary and by this time the Hussars had lost ten tanks.

In 1970 Jean Demota who owned the salvage rights off Courseulles recovered a Canadian Sherman DD from about three miles out at sea. Leo Gariepy had settled in France after the war and he, in conjunction with the Mayor of Courseulles, helped to raise money for the venture. Once on shore Canadian Army Engineers from Germany moved and restored the vehicle and in 1971 it was dedicated in the position it is in today. Leo Gariepy was present, although sadly he died a year later.

Churchill AVRE, Graye-sur-Mer

Comité du Débarquement Monument Signal, Graye-sur-Mer

There are a number of memorials within walking distance of the Sherman, now named Bold (Audacieux), *which has a talking machine and notice board explaining its history. All except the dagger are around the car park.*

Plaque describing the action on JUNO Beach.

A memorial commemorating de Gaulle's landing here on 14 June.

A plaque on one side of the beach entrance to the 1st Canadian Scottish Regiment erected on 6 June 1969.

A plaque on the other side of the beach entrance to the 458 officers and men of the Regina Regiment who fell from 1939 to 1945.

A memorial to the French destroyer *la Combattante*. She was part of the supporting Bombardment Group and was built in 1942 at the Fairfields Yard in Glasgow. On 23 February 1945 she disappeared in the North Sea. Sixty-five French and two Royal Navy sailors were lost.

Some 200yd to the west along the promenade is a huge memorial dagger to the 'Little Black Devils', the Royal Winnipeg Rifles, erected on 6 June 1964.

Memorial commemorating the landing of General de Gaulle at Courseulles

A D-DAY MEMORY

Sergeant Howard Roy (John) Clewlow. 13th/18th Hussars, Turret Gunner DD tank. Landed on SWORD beach.

"We had to do this DD training in Yarmouth and then right to the north in Scotland to Fort George. We did practice landings in these DDtanks. The problem was ... it was a bit of a hairy scary thing. We were sometimes under the submarine command ... we had to have Davis escape apparatus ... if the tank sunk we had to put on the Davis escape apparatus, a bottle on our front, we had the bag on our chest, we had a nose-clip where we took the oxygen in. The submarine lieutenant there said 'it's only to give you a bit of buoyancy, if you sink in these things, you'll go down so fast you'll get the bends.' I think it was in Yarmouth that they stuck us in a big tank, a big pit, and the water just flowed in and the water came up your body that quick ... you had to put the Davis escape apparatus on. The water went all the way over you and went up about twenty or thirty feet and you had to get out. If you couldn't swim you were a bit panicky.

DD tanks were compulsory. The regiment I was in did the charge of the Light Brigade and that was it, the charge of the Light Brigade came all again — officers with big moustaches and they all thought they were charging at Balaclava .... DD tanks were a bit weird. All it was was a canvas screen and that kept the tank afloat. There were about thirty-two air pillows. The canvas screen came up — there was a mesh that kept it up. So all there was between you and the bottom of the sea was this

Continue on the D514 following signs to Bernières and Ouistreham. As the road returns to the coast on entering Bernières there is a large clearing on the left with an armoured car and memorial. Stop.

Bernières

This was the centre of the assault area of the 8th Canadian Brigade Group and the sector here is NAN White. The assault regiment was the Queen's Own Rifles of Canada and they had the largest D-Day casualties of any Canadian unit. The Germans had constructed a '*Widerstandsnester*', a resistance nest, with mutually supporting weapons and good fields of fire using concrete bunkers and connecting trenches.

The Queen's Own landed at about 0815 hours without tank support (it was too rough to launch the DDs), and some 200yd east of its target — right in front of the *Widerstandsnester*. The leading company lost half its strength running over the beach to the sea wall, but thanks to the

canvas screen. The drive from the engine was transferred from two propellers at the back. You pulled a lever and it turned these two propellers and you went around 5 knots an hour and when you got heavy seas you really rocked .... In training we lost about three crews up in Scotland, they went down in about three hundred feet of water and we never saw them again. It was a bit weird when you thought what might happen on D-Day, but we took it philosophically ....

On D-Day there was a hell of a swell on ... we launched three miles out and the waves came up that high that we had to get out of the tanks and hold the canvas screen up, what a way to land .... We were awash with water, we were sea-sick, we had the Davis escape apparatus on, we had the ear phones on, you'd got a mike, you'd got a Mae West on, you didn't know which to pull next.

The real panic came when the other stuff started to back up on us. We were supposed to be ahead of it but we were going that slow that the other stuff was catching up on us. If we got too close the landing craft just ploughed into you and sunk you. They didn't worry. Their idea was to get to the shore and if you were in the way that was just your hard luck. Being outside the tank instead of inside we could see these landing craft coming closer and the stuff was going over from the battleships, the fifteen inch shells, sixteen inch shells. The air force was flying around at about five hundred feet. You didn't know what to do and you were sick and you'd got all this gear on. People say, 'Were you panicky?' There was that much confusion you hadn't got time to feel frightened."

support of a flak ship which came almost to the beach, the Germans were so effectively silenced that only snipers were active when the Regiment de la Chaudière began to land fifteen minutes later. The Canadians headed inland towards the D79 leading to Bény but German 88mm guns and machine guns stopped the advance. The divisional commander, not aware of the hold-up inland, ordered the follow-up brigade, the 9th, to land at Bernières on NAN White, and by mid-day the whole area was packed solid with men and equipment. It was one huge traffic jam and the 9th could not get moving until around 1600 hours. Without the jam the 9th might have reached Carpiquet that night before the 12th SS, and the battle for Caen *might* have been quite different.

On the beach here a sapper bulldozer driver silenced one pillbox by driving up behind it and filling it with sand and on 7 June Lt Fairbrother RE won the George Cross for moving ammunitions during an air raid.

*Comité du Débarquement Monument Signal and
Queen's Own Rifles armoured car, Bernières*

There is a six-wheeled armoured car of the Queen's Own Rifles and a Comité du Débarquement Memorial. 250yd to the east along the promenade is a German bunker in an area called Place du Canada and on and beside it are badly corroded memorials to the Queen's Own Rifles of Canada and Le Régiment de la Chaudière. The latter mentions the CO of the Regiment, Lieutenant Colonel Paul Mathion DSO ED, and 0700 hours as the landing hour. The official history says 'about 0830'.

General Keller, the Divisional Commander, left his HQ ship HMS *Hilary* at 1145 hours and by 1435 hours held his first conference in France in a small orchard outside Bernières. The press had established themselves in the centre of Bernières even earlier — at the Hotel de Grave (now in the 'Rue du Régiment de la Chaudière) by 1030 hours and there is a plaque there to commemorate 'The first HQ for journalists, photographers and moviemakers ....' One thing in particular surprised the local inhabitants. The 'Tommies' spoke French.

Continue on the D514 to St Aubin keeping to the sea front and stop by the German bunker.

St Aubin

The area to the east of here has no suitable beach for a major landing until la Brêche d'Hermanville is reached some four miles away. This

Bunker with Régiment de la Chaudiére plaque and
Queen's Own Rifles of Canada Memorial behind

dangerous gap was planned to be filled by rapid movement inland along the coast by special forces such as commandos. 48th RM Commando were to land at St Aubin and to move east, while 41st RM Commando were to land at Lion-sur-Mer and move west. They were to meet at Petit Enfer two miles east of Langrune, which was a German strongpoint.

The North Shore Regiment of Canada who landed here found that the German strongpoints were still in action despite the bombardment and it was thanks to their DD tanks, and AVREs using their petards, that they overcame the pillboxes. One bunker, silenced by a Royal Marine Centaur, had some seventy empty shell cases inside it as witness to the determination of the defenders. About four hours after landing the beach was clear except for one strongpoint and a number of snipers. The Commandos struck out to Langrune two miles east where they were held up until the following day by stubborn German opposition.

To the left of the bunker are memorials to the North Shore Regiment, 48th RM Commando and to Maurice Duclos, a French secret agent code-named 'Saint Jacques' who landed here on 4 August 1940. One hundred yards to the right of the bunker is a stone memorial to the Fort Garry Horse Regiment, erected in 1965.

Continue on the D514 to Langrune and stop in the open space on the promenade.

Canadian troops pour ashore on D-Day carrying bicycles and motor scooters on JUNO Beach, St Aubin

Langrune

This seafront road and the parallel one behind it, had been strongly fortified by the Germans. The sea wall was covered in barbed wire and there were trenches running along this road, while the parallel one inland had inset concrete machine gun positions. Lateral roads were blocked, the windows and doors of all the buildings were bricked up, and there were connecting underground passages. Coming in on the parallel road from St Aubin the Commandos enlisted the help of a naval bombardment and a Centaur tank of the Royal Marine Armoured Support Regiment to help them break through to the seafront. The Centaur ran out of ammunition and was replaced by another. That blew up on a minefield. Further efforts involved an anti-tank gun and a Sherman tank, which was also immobilised. It was a bitter hand-to-hand battle, which was not won until late on 7 June, when thirty-one German prisoners were taken. The memorial stone commemorates 48th RM Commando on one side and on the other, under the coat of arms of Langrune and the Croix de Guerre, carries the command '*Souviens-Toi* [Remember]'.

Continue on the D514 to Luc-sur-Mer and stop at the eastern end of the sea front.

48th (RM) Commando Memorial, Lagrune

Luc-sur-Mer/Petit Enfer

This is the boundary between JUNO and SWORD Beaches, the town itself being in SWORD. It was to here that the small detachment of 21st Panzer advanced on the evening of 6 June to find the defences intact, and it was the arrival of 6th AB Division's follow-up glider force that so stunned 21st Panzer's commanding general that by the time he recovered it was too dark to reinforce the advance. By the following day it was too late. The German strongpoint at Petit Enfer was cleared by 46th RM Commando who landed here at 0900 hours on 7 June without casualties. They were later joined by 41st RM Commando who had moved west from their landing at Lion-sur-Mer.

In front of the Hotel Beau Rivage at the eastern end of the sea front is a memorial commemorating *'le premier commando allié en Normandie, 28 Septembre 1941'* — the first allied commando raid on Normandy September 1941. The raid referred to was carried out on the night of 27 September 1941 by 5th Troop of No 1 Commando. As they landed a machine gun fired at them and the troop leader, Captain Davies, led an assault over the sea wall. Two more machine guns joined in and the commandos had to withdraw. Two commandos were missing and one was wounded. However, there is some confusion about where this took place and whether a German bicycle patrol had been involved. One

Memorial to the first Allied Commando raid on Normandy, 1941 Luc-sur-Mer, and Liberation 1944

account says that the commandos were heading for Courseulles and mistakenly landed at St Aubin. Whatever the truth, the memorial is here.

On the southern approach to the town (although not on this route) is a poorly maintained memorial to General Leclerc and his French Armoured Division.

Continue on the D514 to Lion-sur-Mer. The road curves inland and the village is easy to miss. Park as near as possible to the sea and walk through the houses to the centre of the promenade.

Lion-sur-Mer

41st RM Commando landed here having crossed the Channel in 'LCI(S)' — Landing Craft Infantry (Small) — and it was not until they had begun their far from comfortable journey that they found out their exact destination. At about 0845 hours the LCIs hit the sand some 200yd out under intense mortar and shell fire and not exactly on target. Lieutenant Colonel T.M. Gray, CO of 41st RM Commando, sent part of his force to the east to make contact with the South Lancashire Regiment and part into the town. Three tanks brought up in support were quickly knocked out. Between 1600 hours and 1800 hours destroyers fired upon German positions in the town but the defenders were still there the following morning. Just before a set-piece attack by a battalion of Lincolnshires

Lion-sur-Mer Memorial

supported by the Royal Ulster Rifles and 41st Commando, a raid by three Heinkels wounded the CO and some of the HQ staff. The attack was successful however, and that evening 41st Commando moved on to Luc-sur-Mer to join up with 46th Commando.

The memorial here, raised by the people of Lion, honours the memory of their liberation and French civilians who died in the fighting.

Continue on the D514 to the crossroads with the D60 to Hermanville sur Mer. Turn left up a road to a car park with a memorial in the centre.

La Brêche d'Hermanville

The upright memorial acknowledges a number of formations on either side:

'Pionniers alliées. Le 5 juin 2300 heures'. Presumably this acknowledges the work of the two midget submarines X20 and X23 that marked the edges of the British beaches, though they were actually in position by 2300 hours on 4 June in anticipation of   the   original date for D-Day of 5 June.

3rd Division. 27th Tank Brigade. Royal Marine Commandos. 101st Beach Sub Area. Commanded by Major General T.G. Rennie.

A D-DAY MEMORY

Lance Corporal P.L.M. Hennessey. A Sqn 13th/18th Royal Hussars DD tank. Landed on SWORD beach.

"My Regiment led the assault on SWORD Beach, at Lion-sur-Mer, in amphibious tanks, (DD), swimming in from 5,000 yards in a very rough sea. On the beach we dropped our canvas screen and opened fire. The tide was coming in and the water where we stood was getting deeper. We could not move further inland because the mines had not yet been cleared. A large wave swamped the engine, the tank was immobilised and was becoming flooded. We took to the rubber dinghy, but, hit by machine-gun fire we were sunk and obliged to swim for the shore, now some 300 yards away. Halfway there I clung to a post sticking up out of the water and glancing up I saw a large black Teller Mine attached to the top of it — I swam on.

We reached dry land where we lay wet and exhausted. One of our tanks came up beside us and the commander threw us a tin of self-heating soup, which we gratefully shared between the five of us. The beach was now an inferno of machine-gun, shell and mortar fire, but we reached the promenade behind it and met up with some other un-horsed tank crews. Later we were directed to make for the village of Hermanville where we found the survivors of 'A' Squadron and our five remaining serviceable tanks."

Ships making up the Gooseberry off SWORD Beach including the Courbet, the Centurion, the Durban and the Sumatra.
The phases of the Liberation.

In the ground before the memorial is the triangular emblem of the Division, to the left a Churchill AVRE presented on 6 June 1987 by 3rd British Armoured Division and in the small hut a model of the SWORD Beach Gooseberry.

3rd British Division's task on D-Day was to capture Caen. The plan was to land on a one-brigade front on QUEEN Beach using 8th Infantry Brigade who were to secure the landing areas and the high ground of the Periers Ridge just inland. Then, by moving both east and west, it was to link up with 6th AB Division and Canadians respectively. 185th Infantry Brigade, the follow-up force, was to pass through 8th Brigade and seize Caen eight miles inland. The assault brigade plan was to attack the beach on a two-battalion front supported by DD tanks.

Walk to the edge of the beach.

A D-DAY MEMORY

Lieutenant Commander Rupert Curtis RNVR Commander LCI (S)519.
Ferried Lord Lovat's Commandos ashore onto SWORD beach.

"My mind concentrated on finding a path through the underwater obstructions. Fortunately at that state of the tide, the tops of many of them were still visible sprouting above the surface of the sea, many with lethal attachments.

Working completely by instinct ... I felt I could discern a clear path through the menacing stakes. It looked a bit of a zig-zag but I backed my instinct and took 519 through with rapid helm orders. We emerged unscathed and I called for more power from the engine room to thrust our bows hard on to the beach to ensure as dry a landing as possible. Then we kept both engines running at half ahead to hold the bows in position. At that moment we were hit by armour-piercing shells which zipped through the port Oerlikon gunshield but fortunately missed both gunners and our Commandos. 502 (Lieut John Seymour, RANVR) carrying the remainder of Brigade Headquarters, beached very close on our port hand and as she did so she was hit by armour-piercing shells which penetrated four petrol tanks and hit the port engine and put it out of action. Perhaps I should explain that each of our craft carried 4,000 gallons of high octane petrol in non-sealing tanks just abaft the bridge. Had the enemy used incendiary or high explosive ammunition 502 would have blown up and disintegrated in a sheet of flame which would have engulfed them and us in 519. The Brigade would almost certainly have lost its trusted leader, Lord Lovat, and most of the Headquarters group. At the end of the day I estimated that half of the Brigade might not have got ashore but for the fact that the Germans used solid shot on us which was really meant for tanks.

I gave the order for our troops to land. The ramps were manhandled over the bows by our well trained ramp crew under Sub-Lieutenant Stephen Garrett, RNVR, and our Commandos began to land in about three feet of water as calmly as though on exercise. Each man carried some 80lb of weaponry and gear and clambering down our narrow landing bows on to a danger-laden strip of sand could have been no fun.

We bade goodbye to Lord Lovat and wished him good luck .... As the Commandos crossed the fireswept sands the skirl of Bill Millin's pipes gave heart and encouragement to all. Then we began the tricky task of coming off the beach stern first through the obstructions to make way for our second wave of LCI (S) to come in to land No 3 Commando and No 45 Commando Royal Marines."

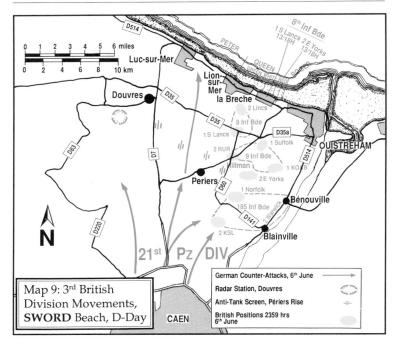

Map 9: 3rd British Division Movements, **SWORD** Beach, D-Day

German Counter-Attacks, 6th June
Radar Station, Douvres
Anti-Tank Screen, Périers Rise
British Positions 2359 hrs 6th June

You are now approximately in the centre of SWORD Beach, on QUEEN sector. To your left is QUEEN White. To the right is QUEEN Red. The assault infantry on QUEEN White was the 1st South Lancashire Regiment, and on Red, the 2nd East Yorkshire Regiment. The sight that faced the defenders in the early light of 6 June 1944 must have been terrifying. The sea was full of ships, the sky alive with aeroplanes. In the gap between flew hundreds of barrage balloons, while, driving rapidly towards the shore, were landing craft carrying the infantry. In front of them were the DD floating tanks of the 13th/18th Hussars.

SWORD Beach stretches for about $1\frac{1}{2}$ miles in each direction, and it received the most concentrated pre-assault bombardment of all beaches, being drenched with fire from every gun available to the 3rd Division. The area between here and Ouistreham was thought to be under observation from the big guns at le Havre. Bomber Command destroyed the 16in guns before D-Day and the 11in guns were blanked off by a smoke screen out at sea. In the bad visibility, a group of LCTs lost their direction and cut across the main axis, hitting and sinking two

Churchill AVRE, la Brêche

DD tanks. Twenty-one DDs made it ashore, and it was these tanks, and the other specialised armour of Major General Sir Percy Hobart's 79th Armoured Division, that enabled major exits to be cleared from Red and White sectors within 2 hours. Further west, the Americans would regret that their Army Commander, General Omar Bradley, had decided to do without 'Hobart's Funnies'. There were no minefields on the beaches here, though the lateral and exit roads were heavily mined. All minefields were clearly marked and many turned out to be dummy ones — probably one of Rommel's ideas. There was, however, a double row of ramps out at sea, and a large number of 'hedgehogs', many of which were mined. Following the initial landings just after low tide, the sea came in rapidly, hiding the obstacles and making their clearance difficult. The water pushed those troops ashore up against the promenade where you now are, and they suffered heavily from enemy machine-gun and small-arms fire, particular on Red from the 3 o'clock direction. Into this turmoil at 0820 hours came No 4 Commando, complete with Piper Bill Millin, playing *Highland Laddie*, and stormed their way past the German shoreline defences, re-organised, then moved off to Ouistreham, which can be seen to the right. There the Free French took the Casino, which was a German strongpoint covering SWORD Beach, and, with its capture, the assault infantry were better able to move off the beaches.

As the troops and equipment poured ashore, the incoming tide reduced the width of the beach available and shore and exits became jammed. Orders were given to delay the landing of follow-up units, but, before the congestion could ease, accurate German artillery fire began to fall. It was a puzzle trying to decide how the Germans were working out where to aim their guns. Suddenly someone realised that they were ranging on the barrage balloons, which were being put up on the beaches against low level aircraft attack. The balloons were quickly lowered. They were no loss. The only significant air attack came from eight aircraft the following morning. One was shot down and crashed 300yd away to the right from the beach exit. Slightly right of centre, 1,100yd out to sea, was the wreck of the French Cruiser, *le Courbet*. She had last helped the British by covering their evacuation from Cherbourg in June 1940. The old ship, without engine or guns, and filled with concrete, had to be towed across the Channel to be sunk as a Gooseberry blockship to provide protection for craft landing on SWORD Beach. There she proudly flew the Tricolore and the Cross of Lorraine, making her a favourite target for the Germans, ignorant of her helplessness. She was shelled, bombed and attacked by human torpedoes. German radio on 8 July claimed that their attacks had driven the *Courbet* ashore. The illusion of her importance was fostered by other Allied ships, which fired from directly behind her cover. Each of the five invasion beaches was provided with a temporary harbour named a Gooseberry. The shelter was formed by sinking old ships in a line off the beach. Over sixty were sunk altogether. The majority were merchantmen, though a few warships were used — the battleship *Courbet*, the British battleship *Centurion*, the cruiser *Durban*, and the Dutch cruiser *Sumatra*.

The order of landing of 8th Infantry Brigade Group from H-Hour at 0725 hours was:

1 A and B Squadrons of 13th/18th Hussars. DD tanks.
2 Eight Royal Engineer obstacle-gapping teams, each one made up of two flail tanks of 22nd Dragoons, three AVREs and one bulldozer.
3 Two obstacle-clearing teams, each of four flail tanks and four AVREs.
4 The assault infantry:
   QUEEN White — two companies of the 1st South Lancashire Regiment.
   QUEEN Red — two companies of the 2nd East Yorkshire Regiment.
5 At 0745 hours the HQ elements of the assault infantry plus their remaining two companies.
6 At 0810 hours HQ and C Squadron 13th/18th Hussars.
7 At 0825 hours the 1st Suffolk Regiment, the reserve battalion, plus 8th Brigade alternative Main HQ.
8 At 1000 hours the 185th Brigade.

A D-DAY MEMORY

Piper Bill Millin. 1st Special Service Brigade. Landed on SWORD Beach.

"Lovat got into the water first ... I followed closely behind him ... he's a man about six feet tall and, of course, the water came up to his knees ... I thought it would be alright for me so I jumped into the water and it came up to my waist ... anyway I managed to struggle forward and then I started to play the bagpipes. I played *Highland Laddie* towards the beach which was very much under fire. At that time there were several ... three ... burning tanks, there were bodies lying at the water's edge, face down floating back and forward. Some [men] were frantically digging in ... others crouched behind a low sea wall. No one could get off the beach. The road and the exits were under heavy fire. I made for cover at an exit ... a narrow road and I just got there behind a group of soldiers and they were all cut down ... about nine or twelve of them .. they were shouting and seeing me with the kilt and the bagpipes they shouted, 'Jock! Get the medics'.

Then I looked around and to my horror I saw this tank coming off a landing craft with the flails going and making straight for the road. I tried to catch the commmander's attention ... his head was sticking out of the turret ... but he paid no attention and went straight in and churned all the bodies up. Then I saw Lovat and the Brigade Major standing at the water's edge. Everyone else was lying down. So I joined them. He [Lovat] asked me to play. That sounded rather ridiculous to me to play the bagpipes and entertain people just like on Brighton sands in peacetime. Anyway ... I started the pipes up and marched up and down. This Sergeant came running over, 'Get down you mad bastard. You're attracting attention on us'. Anyway I continued marching up and down until we moved off the beach."

Inevitably there was overlapping between the phases, but for over four hours the landings went to the timetable. Then because of crowding on the beaches a half-hour delay was ordered. However, despite the loss of the officer commanding the beach clearance who was killed on landing and over 50 per cent casualties to the armoured vehicles, nine beach exits were opened by 1130 hours. Meanwhile the German resistance on Periers Ridge was holding up movement inland, preventing the 185th Brigade from getting on towards Caen. There has been criticism of 3rd Division's performance following its successful landing. It has been suggested that their hearts and minds had been set on breaking the Atlantic Wall, and when that had been achieved relatively

Piper Millin with friends on the beach where he landed, at La Brêche

easily, the Division was left without a clear purpose. Troops accustomed to a defensive mentality in England since Dunkirk favoured digging in instead of aggressive forward movement. The German resistance on the Periers Ridge, and at the strongpoints named Hillman and Morris, leeched away the armour strength needed for the drive to Caen, where the 21st Panzer Division was gathering itself to strike. General Bradley, commanding the United States First Army, expressed himself as 'keenly disappointed' at the performance of General Dempsey's Second British Army. In September 1944, lack of drive of the ground forces was said to have been one of the reasons why the 1st AB Division was cut off at Arnhem. General Dempsey was again the Army Commander.

Continue on the D157 for just under half a mile to the junction of the 'Place 6 juin' on the left and 'Boulevard du 3me Division' on the right. Turn right and continue to the village outskirts. Stop by the memorial.

De Gaulle Memorial
It was from this spot that Roger Weitzel, the captain of the *Courbet*, took a sample of French soil on 7 June which he later presented to de Gaulle.

Return to the D514 and continue to the traffic light junction at Colleville-Montgomery Plage. Stop on the verge. There are now a number of choices.

Museum to No 4 Commando, Ouistreham

Colleville-Montgomery Plage
To the left on either side of the road leading to the beach are two memorials. One erected on 6 June 1945 commemorates the first British graves of 6 June 1944, the Anglo-French forces of General Montgomery and Capitaine Kieffer (of No 10 Inter Allied Commando) and the decision of Colleville-sur-Mer to change its name to Colleville-Montgomery. On the other side of the road is another memorial to Commandant Kieffer

A D-DAY MEMORY

Major Patrick A. Porteous, VC. RA No 4 Commando. Landed on SWORD beach.

"0600hrs, 6th June 1944. Reached lowering position — grey sky — sea very choppy — ships of every shape and size as far as the eye can see.

As my landing craft hit the water, we took a large wave over the side. A foot of water swilling round our feet. Get pumping — Damn! The bilge pumps not working, so get bailing with tin hats. Difficult in very cramped conditions on board, especially as some men being sick. Still making water as every wave slops some more in. Approaching the beach all hell going on but anything preferable to this horrible boat. As the front ramps went down, she finally sank in three feet of water."

and the French forces of No. 4 Commando. Also on the left is a private SWORD landing museum which may, or may not, be open. The road to the right leads to Hermanville where there is a Commonwealth War Graves Commission cemetery. At the entrance road to the cemetery there is a well with a plaque which explains that the well was operational from D-Day and thirty or so taps along the church wall supplied over 7 million litres of water during the month of June 1944. Opposite on the wall of the Mairie two plaques record that 3rd Infantry Division set up its HQ there on D-Day and that the area became a major medical facility.

Continue on the D514 to the western edge of Ouistreham where the road leads into a wide, open space, with the large Casino building on the left and the Musée de No 4 Commando on the right.

Ouistreham-Riva-Bella

The central task of 1st SS (Special Service) Brigade was to land in the Ouistreham area, to clear the town and then to move on to link up with the airborne forces at Pegasus Bridge. The Brigade, under command of 3rd British Division was made up of:

Brigade Commander. Brigadier The Lord Lovat, DSO MC
No 3 Commando. Lieutenant Colonel P. Young, DSO MC
No 4 Commando. Lieutenant Colonel R.W.F. Dawson.
No 6 Commando. Lieutenant Colonel D. Mills-Roberts DSO MC.
No 45 RM Commando. Lieutenant Colonel N.C. Ries
No 1 and No 8 French Troops of No 10 Inter-Allied Commando. Captain Philippe Kieffer.

In addition, No 41 RM Commando (Lieutenant Colonel T.M. Gray) also came under command but had an independent role at Lion-sur-Mer.

No 4 Commando landed at 0820 hours on QUEEN Beach Red sector and came under heavy fire, suffering about forty casualties. Lieutenant Colonel Robert Dawson was wounded in the leg and in the head but No 4 Commando reached the D514 and set off in the direction that you have driven towards Ouistreham, led by Philippe Kieffer. A local gendarme whom they met on route gave them details of German strengths and positions and after a fierce fight, in which both sides sustained many casualties, Kieffer's men took the Casino. No 4 Commando then moved on towards Pegasus Bridge.

Lord Lovat, SS Brigade HQ and No 6 Commando landed on QUEEN Beach Red sector at 0820 hours, piped ashore by Piper Bill Millin. Artillery and mortar fire was considerable and three of their landing craft were hit. They moved rapidly inland, heading for Breville to the east of Pegasus Bridge, clearing two pillboxes on the way. As they approached the bridge they waved a Union Flag in order to establish themselves as 'friendly forces' and were met by Brigadier J.H.N. Poett, the Commander of 5th Parachute Brigade. 'We are very pleased to see you', said Nigel Poett. 'I am afraid we are a few minutes late sir,' was the reply. Bill Millin then piped the party over Pegasus Bridge to the cheers of the paratroopers and attracted considerable fire from German snipers.

No 3 and No 45 RM Commando landed at 0910 hours and moved inland and across the bridges over the Orne river and canal. No 45 went on to Merville while No 3 formed a protection force at Ranville for 6th AB Division HQ.

By the end of the day the 1st SS Brigade had not occupied the high ground east of the Orne, but they had cleared Ouistreham and fulfilled their main task of linking up with the airborne forces. They had also found out that French civilians were not too enthusiastic about their shoulder patch, which said 'SS'. It was later changed.

200yd to the west of the Casino on the dunes is a memorial to the memory of ten members of Kieffer's Commandos and to No 4 Commando. It is a symbolic flame erected in 1984 on top of a German blockhouse cupola. 200yd to the east of the Casino in the point of the 'Y' junction is a bas relief memorial to Commandant Philippe Kieffer.

Continue past the museum and take the road 'Boulevard 6 juin' to the right of Kieffer's memorial. 200yd later there is a large concrete building/ museum on the left. Stop.

Musée le Mur de l'Atlantique

This is the only major German work left in Ouistreham and is surrounded by new houses. It was a flak tower designed to control anti-aircraft defence of the harbour and since 1987 has been a museum. Opening times are temperamental.

Continue through Ouistreham (West Ham) following signs to Caen.

In the church on the hill in the town are two beautiful stained glass windows. One is to the commandos and the other to the 51st Highland Division, the follow-up formation in I Corps that was to have bloody battles east of the Orne in the fight for Caen.

In the roundabout on leaving Ouistreham on the D514, is a Comité du Débarquement Signal Monument, which until 1987 stood on the Harbour at Ouistreham. At the back of the memorial is a plaque to the French and British commandos of No 4 Commando.

Memorial to Cdt Kieffer's Commandos, Ouistreham

TOURIST INFORMATION

TOURIST OFFICES

Caen
Departmental tourist office for Calvados.
Place du Canada.
Everything the tourist needs to know about the area. Bookings made for all kinds of accommodation.
☎ 31 86 5330

Caen Tourist Office. Place St Pierre. Information, reservations and guided tours. Lists of hotels, hostels, bed and breakfast, restaurants, etc.
☎ 31 86 2765

Courseulles
54 rue de la Mer
Open: everyday 1 June-20 September, and weekends in springtime.

Details of the many regattas and other events which regularly take place in the summer. Bookings for hotels, self-catering, camping.
☎ 31 97 4680 (all year)

Ouistreham-Riva-Bella
Jardins du Casino.
Open: summer Monday-Saturday 1000-1830, Sunday 1030-1800. Winter Friday afternoons, Saturday and Sunday mornings.
Tourist information, sporting events (regattas etc), casino, discos.
☎ 31 97 1863

Most of the smaller coastal resorts between Courseulles and Ouistreham (Bernières, St Aubin, Langrune, Luc, Lion and Hermanville) have small, seasonal Syndicats d'Initiative.

Flak tower and Museum, Ouistreham

MUSEUMS

Caen
Memorial Museum
This impressive, modernistic museum makes use of the latest audio-visual devices to tell its story, with huge screens, videos, sound effects and computers. It has research facilities, archives and library, cafeteria, restaurant, nursery, bureau de change, and a well-stocked shop with books, videos, cassettes, maps and souvenirs. Allow 2 hours to visit it properly.
Opening Times: 14 July-31 August, 0900-2200; 1 September-30 September 0900-1900 (2000 on Fridays); 1 October-24 March, 1000-1800 (2000 on Fridays)

Entrance fee payable. Reductions for children, senior citizens. No charge for World War II veterans.
☎ 31 06 0644 (a very appropriate 'phone number!)

Ouistreham
No 4 Commando Museum
Opposite Casino.
The exhibits have grown, despite the setbacks of robbery which seems a natural hazard of war museums in Normandy, concentrating on the commando exploits (including the French under Commandant Keiffer) at Ouistreham.
Open: 1 June-30th September, everyday 0930-1800; Easter-31 May, weekends 1000-1200, 1400-1730.

Entrance fee payable. Reductions for children and groups.
☎ 31 96 3610.

Atlantic Wall Great Bunker Museum
Avénue de la Plage.
This enormous flak tower has been converted into a private museum.
Open: advertised as everyday 0900-1900.
Entrance fee payable. Reductions for groups.
☎ 31 97 2869.

Colleville-Montgomery
SWORD Museum
At corner on Avénue de Bruxelles, in the basement.
Privately owned collection of invasion artefacts found in the area by the proprietor, M. Chauvin-Doisy, and some vehicles.
Open: usually everyday all day in June; weekends rest of year.
Entrance fee payable.

HOTELS

Caen
This important city, capital of la Basse Normandie and of Calvados, was rebuilt after its 70 per cent destruction in 1944, with a good range of hotels. The 40th anniversary of the D-Day landings in 1984 and the opening of the new Memorial Museum in 1988, triggered further spates of hotel chains to open here, especially 2-star hotels and in the Hérouville St Clair/la Folie Couvrechef areas near the Ring Road.
*** Novotel
Off Ring Road (*Périphérique*), Ave. Côte du Nacre.
Smart, well-run, with outdoor swimming pool. Very popular

business and tourist hotel. Advance booking essential.
☎ 31 93 0588.
*** Mercure
Near the Bassin St Pierre, rue de Courtonne.
Beautifully designed and well-equipped.
☎ 31 93 0762
*** Moderne
Blvd Maréchal Leclerc.
Recently renovated.
☎ 31 86 0423
** Campanile
Hérouville.
Small, but well-equipped rooms. Family run.
☎ 31 95 2924.
** Ibis.
Hérouville.
Small rooms but attractive décor.
☎ 31 93 5446.

Courseulles
** Hotel de Paris
Place 6 juin
Overlooking most of Courseulles' D-Day Memorials. Logis de France.
☎ 31 97 4507.
** Hotel La Crémaillerie.
Next to the Royal Winnipeg Rifles Dagger Memorial.
Overlooking the beach. Logis de France.
☎ 31 97 4673.

Ouistreham-Riva-Bella
Now Brittany Ferries dock here, this popular holiday resort is even busier.
** Hotel Brôche d'Argent
Place Gen de Gaulle
Well-placed, overlooking port, near car park. Insist on a room in the main building.

RESTAURANTS

Caen

Caen prides itself on its gastronomy — its best known dish being the famous *Tripes à la Mode de Caen*! There is a wide range of eating opportunities — from the grand gourmet to bistrots, brasseries, pizzerias and *crêperies*. Most of the hotels (eg the Mercure, Moderne) have restaurants. Gourmet regional and foreign dishes (eg *couscous*) are all readily to be found. Menus with prices are posted up outside the establishments.

Courseulles

Again there are many options. Remember that the oyster is king in Courseulles, and has been for 300 years, exporting 10 million to Paris each year. Try them in gourmet restaurants like La Crémaillerie (see hotel above), and La Pêcherie, Place du 6 juin. There is a host of cheaper eating places too, round the busy port with rows of beautiful yachts.

Ouistreham

A large choice in this attractive harbour area, from serious restaurants to *crêperies*, to 'quick snacks'.
La Brôche d'Argent,
Place Gen de Gaulle.
Seafood specialities, pretty dining room.
Le Channel,
Ave M. Cabieu.
Excellent *gallettes*.

Côte du Nacre

Each little resort between Ouistreham and Courseulles is well served with restaurants during the season. Many close for the winter.

SOUVENIRS AND SHOPPING

Caen is an excellent shopping centre — from big department stores to street markets. The new Memorial Museum's shop is a military buff's delight. Ouistreham makes a good supply stop with supermarket, chemist, shops selling film and fish and vegetable markets if you are self-catering.

OTHER ATTRACTIONS

Caen

Offers historic guided tours, cinema, theatre, concerts, discos — see tourist office.

The Côte de Nacre

Offers a variety of leisure and sporting facilities (water and land, eg tennis, shooting, horse riding) and superb, safe sandy beaches.

Route de Moulins

(Old Mill itinerary) see tourist office.

CHÂTEAUX

Fontaine Henry — beautiful Renaissance building with spectacular pointed slate roofs.
Courseulles — historical building, restored in 1950 (after it was hit by incendiary bombs in 1944).
Lantheuil — fifteenth century.

CHURCHES

Ouistreham — twelfth-century fortress church with Commando and Highland Division stained glass windows.
Douvres la Délivrande — neo-gothic basilica with famous Black Madonna.

9

THE BRITISH AIRBORNE LANDINGS

The Germans had begun to organise airborne forces in 1936. The Americans are said to have considered an airborne assault in 1918 at St Mihiel. The British began their airborne forces in 1940 at the instigation of Prime Minister Winston Churchill, and the early paratroopers were volunteers from No 2 Commando. In May 1943 6th Airborne Division was formed under Major General R.N. Gale and, with 1st Airborne Division under Major General R.E. Urquhart, comprised the Airborne Corps commanded by Lieutenant General Sir F.A.M. ('Boy') Browning. Within the organisation, and an integral part of it, was the 38th Wing of the Royal Air Force.

As early as August 1943 COSSAC had proposed the use of airborne forces in the invasion. At that time a direct assault on Caen was being considered. General Montgomery's appointment brought drastic changes to the plan. His idea was to seal each end of the sea assault using airborne troops. Their prime task was flank protection.

There were two types of airborne soldiers, classified according to the way in which they landed — by parachute or by glider. Thus there were two types of zones in which they would come down — *dropping* zones for parachutists and *landing* zones for gliders. Parachute troops can be widely dispersed by wind, which is a considerable disadvantage, while glider-borne forces can be more readily directed or aimed at small targets and can bring with them heavy equipment like field guns and small vehicles.

Gliders, however, are more vulnerable to obstacles such as the poles, known as 'Rommel's asparagus', that the Germans were erecting on potential landing grounds along the French coast. Therefore, the mix of glider and parachute forces, and the tasks allocated to them, could decide the outcome of the airborne assault.

Six weeks before D-Day, over a three-day period, 6th Airborne Division carried out an airborne exercise. They did not know that it was a dress rehearsal for Normandy.

6TH AIRBORNE DIVISION LANDINGS

Drop Time:	0020 hrs *Coup de Main* on Pegasus bridge.
	0050 hrs 3rd Para Brigade & 5th Para Brigade.
Leading Formations:	3rd and 5th Parachute Brigades of 6th
	Airborne Division.
6th AB Division Commander:	Major General R.N. ('Windy') Gale
German Defenders:	716th Infantry Division
716th Division Commander:	Lieutenant General Wilhelm Richter

The Plan (map 10, page 194)

The airborne plan was scheduled to begin before the main landings, and in darkness, in order to achieve the maximum surprise. The earliest troops into Normandy were, where possible, to be paratroopers who would be less sensitive to obstacles than their comrades in gliders. The paratroopers were to clear landing areas for later glider landings. The tasks were distributed between two brigade groups on a geographical basis as follows:

5th Parachute Brigade Group (Brigadier J.H.N. Poett) comprising the 7th, 12th and 13th Parachute Battalions, D Company of the Oxfordshire and Buckinghamshire Light Infantry and supporting arms and services was to:

1   Seize the bridges over the Orne using six gliders manned by the Oxfordshire and Buckinghamshire Light Infantry and

2   Seize and hold the area of Pegasus Bridge and Ranville and clear the LZs (landing zones) north of Ranville for glider reinforcements.

They were to land on DZ 'N' with elements of the 7th Parachute Battalion on DZ 'W'.

3rd Parachute Brigade Group (Brigadier James Hill) comprising the 1st Canadian Parachute Battalion, 8th and 9th Parachute Battalions and supporting arms and services was to:

1   Destroy the Merville battery $1\frac{1}{2}$ hours before the first landing craft were due and

2   Destroy a number of bridges (eg at Varaville, Robehomme, Bures and Troarn) over the River Dives and thus prevent the enemy from attacking Ranville from the eastern flank.

They were to land on DZ 'K' and DZ 'V'.

In each case the airborne brigades would be spearheaded by pathfinders scheduled to drop at 0020 hours on 6 June. The main troops were due to come in about thirty minutes later.

WHAT HAPPENED ON D-DAY

The leading planes of 38th and 46th Groups of the Royal Air Force carried men of the 22nd Independent Parachute Company whose job it was to mark the dropping and landing zones. With them went the RAF Commander, Air Vice Marshal L.N. Hollingshurst, and on time the pathfinders jumped out into the night sky. One of the first to land was Lieutenant de Latour who featured in a *Picture Post* story on 22 July as the 'first' Allied soldier to land in France. On 9 September the same magazine carried a sad postscript — a picture of de Latour's grave with a temporary wooden cross. He was killed on 20 June, then a captain and is now buried in Ranville CWGC.

At the same time as the pathfinders flew over their objectives the *coup de main* party of Oxs and Bucks led by Major John Howard landed three of their gliders beside the Orne canal, between the two bridges. In ten minutes Pegasus bridge was theirs.

Thirty minutes later at 0045 hours the main bodies of the para brigades arrived and then, less than three hours after that, gliders brought in the heavy equipment and General Gale, the division's commander.

By the end of the day both Orne bridges were in Allied hands, despite German counter attacks, Ranville and the DZs were secure, a link-up had been made with Lord Lovat's Special Service Brigade from SWORD Beach, bridges over the River Dives at Troarn, Bures, Robehomme and over a tributary of the Dives at Varaville had been blown and the Merville Battery had been put out of action, despite a bad start. Only seven of over 260 parachute aircraft used in the assault were missing, but twenty-two of the ninety-eight gliders did not reach their LZs. Some never made it to France due to broken tow ropes, and many landed in the wrong place. Of the 196 members of the Glider Pilot Regiment involved in the operation seventy-one were casualties. Some of the drops were very scattered so that only about 3,000 of the 4,800 men who landed fought as planned. 6th AB Division had achieved its objectives but it was thinly spread. The 6 June may have been the longest day for the men of the airborne forces but there was another one tomorrow and the Panzers were coming.

BATTLEFIELD TOUR F

The tour first covers the actions of 5th Brigade and then the actions of 3rd Brigade. It starts at Pegasus Bridge and its museum in Bénouville and continues to the GWGC cemetery at Ranville. Then, after crossing DZ 'N' and visiting the commando memorials at Amfréville, it continues to the Merville Battery. After Merville a number of airborne memorials,

A D-DAY MEMORY

Brigadier Nigel Poett, Commander 5th Parachute Brigade. Dropped with the pathfinders east of the Orne.

"My brigade task was to seize, intact, the bridges over the River Orne and the Canal de Caen at Bénouville and Ranville and establish a bridge-head.

As my small aircraft skimmed over the defences of the Atlantic Wall, not a shot was fired. The red light came on and then the green. I was 'out', seconds later a bump. It was the soil of France. The time some 20 minutes after midnight on the 5/6 June 1944. The darkness was complete; the silence unbroken except for the sound of my disappearing aircraft.

A few minutes later the sky to the west lit up — firing, explosions, all the sights and sounds of battle. It was John Howard's assault. He also had been timed to land at 20 minutes after midnight.

Now I must get to the bridges as quickly as possible and be able, if need be, to adjust the Brigade plan.

Would the bridges be in the hands of friend or foe? Intact or damaged? Indeed Howard's Company had achieved a splendid success. The bridges were in our hands, intact. All was well!"

including Canadian ones, are visited and the tour ends at a small private memorial in Touffreville.

Total distance:45km (28 miles). Total time: 4 hours.

Map: IGN 1612, 1:50,000 'Caen'.

Pegasus Bridge may be found from Caen by taking the D514 road north from the ring road (Periphérique, N13) and following signs to Bénouville.

Pegasus Bridge

The bridge, over the Orne canal, was captured by the British airborne forces on D-Day, and subsequently named after the Flying Horse emblem of the Airborne Division. 300 yards away to the east is a second, not original, bridge. Both bridges were to be captured by a special *coup de main* party of six gliders commanded by Major John Howard.

It was in 1942 that one-time soldier and former Oxford policeman John Howard, joined the airborne forces. He had been recalled in 1939 at the outbreak of war, commissioned and posted to the Oxfordshire and Buckinghamshire Light Infantry, which was chosen to be glider-borne. In May 1942 he was promoted to major in command of D Company.

In late 1943, General Gale, knowing that the Orne bridges had to be

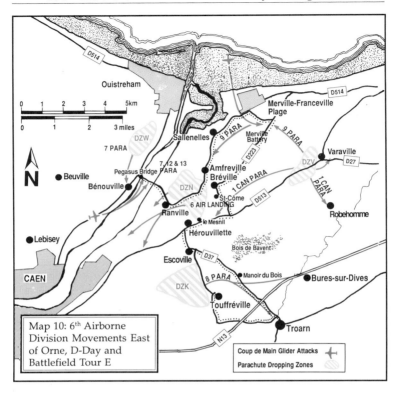

Map 10: 6th Airborne Division Movements East of Orne, D-Day and Battlefield Tour E

captured by his airborne soldiers, and influenced by the German success at Eben Emael, decided upon a *coup-de-main* operation. He chose D Company of the Oxs and Bucks to carry it out and added two extra platoons to the normal complement of six. In the spring of 1944 training for the operation began, though neither Major Howard nor his men knew anything about Normandy and the task that was to be theirs. Night exercises were frequent and sixteen pilots were intensively trained to fly by moonlight and to land their Horsa gliders in a precise pattern.

In May 1944 John Howard found out what he and his company were being trained for — 'to capture and to hold the bridges over the Orne until relieved by the 7th Parachute Battalion', though he was forbidden to share this knowledge with any of his officers and men. He immediately began a detailed training programme on Salisbury Plain, using tapes to lay out a full-scale model of the bridge area. If the operation was to succeed the bridges would have to be captured in a few minutes, and that meant that the gliders needed to land almost on top of them. John Howard told his glider pilots that he wanted the leading machine to land within 50yd of the canal bridge. Three gliders were to go for one bridge and three for the other. Howard himself was to be in the force attacking the canal bridge with a platoon of some thirty men in each glider. His plan there was that the platoon in No 1 glider, commanded by Lieutenant Den Brotheridge, would silence the pillbox and weapon pit at the eastern end of the bridge and then dash across the bridge to seize the other end. The platoon in No 2 glider, commanded by Lieutenant David Wood, was to clear enemy from trenches on the east bank and No 3 glider, under Lieutenant Sandy Smith, was to do the same for the west bank. All the while the men were to shout out 'Able', 'Baker', or 'Charlie' to identify themselves as friendly and hence avoid being shot up in the darkness by their own side.

Final training took place at Tarrant Rushton where the Oxs and Bucks studied aerial photographs of the bridge defences. The steady increase in the erection of Rommel's asparagus in the fields around the bridges was worrying evidence of the Field Marshal's influence on the state of readiness of German defences. Howard confided his concern to Jim Wallwork, the pilot of his glider. To Howard's surprise, Wallwork was pleased. The poles, he said, would help the gliders to stop.

On 3 June General Montgomery visited Tarrant Rushton, had a look at the gliders and talked to John Howard. On 4 June the attack was postponed for 24 hours but at 2256 hours on 5 June the little armada, towed by Halifax bombers, took off. In glider No 1, flown by Jim Wallwork, John Howard sat beside Den Brotheridge and they all practised the code words meaning that the bridges had been captured—'HAM' for the canal bridge and 'JAM' for the river bridge.

The journey over was uneventful and some seven miles from the bridges the tugs released the gliders. Now it was up to the pilots, and this is how John Howard remembers what happened from then on:

I was behind Staff Sgt Ainsworth but could see Jim Wallwork in profile and could see the beads of perspiration on his forehead and face as he struggled to maintain control of that damned great monster he was driving. I knew that the arrester parachute in the tail would operate any moment now to help slow down the glider as it hurtled in to touch down at anything around 100mph. Everybody had automatically carried out the landing drill soon after we had done our second turn. This was to link arms down each side of the glider with fingers locked into what was known as a butcher's grip. Legs up under your chin to avoid breakages when the floor disintegrated, as we expected it to on that bumpy field. Then all you could do was pray to God for a safe landing.

My thoughts were many. Firstly the damned poles. Would collision with one of them cause just one of the many primed grenades we were all carrying to explode and everything else in the glider go up through sympathetic detonation — it had happened many times in Sicily! Were the enemy standing-to and perhaps reinforced with MGs [machine guns] trained on the landing zone? Where would the other gliders land? It was all flashing through my mind as we experienced the first terrific bump! The glider seemed to take it well because we were momentarily airborne again — crash again but this time on skids because the wheels had gone — this was a lot noisier and damaging as the skids seared through the ground and sent up sparks as the metal skids hit flints and it looked like tracer fire flashing past the door causing inevitable thought of surprise lost. Airborne again and suddenly there was what was to be the last searing God Almighty crash amidst smashing plywood, dust and noise like hell let loose, followed by sudden silence as we came to a halt. The dazed silence did not seem to last long because we all came to our senses together on realising that there was NO firing. There WAS NO FIRING, it seemed quite unbelievable — but where were we? Everyone automatically released safety belts and felt their limbs for breakages. I realised that everything around me had gone very dark and my head was aching. My God I can't see! I clutched at my helmet and found that I must have hit the top of the glider during that last helluver crash and all that had happened was that my battle-bowler had come down over my eyes. What a relief! I quickly pushed it up and saw that the cockpit and door had telescoped and we would have to break our way out. I could hear the GPs [glider pilots] moaning and knew that they must be hurt, but they seemed to be breaking out of the front and in any case the drill was to get the hell out of it before any machine guns had time to get into action. Everyone was doing the same and considering the situation, commendably quietly. I did not know whether Den was out before or after me. All I can remember was as I stood clear of the mangled glider I saw the tower of the canal bridge no more than 50 yards away, and the nose of the glider right through the enemy wire defences — precisely where I had asked the GPs to put it during briefing. To cap it all there was NO enemy firing. The sense of complete exhilaration was quite overwhelming! I automatically looked at my watch, it had stopped at 0016 hours.

As I experienced that never-to-be-forgotten moment, the leading section moved quietly up the small track leading to the bridge to their vital task of putting the pillbox out of action. As I moved up myself I heard the dull thud of the phosphorus bomb and saw the greenish cloud of smoke which the section quickly dashed through to lob short-fuse HE [high-explosive] grenades through the gun slits of the pillbox. In the meantime Den was moving up to the near end of the bridge with the rest of his platoon at his heels and as he and his men charged across the bridge we heard three or four ominous thuds inside the pillbox indicating that the grenades had done their stuff.

Then the battle really started, enemy firing came from all directions but the first shots were from the direction of the Gondrée café, clearly aimed at Den and his platoon as they came off the far end of the bridge. Our chaps replied with gusto, no doubt running and firing guns from the hip. I simultaneously heard two more crashes which sounded like gliders pranging and I could hardly believe my ears. Within a very short time it seemed David Wood came steaming up from the landing zone with his platoon hard on his heels and I straightaway confirmed task No 2. As soon as he got into the trenches enemy firing started from several new directions. A runner came from the other side of the bridge with the sad news that Mr. Brotheridge had been seriously hit in the neck during the opening burst of enemy firing as he came off the bridge and he was lying unconscious. I was just about to go over when Sandy Smith arrived with his platoon. He said his glider had had a very bad landing and there were several casualties. I then noticed that one of his arms was hanging limply and tucked into his battle-dress blouse. He was also limping badly. He assured me that he was fit enough to bash on so I confirmed No 3 task and as Den was out of action said he was to co-ordinate things on the other side of the bridge until I could arrange a relief. So off he went and skirmishing went on all round the bridge. Very soon after I learnt that David Wood, his Sgt and radio operator, had all run into enemy MG fire and were out of action the other side of the pillbox. They had apparently caught a German laying booby-trap mines in the trenches. I thus had only one of my three canal bridge platoon commanders on his feet and he had an injured arm and leg.

Apart from the firing going on a great deal of noise emanated from platoons shouting code-names to identify friends in the dark and there was an unholy rabble of Able-Able-Able, Baker-Baker-Baker, Charlie-Charlie-Charlie, and Sapper-Sapper-Sapper, coming from all directions; on top of automatic fire, tracer and the odd grenade it was hell let loose and most certainly would have helped any wavering enemy to make a quick decision about quitting.

The most spectacular operation of D-Day had lasted barely 10 minutes. Total casualties were two killed and fourteen wounded. The airborne had taken Pegasus Bridge and the Germans never re-took it.

Park in the museum car park and visit the museum first. The story of the capture of the bridges is well told via a table model and slide presentation. There are many exhibits donated by former airborne soldiers, including General Gale. The museum cost £80,000 to build and the money was donated by the Comité du Débarquement, whose President is Mr. Raymond Triboulet. The designer was François Carpentier, who designed the museums at Arromanches and at Ste Mère Eglise. It was opened on 5 June 1974 by General Gale and has a small stock of books for sale, including one by Huw Weldon who landed by glider on the evening of D-Day. Captain (later Sir) Huw Weldon of the Royal Ulster Rifles won an MC for his actions the following day and after the war became Managing Director of BBC Television. There is a toilet in the museum but it is underneath the building with a separate entrance and

A D-DAY MEMORY

Lieutenant D.J. Wood, 24th Platoon Commander, D Company, 2nd Battalion Oxfordshire and Buckinghamshire Light Infantry. *Coup de main* group for Pegasus bridge.

"We were seated, arms interlocked, facing each other in silence, lest the enemy below were alerted by our voices. Not a sound, except for the swishing of air rushing past the open door of the Horsa glider, flying through the night at 90mph over Normandy just after midnight on the morning of D-Day. Without warning, the pilot shouted, 'Christ, there's the bridge!' The glider's nose tilted sharply down and sparks, which we thought were enemy tracer, flew from the skids as they struck the ground. A series of violent bumps and the sound of splintering wood, followed by my being ejected through the side of the aircraft. Relieved to find I was still in one piece, still holding the sten with its bayonet fixed and gratified that none of the extra grenades, which I was carrying in my camp kit canvas bucket, had gone off. Pulled myself together, collected my platoon and doubled off to report to my Company Commander."

usually a key has to be obtained from the curator.

There are a number of interesting things to see near Pegasus bridge:

Some 300yd to the west at the cross roads with the D514 (N814) is the *Mairie*, outside of which stands the Bénouville First World War Memorial. On the gate post of the *Mairie* is a plaque commemorating it as the first *Mairie* to be liberated. Gallic enthusiasm insists that liberation came at 2345 hours on 5 June '*par les parachutistes anglais.*'

On the corner diagonally opposite is a religious stone memorial to 'Peace 6 June 1944', at the bottom of which is a plaque in memory of the 7th Light Infantry Battalion of the Parachute Regiment. Their drop zone was divided by the Orne between DZ 'N' and an area to the north of Bénouville. They were the scheduled reinforcements for John Howard's men at Pegasus Bridge. The strong winds scattered the men, many of whom were shot in the air on the way down. Their CO, Lieutenant Colonel Pine-Coffin, landed north of here about half-way to Ouistreham and by using his bugler who dropped with him, managed to rally a force of about 200 men. By 0300 hours the 7th Light Infantry Battalion had established a defence perimeter around the bridge.

The road from the Mairie to the bridge is named 'Avénue du Commandant Kieffer'.

Pegasus Café. As Den Brotheridge led his men over the bridge, George and Madame Gondrée, the owners of the café, looked excitedly

Memorial to the first mairie *to be liberated, Bénouville*

out of the top windows. They may well have been the first French people to greet the Allies on French soil. In the fire fight that followed between the airborne troops and men of the company of 736th Grenadier Regiment of 716th Infantry Division, that were guarding the bridge, several soldiers remember George Gondrée shouting loud encouragement from his window. When, during the day, John Howard set up a first-aid post in the café, George Gondrée dug up ninety-nine bottles of Champagne which he had hidden in the garden and much celebrating and reporting sick went on. After the war the café became a focal point for veterans and their families and took the name Pegasus Café, with the Gondrées and their three daughters, Françoise, Georgette and Arlette, being a vital feature of every pilgrimage visit. The walls were covered with mementoes and all veterans signed a book of honour. Madame Gondrée outlived her husband to see the ceremonies connected with the 40th anniversary of D-Day in 1984, but died later that year. Sadly, following her death, the sisters had a disagreement about the future of the café, with Françoise (who had been closely involved in setting up the museum on café land) on the one hand, and Georgette and Arlette on the other. A series of negotiations and two auctions in 1988 led to a complicated situation. Supported by donations from veterans' organisations, British national newspapers and well-wishers, the two sisters bought the cafe for £160,000 (probably five times its value as real estate) at the second

Major John Howard and Arlette Gondrée-Pritchett at the Gondrée Café, Pegasus Bridge

of two auctions in December 1988. Biddings were allowed to continue while three candles burned. Francoise's lawyer appealed against the sale, claiming that the candles had not completely burned out when Arlette and Georgette made the seventy-sixth and final bid. His appeal was unsuccessful. Now Arlette and Georgette intend to restore the café as a place of pilgrimage for veterans and future generations, but are still grateful for donations to make up the huge purchase price.

The Airborne Assault Normandy Trust, formed by General Sir Richard Gale and the Normandy Veterans' Association, support the retention of the café as a memorial and the French authorities have recognised the building as one of 'historic importance'. The café, like the *mairie*, was also liberated 'in the last hour of 5 June 1944' according to a plaque which may, or may not, now grace its entrance.

Walk over the bridge and continue some 20 paces beyond the gun pit on the canal bank. Face away from the canal by the great stone Comité du Débarquement Monument Signal

In the low ground ahead are three lectern-like glider markers. They show exactly where each of John Howard's gliders landed, and give

Pegasus Bridge from the east bank, with the Comité du Debarquement Signal Monument

details of their crews and passengers, and precise time of landing.

Walk forward and read the details. (It will probably be wet under foot). Return to the 'Esplanade Major John Howard' on the canal bank and stand behind the gun pit, facing the Gondrée Café. Take that direction as 12 o'clock.

From this point UTAH Beach, effectively the other extreme end of the invasion area, is 47 miles away in a straight line, at 12 o'clock. Major Howard's glider PF800 landed at 0016 hours, where the first marker stands at 7 o'clock. It is 47yd from the bridge. The leading section moved up, past where you are now standing, and threw grenades into a pillbox, which was located where the house now stands at 3 o'clock. The house is built over the old pillbox.

At one o'clock, on top of the counterweight of the canal bridge, is the dent caused by a bomb from a German aircraft. Luckily it did not explode.

250yd behind you, at 6 o'clock, is the bridge over the river. (The canal bridge is the original one — although there are plans to replace it with a new one — the river bridge is not.) The enemy defending it had run away leaving their weapons behind. The first glider carrying the three platoons for the assault on the river bridge came down at 0020 hours about 190yd away from it and, led by Lieutenant Fox, rushed it. Little more than a minute later Lieutenant Tod Sweeney's platoon landed some 400yd

A D-DAY MEMORY

Lt H.J. ('Tod') Sweeney. 2nd Battalion Oxfordshire and Buckingham-shire Light Infantry. *Coup de main* group for the Orne river bridge.

"As the glider in which I was travelling broke through the clouds I saw clearly in the pale moonlight the River Orne, the Caen canal and the two bridges we had to capture—exactly as on the model we had studied so carefully over the last few weeks. The glider pilot called out 'There's the bridge straight ahead, better strap up.' But I had one more task to carry out before I sat down and strapped up — to open the door for a quick exit. I struggled with the door for a few seconds and then it shot up. As it did so, to my horror, the glider made a final bank to the left and I found myself peering down at the fields and cattle 100ft below. Luckily my batman grabbed my belt and clung on to me until the glider righted itself and I was able to get into my seat. A minute later we were bumping over the fields of France towards the bridge over the River Orne. We had arrived, and for me and my platoon the invasion had started."

away and he too led his men directly to their objective.

A radio message was sent to John Howard to tell him that the river bridge had been captured intact and at almost the same time Howard learned that an inspection had shown that there were no explosives under the canal bridge. The first part of his task was complete. He ordered his men to take up defensive positions and despatched a patrol to secure the landing zones. Then he sent out the radio signal for success, 'Ham and Jam — Ham and Jam.' 'As I spoke', he said, 'I could hardly believe that we had done it.'

Just before daylight three German tanks rounded the corner by the *mairie*, at 12 o'clock, and headed slowly towards the bridge. The paratroopers' PIAT (Projector Infantry Anti-Tank) destroyed the first tank, which burst into flames and started exploding like fireworks. The noise it made probably persuaded the enemy that it was too dangerous to counter-attack until daylight. Some time after this, a German motor cycle and car approached at speed from behind you along the road. They were shot up by Lieutenant Tod Sweeney and his men on the river bridge, and crashed in the ditch between the bridges. An officer in the car turned out to be the bridge commander, Major Hans Schmidt, who asked to be shot, because he had 'lost his honour'. Whether his loss was related to 6th Airborne's capture of the bridges, or to the ladies' lingerie and perfume found in the car, was never established.

Centaur tank at Pegasus Bridge

The gun in front of you is in a simple 50mm Tobruk-type emplacement, believed to be the original there on D-Day. The area around the gun and the memorial is known as the 'Esplanade John Howard'.

Despite troublesome snipers in the woods, General Gale, Brigadier Poett, (who had dropped with the pathfinders at 0021 hours and was therefore the first general officer to land in Normandy) and Brigadier Kindersley (commanding 6th Air Landing Brigade) crossed the bridge (coming from 6 o'clock) on a tour of inspection around 0930 hours.

Other snipers were in the large building seen at 10 o'clock across the canal. It seemed likely that there was an artillery observation officer there too, because accurate mortar fire was coming down. However, it was thought that the building was a maternity hospital, and the paratroopers were forbidden to return the fire. To the right of the building, at 11 o'clock, there was a water tower, from which snipers were also operating, and, around mid-day, Major Howard agreed that one shot could be fired at the tower, using the 50mm German anti-tank gun in the pit in front of you. It scored a direct hit and everyone cheered. An even stranger sound was heard later, when Lord Lovat and No 6 Commando were led up to the bridges by Piper Bill Millin, en route to Amfréville, the village over the rise at 5 o'clock. He had piped them off from Spithead at 2100 on 5 June, and over the Ouistreham beaches at 0820 hours that morning. His pipes, which were 'wounded' in the attack on Amfréville, are in the museum.

For many years after the war, Major Howard accompanied many student officers of the British Army's Staff College on their annual battlefield tour. One of the innumerable stories which he told so well was of the two Italians that were taken prisoner near the bridge. Their job had been to put up the anti-glider poles in the fields. 'I didn't have the time to deal with prisoners,' he said, 'so I let them go. Do you know what they did? The silly sods went back to putting up the poles!'

Note at 9 o'clock the Centaur version of the A27M Cromwell tank used by Royal Marine Commandos. This example came ashore at la Brêche d'Hermanville, where it was put out of action. It was recovered in November 1975 and placed here in June 1977.

One of those who jumped into Normandy that morning was Richard Todd who landed just before 0100 hours. Both he and Lt Sweeney told the same story about how they met each other on Pegasus Bridge on 6 June. Lt Sweeney's version was, 'I met this chap on the bridge and he said "Hello, my name is Todd and they call me Sweeney", so I replied "Hello, my name is Sweeney and they call me Todd"'. Richard 'Sweeney' Todd went on to become a very well known actor while 'Tod' Sweeney, who later took part in the assault on Hamminkeln during the Rhine Crossing, became the head of the Battersea Dogs' Home and the subject of a *This is Your Life* programme in the 1980s.

Brigadier Peter Young once wrote 'Much of what passes for military history is little more than fiction'. In the continuing struggle to achieve recognition as the 'first' to have done something or the 'first' to have been liberated some stories 'improve' with time. In a letter to the authors, Brigadier, now General, Sir Nigel Poett wrote, 'Pegasus Bridge was the first engagement of D-Day. This is beyond dispute'. That at least we can be certain of but it would be unwise to be dogmatic about timings.

Continue east on the D514 (N814) over the new river bridge and take the D37, the first turning right signed to Ranville.

Notice as you turn that below the town sign on the right of the road is a black-on-white sign commemorating the liberation of the commune of Ranville by the 6th Airborne Division on the night of 5/6 June 1944.

Take the next turning right and then immediately left heading for Ranville church. The tower of the church had been a recognition feature for the paratroopers but many failed to see it in the darkness.

Drive to and just beyond the church to the Commonwealth War Graves Commission Cemetery. Stop.

Ranville CWGC Cemetery and Area

The capture of the Ranville area was the responsibility of the 13th (Lancashire) Parachute Battalion of Nigel Poett's 5th Brigade. First they

Ranville CWGC Cemetery

had to improve and protect landing strips on DZ 'N' in anticipation of the arrival of the glider waves at 0330 hours and of the 6th Airlanding Brigade at 2100 hours, and then move on to Ranville. Accompanying them, in order to prepare the landing strips, were sappers of the 591st Parachute Squadron RE, who dropped at 0030 hours. The first landing strips were cleared by 0330 hours and resistance by the 125th Panzer Grenadier Regiment of 21st Panzer Division was over by 0400 hours.

There are a number of visits that can be made on foot.

Stand squarely in front of the main entrance to the CWGC Cemetery and take that direction as 12 o'clock.

The cemetery was begun by Royal Engineers of 591st Parachute Squadron RE, who put up wooden crosses, which remained until after the war. By 21 June there were twenty-seven graves, left in the care of a 9-year-old French boy called Claude, who promised the Sappers that he would look after them. Today there are 2,563 burials, including 323 Germans. To the left of the War Stone almost in the centre of the cemetery is a stone cross bearing a bronze plaque with the emblem of the Airborne Forces on it and remembering simply, 'June 1944'. This was erected in September 1944 by Royal Engineers of 1st AB Division. The chains surrounding it are glider lashing chains and the shell-like supports are brake fluid casings. At the multi-denominational service of inauguration were the Count and Countess of Ranville. At 2 o'clock is Ranville church. The old ruined tower is to the left of the main building. Following the immediate shock of the invasion, the Germans reacted quickly. The town of Colombelles (known to the troops as 'steel city' because of its tall metal chimneys) some two miles away at 6 o'clock, became a forming-up area for German counter-attacks. On D+5 naval spotters were sent up the tower to direct the fire of HMS *Belfast* (now floating on the River Thames near Tower Bridge, part of the Imperial War Museum in London) onto Colombelles and the shells could be heard whistling overhead here. The Germans replied with 88mm artillery fire onto the church, which was badly damaged. The civilian cemetery was destroyed, and so the first soldiers' graves were dug in the field, which is now the CWGC Cemetery. To allow access to the graves from the church, a hole was knocked in the boundary wall. Today the hole is a gateway between the two. Just before the gateway is a seat with a memorial plaque to 8th Parachute Battalion which was donated in June 1987. Another unmarked seat in the cemetery was presented by the Thanet Branch of the Airborne Forces Association in June 1986. It matches one they presented to the Airborne Cemetery at Oosterbeek in Holland. Around the inside of the wall on the far side of the church, there are also some war graves, including one German and two French soldiers and Lt Den Brotheridge, who was killed at Pegasus Bridge. Behind Brotheridge's headstone is a commemorative plaque placed by the Gondrée family acknowledging him as the first Allied soldier killed during the landings.

The general area outside the church is known as the 'Place General Sir Richard Gale' and immediately opposite the entrance to the CWGC Cemetery is a low wall on which is a map and a concise summary of the airborne operations in the area. This memorial, erected by the people of Ranville, also lists the units involved in the actions. In the field beyond the wall, which faces the local school, Sergeant Ken Routman of the 591st Squadron organised a football match against the 13th Parachute Battalion on 9 June. The result is not recorded. On the other side of the entrance to the cemetery is a stone tower on the southern side of which is a plaque in memory of the Belgian Piron Brigade which formed an 'Allied' element of the 2nd British Army together with a Czech armoured brigade, a Netherlands brigade and a Polish armoured division.

General Gale, the Airborne Division Commander, had arrived at about 0330 hours by glider and moved with his HQ to an area just to the west of the village of Ranville called le Bas de Ranville. On route he commandeered a white horse and many soldiers remember him riding it. Later it saved his life by being between him and a mortar shell. The area of le Bas de Ranville, which was being defended by the 12th (York-

Lt Den Brotheridge's headstone, Ranville

shire) Parachute Battalion, came under intense German counter-attacks, and when Lord Lovat's Special Service Brigade arrived at Pegasus Bridge at 1300 hours the leading Commando was diverted from its main task and sent up here.

Drive down the road past the school to the first crossroads in the village. There is a wall plaque in the area known as 'Place du 6 Juin'.

13th Parachute Battalion Memorial

The memorial, which has in bas relief an Airborne Division cap badge, asserts that Ranville was the first French village to be liberated and gives the time as 0230 hours. Paratroopers re-visiting the area often discuss which was the first *mairie* to be liberated, or the first house to be liberated, or the first village, or the first town, but the most enthusiastic conversation always centres around the first Frenchwoman they liberated. Whoever it was, and wherever, the ties between the local people and the British paratroopers remain very strong. The first Airborne Division pilgrimage here was led by Brigadier James Hill in June 1946 and the 29 June issue of *Illustrated* carried a full photographic report.

Drive along the D223 which leaves the crossroads to the north-east following signs to Amfréville.

The road bisects DZ 'N' on which the 5th Parachute Brigade and later the 6th Airlanding Brigade landed. The pathfinders of the Independent

A D-DAY MEMORY

Major Tony Dyball commanding D Company Royal Ulster Rifles 6 Airlanding Brigade. Landed east of the Orne.

"I had a most unfortunate experience when we got into the gliders. If you can imagine — they were all lined up astern down the runway with the tug aircraft and then the glider. When we were about 100ft off the ground the tow rope broke and so we had to land — an emergency landing — on the grass. We just sat until some kind person brought round a tractor to drag us back and there we were at the end of the queue. Now perhaps you should understand that in those days we had six gliders for one company. At that particular time I was commanding D Company of the Royal Ulster Rifles. I had six officers and 128 riflemen. Anyway there I was and half an hour later I got off with another tug aeroplane. Well you can imagine what was going through my mind. What am I going to do? They've all gone there. I'm going to arrive. I don't know if I've got a company or anything at all. So I talked to the tug aeroplane and said 'Could you catch up?' He said, 'Well, I'll do my best. I'll slide down 400ft and I'll give full throttle.' So there we were chugging over Brighton, everybody waving away like mad. Then he said 'We've got to get up a bit because I've got to let you off over Ouistreham.' There were a few puffs of anti-aircraft fire but nothing serious. We got up and released and landed exactly where I'd shown the pilot on an aerial photograph that I'd wanted to be. There was the Company all lined up and ready to go. The Second in Command came up to me and said, 'What kept you?' "

Parachute Company had had a scattered drop and were unable to set up their markers properly. One section operated its beacon thinking that DZ 'N' was DZ 'K' and attracted a number of 3rd Brigade units before the mistake was discovered. Therefore, as the Horsa gliders began to come in at 0330 hours, many pilots were unable to locate their correct strips or even be certain about which way they were supposed to land. One Sapper who was working on the landing strips remembered that 'the gliders came from all directions ... some passed within thirty or fifty feet of each other going in opposite directions.'

Continue to Amfréville. On entering the village the road divides either side of a green in the centre of which is a church. Stop at the division.

No 6 Commando Memorial
You have just passed the memorial, which is 100yd behind you. The

13th Parachute Batallion Memorial, Ranville

bridgehead established by the Airborne Forces and reinforced by the 1st Special Service Brigade (re-named the 1st Commando Brigade in June 1944) was under constant counter attack for almost two months.

No 6 Commando led the way over Pegasus Bridge and their objective was the high ground over which the road you have driven along runs. The road which behind you leads to Bréville, not to Ranville, also runs along the feature attacked and captured by No 6 Commando on the morning of 7 June, though since the whole Commando Brigade was involved in fighting in the area it is impossible to be absolutely certain about who was where. The area taken formed a salient into enemy lines pointing back in the direction from which you have come and at the tip was the village of Bréville, still held by the Germans. The commandos took heavy casualties from artillery fire over the coming days.

The buildings beyond the memorial belong to farmer Bernard Saulnier who, during the fighting around Amfréville, was asked by Lieutenant Colonel Peter Young of No 3 Commando to lop branches off some of the trees so that his soldiers would be able to see the Germans more clearly. Peter Young went on to become a brigadier, a renowned military historian and to found the 'Sealed Knot' a 'Cavalier and Roundheads' re-enactment organisation. He died in 1988.

On 12 June a major offensive was launched through Amfréville's

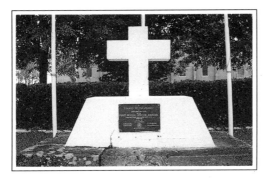

1st Special Service Brigade Memorial, Amfréville, Le Plein

commando positions by 12th Parachute Battalion and elements of the Devonshire Regiment in an attempt to capture Bréville. Lord Lovat was seriously wounded by a high explosive shell and Bernard Saulnier carried him into one of his cowsheds. Each June Bernard holds a dinner for all commandos in the big barn of his farm, 'Commando Farm', and provides free food and drink.

Originally, and for some 20 years, the town of Ouistreham held a day's open house for the commandos and provided free drink and meals with accommodation being offered by local people. Bernard took over the affair and on the 40th anniversary of D-Day in 1984 had about 700 people in his barn. In return the Commando Association presented their old friend with an especially commissioned cut glass decanter and glasses worth over £1,000 bearing the Commandos' insignia.

When Lord Lovat was wounded, Lieutenant Colonel Mills-Roberts took over the brigade and commanded it for the rest of the war. He died in 1980 and in 1988 his ashes were transferred to Normandy and buried by Bernard Saulnier in Bavent, some two miles south-east of here.

Continue left of the church until you reach the church. Stop.

This area is known as le Plein though the name does not often appear on modern maps. To the right of the road and towards the church is a small memorial cross to the 1st Special Service Brigade.

Follow the road around the green.

It is known as the 'Le Plein Place du Commandant Kieffer' and there is a sign over the entrance to the school building to that effect.

Take the north-eastern exit from the green, the D37b signed to Sallenelles, and immediately before the road sign indicating that you are leaving Amfréville, turn left along Rue Oger. Continue to the memorial at the end.

No 4 Commando Memorial, Hoger, Amfréville

Hoger No 4 Commando Memorial
Since 1944 many place names in Normandy have changed or been
amalgamated with others. In British accounts of actions the Anglicised
versions of French names are often used offering yet another spelling
to confuse the reader. The village here, now awash with new houses, was
known in 1944 as 'Hauger' to the British.

This area is also known as le Hoger and on 10 June particularly
intense fighting here involving No 4 Commando led to one troop losing
all its officers. German counter-attacks on the high ground of Hoger —
le Plein — Amfréville had begun on the afternoon of 6 June and continued
incessantly for four days.

The memorial cairn to No 4 Commando is in the 'Place Colonel Robert
Dawson'. Colonel Dawson commanded No 4 but was twice wounded
while landing on the beaches. On 7 June he rejoined the commandos but
on 9 June the medical officer ordered him to the rear. The château over
the wall was, for a time, the No 4 Commando HQ and originally the
memorial was in its grounds, but because it was difficult to get to, it was
moved to its present site. The first Allied occupants of the château had
been Lieutenant Colonel Terence Otway and the remnants of the 9th
Parachute Battalion who made their way here having taken the Merville
Battery. They stayed until late on 6 June, suffering under heavy sniper
fire, until relieved by men from No 3 Commando. No 3 then moved on

Piron Brigade Memorial, Merville-Franceville

to le Plein handing the château over to No 4 Commando.

Return to the D37b, continue to Sallenelles and turn right at the junction with the D514.

Sallenelles Belgian Memorial
Barely 50yd after the turning there is on the left-hand side, on the gate post of house No 13-15, a plaque to the memory of Edouard Gérard of the 1st Piron Brigade. He was the first Belgian soldier to be killed in Normandy — on 16 August 1944.

Continue on the D514 following signs to Merville-Franceville-Plage. At the traffic lights in Merville turn right at the sign for la Battérie de Merville and stop immediately it is safe to do so.

Merville Memorials
There are two memorials in a small clearing on the western side of the road by the traffic lights. One is to the 'Allied Soldiers and the Civilians of Merville-Franceville' who fell during the liberation and the other is to two sergeants and two soldiers of the Piron Brigade killed on 18 August. The two stones flank the main village war memorial.

Continue following signs to the Merville Battery and stop in the parking area by the main gate.

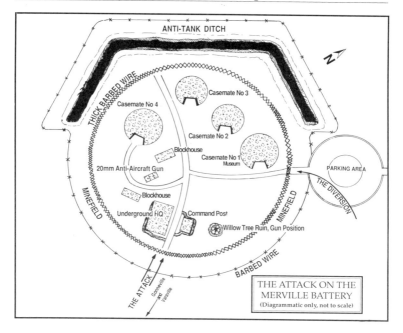

ANTI-TANK DITCH

THICK BARBED WIRE

Casemate No 4

Casemate No 3

Casemate No 2

Blockhouse

Casemate No 1
Museum

20mm Anti-Aircraft Gun

MINEFIELD

Blockhouse

Underground HQ

Command Post

Willow Tree Ruin, Gun Position

PARKING AREA

THE DIVERSION

MINEFIELD

BARBED WIRE

THE ATTACK
Gonneville
and
Varaville

THE ATTACK ON THE
MERVILLE BATTERY
(Diagrammatic only, not to scale)

The Merville Battery

The capture of the battery at Merville was one of the tasks of the 3rd Parachute Brigade. The other tasks, mainly the blowing of bridges over rivers, were widespread and far less concentrated than those of the 5th Parachute Brigade. The capture of the battery here was given to the 9th Parachute Battalion under Lieutenant Colonel T.B.H. Otway whose planned DZ was two miles away near Varaville to the south-east.

In the planning for D-Day great care was taken to identify those aggressive elements of the Atlantic Wall that could threaten the invasion force as it came ashore — its most vulnerable moment. The concrete emplacements of the Merville Battery were thought to house four 150mm guns capable of bombarding the beaches on which 3rd British Division was due to land. It was vital therefore that the guns be silenced by the airborne troops before the sea-borne forces arrived.

The area around the guns had been evacuated by the Germans and the villages of Franceville Plage and Gonneville were used as billets for German soldiers. In the weeks before D-Day the RAF bombed the area several times but with no damage to any of the casemates. The 130 men of 716th Regiment who manned the battery not only had concrete to protect them from aerial attack but any assault on the ground had to penetrate a minefield between two barbed wire fences. On the north-west of the position, which was lozenge shaped some 800yd by 500yd, was a partially completed anti-tank ditch. Within the barbed wire compound were a number of machine-gun positions. To the planners it had the appearance of a fortress and they planned to attack it as if it was.

In April 1944 Major Terence Otway was promoted to lieutenant colonel and appointed to command the 9th Parachute Battalion. In a farmhouse near Netheravon he learned that his battalion had the very special task of neutralising a German battery on D-Day. In the farmhouse was a scale model of the battery with diagrams and aerial photographs, but it was some days before Otway learned where the guns were. It was some weeks before he learned when D-Day would be.

Very quickly Otway decided that the only way that a workable plan could be developed, and train his men to carry it out, was to build a full-scale model of the battery. A 45-acre site was found near Newbury and Royal Engineers with bulldozers worked for seven days and nights reproducing the anti-tank ditch, the paths, the gun emplacements (with steel girders covered with sacking) and the minefield areas.

The plan was complex. The battalion was to divide into two groups. The first, smaller group, was to prepare a rendezvous for the arrival of the main body and also reconnoitre the battery. An attack by a hundred RAF Lancaster bombers was scheduled for 0030 hours and Otway wanted to know the resulting damage before launching his assault. The first group was to jump at 0020 hours and the main body at 0050 hours. The main body comprised most of the battalion including B and C Companies. B Company was given the job of breaching the first wire barrier and clearing a path through the minefield. C Company was the assault force, while the remainder of A Company was to hold a firm base from which the others could begin the assault. C Company was to rush the gap in the minefield and split into four parties accompanied by sappers of 591st Parachute Squadron. Each party was to capture and blow up a casemate. The plan did not end there. Timed to arrive as C Company made its charge through the battery defences, three Horsa gliders were to crash-land inside the perimeter. This party, named like John Howard's force at Pegasus Bridge, as a '*coup de main*', consisted mainly of A Company personnel and a number of sappers. Then if all else had failed, HMS *Arethusa* was standing by to pound the battery with her 6in guns at 0550 hours.

Otway trained his men very hard. He was sparing with his praise and

Merville Battery, casemate No 1

quick to find fault. They rehearsed over and over again — all except the gliders. He could not get gliders to crash land into his dummy battery, so he arranged that the RAF would fly in low as the practice attacks went in. However, the fifty or so paratroopers of A Company had to be retrained as glider troops. They flew over Salisbury Plain and practised accurate landings at Thruxton. Then, finally, the colonel declared himself satisfied and a few days later the battalion was sealed into its pre-invasion camp near Broadwell in Berkshire. There were over seven hundred men, ready, trained and anxious to go.

The first small group took off from RAF Harwell at 2310 hours on 5 June in Albemarles, and dropped accurately and to time at 0020 hours, despite the fact that the aircraft had an uneasy reputation for losing its tail in mid-air. The officer in charge of the rendezvous to which the reconnaissance group and then the main body were to report was Major Allen Parry and on landing he used his 'Ducks, Bakelite' (a whistle device that made a sound like a duck, and the British equivalent to the Americans 'cricket') to locate a friendly face. There was no one about so he set off alone to the rendezvous hearing, en route, the explosions from the Lancaster raid on the battery. It was well off target. Reaching the rendezvous Parry set up his Aldis lamp to guide in the paratroopers and waited for the main body. When they came the aeroplanes seemed to

A D-DAY MEMORY

Paratrooper Les Cartwright 9th Parachute Battalion. Dropped for the Merville Battery.

"I think I should tell you first quickly who we were. Now we were the 9th Para Bn. We were formed out of the 10th Essex Bn and we were designated as a Home Counties Bn therefore most of us came from the Home Counties — Middlesex, Surrey, Essex. That's who we were. The actual boys and myself, the Paras, the average age was 19 to 21. No older. Our officers were a bit older. Our NCOs were a bit older, because 'Windy' (if I speak of Windy that means General Gale) — Windy had nicked a lot of NCOs from the 1st Division who had experience to put in amongst us so as to give us that bit of backing and a bit of experience. Anyway the first thing we knew about this, was we knew something was up, 'cos if you remember we had these little exercises and it always seemed to be guns we were after — up the hill and down the valley, and then one day a little while before Normandy they marched us out and we stopped at the Battalion and the Colonel told us what the job was. Well after that we went down on the plains and the Colonel found a position practically like this (the Merville Battery) and we built a battery and we attacked it night and day for a week. The idea was that first of all to drop would be our pathfinders, then some of the lads would drop and they'd make for the battery, make sure it was alright and then we get to the RV and we do the approach march which was approximately about a mile and a half across the fields. And then when we got here we had three gliders coming in with twenty paras in each who had volunteered to go in, those gliders, to actually crash land in the battery when we put the attack in. That was at the same time that one party came up here to the main gate. They would attack from that position. Well we were to come through and blow the wire in four positions. 'C' Company was the attacking Company. Then once through those four positions we had to take a gun each and blow it. And everything we done just dovetailed, and it was beautiful. We were so confident that we could do it, he'd brain-washed us too much. So anyway, a couple of weeks later, three o'clock in the morning, lights go on in the barrack room. 'Right — get up, get your kit — OUT'. And when we walked out on the square there were all these transporters. Into the transporters, and I think we drove around for about 8 hours, changing drivers here and there, and the last thing we knew there was all these tanks, all the barbed wire round it. In we went, they shut the gate and said, 'You stay there'. And we'd had a big mosaic made of the battery itself, and we had to study that and an officer could stop you any time and say, 'Where is so-and-so in the battery?' And if you didn't know, mate, you were back in there and you were stuck in there an hour, and you had to explain everything to him. So everybody knew — exactly what the other chap was doing and exactly what was in there, and it looked a perfect plan. But come the night, 5 June, we took off just after midnight and we dropped just before one. It was a beautiful flight across till we hit the coast, and we hit the coast and you've never seen anything like it in your life. It was just like going into a firework display and the old duck was going five ways at once and everybody was saying, 'Let's get out of this so-and-so thing'. Anyway eventually the Pilot says, 'Go', and puts the light on and on our way we go. And as I dropped, obviously you look round and I could see other 'chutes coming down and I hit the deck and out of my 'chute, got my sten out, everything going, look round — couldn't see anybody. But there was one thing that got implanted in my mind — we must get to that RV. And the Colonel's orders were 'You were to have no private fire fights. You get to the RV AND THAT IS IT'. And I checked around a bit. I found the road that runs in front of the rendezvous. I didn't know which way to go — right or left — but I heard a fire fight going on up to the left so I thought I'd go up to the right. And I just got along the side of the road looking, and away in the distance I could just see this red light twinkling. And it was one of the officers got up the tree with an Aldis lamp and was flicking this right round in circles to bring the lads in. As soon as I saw that I knew where I was to get. I could see the tree across the fields and I saw a bod just in front of where I knew the RV was and I yelled the password out and he yelled it back and I looked at him and it was the Colonel. He was standing there waiting to bring the lads in. He tapped me on the shoulder and he said, 'well done, lad. What company?' 'C Company.' 'Down there.' I went down there and ... I dropped down beside my Lieutenant (Jackson) and had a little word with him, you know. At the time I thought, well there don't seem many of us here, but you know most of us thought that but we didn't say it. 'Cos there's 100 of us in the company. It didn't look 100, but you didn't want to say anything because you didn't want to upset anybody. Any rate we was sitting there and we knew the timetable, knew we ought to be moving now. We ought to be moving and eventually the Colonel said 'Move', and it wasn't until years afterwards I found out that out of the 550 who jumped in our battalion, only 150 got to the rendezvous."

be spread out and as their engine noise faded away he began to flash his Aldis signal. But two hours after the drop only 150 men, including Lieutenant Colonel Otway, had arrived. It was less than 25 per cent of those that had set out. There were no Royal Engineers and apart from sidearms, they had only one Vickers machine gun and twenty Bangalore torpedoes between them. Otway decided to make for his objective and at 0250 hours set out, reaching the firm base area 500yd from the battery at about 0420 hours. Parry, originally in charge of the rendezvous, was given command of the assault party and divided his allocation of fifty men into four units in imitation of the original plan. Now they would wait for the *coup de main* party. When that arrived smack into the middle of the battery, they would attack.

Things went wrong again. One of the three gliders broke its tow rope just after take-off, the second landed several miles east of the battery and the last one, although it actually flew over the battery, crashed in an orchard about 100yd away to the south-west having been hit by anti-aircraft fire. The third glider did however distract the attention of some German machine gunners who had been causing casualties from their position outside the defended perimeter as well as intercepting a German patrol that was moving up to reinforce the battery. Otway decided to get on with the job. Without engineer support or any mine clearing equipment it was a case of charging both the wire and the minefield. The paratroopers went forward firing their sten guns from the hip, using the gaps in the wire and minefield caused by the bombing and blowing two more gaps using the Bangalore torpedoes. At the main gate a small party opened fire hoping to cause a diversion. The Germans fought well, coming out of their bunkers to counter-attack. It was a short and bloody scrap in which Allen Parry was wounded. The cost to the battalion was heavy — seventy officers and men killed or wounded. The battalion was down to eighty. The German garrison was reduced to twenty-two prisoners, all the rest were killed or wounded.

When the casemates were examined the guns were found to be old French 75mm weapons on wheels. The anticipated heavy weapons had not been installed. Nevertheless the guns were put out of action and the victory signal was made both by pigeon and by smoke flares just thirty minutes before 0530 hours when the *Arethusa* was due to begin her bombardment. The 9th Parachute Battalion had not finished its task however. Now they had to head for the high ground around Amfréville. Otway led his men off and later in the day a combat group of the German 736th Grenadier Regiment regained Merville only to lose it the following day to an assault by two troops of No 3 Commando. Once again it was a fierce battle in the casemates and in the tunnels that linked the different bunkers, but the Germans were overcome. Almost immediately the enemy counter-attacked using self-propelled guns and drove the commandos out and back to le Plein.

9th Parachute Battalion never collected all of its men. The initial drop which was supposed to have been contained within an area of $1\frac{1}{2}$ square miles was spread over 50 sq miles. There were a number of reasons for this: the aircrews carrying out the drop were inexperienced, having only been formed into a Group (No 46) in January 1944: the leading aircraft of each formation did the navigating and signalled to the others when to drop so that single aircraft, when disorientated by trying to avoid flak on the way over, led groups of others to the wrong place, while others confused the rivers Dives and Orne. Hundreds of men were dropped into the flooded areas of the Dives and many were drowned.

The museum here is not always open and its times can be erratic. It is controlled from the museum at Pegasus Bridge. It was established on 6 June 1982, thanks to the energy and enthusiasm of General Sir Nigel Poett, who, as Brigadier Poett, commanded the 5th Parachute Brigade on D-Day. It is partly funded by Airborne Assault Normandy, a charitable trust established to commemorate the 6th Airborne Division's achievements in Normandy. At the entrance where the diversionary action was made, there are a number of notice boards and diagrams explaining what happened, but these weather badly and may not be legible. Like Pegasus, this museum has suffered from a number of thefts, and it is kept tightly closed during most winter months. The ground, however, and the casemates themselves are always accessible.

Return to the T junction and turn right continuing in the original direction of travel to Descanneville. There turn right on to the D223. Drive to the crossroads by the church in Bréville and stop.

Bréville

To best understand the importance of Bréville, the traveller is advised to consult map 10 on page 194 and to ascertain the general direction of Amfréville/le Plein/Hoger and the château of St Côme.

During one of his inspection tours, Rommel had visited Bréville, planning his defence of the high ground from a viewpoint at the crossroads where you now are. That defence was formidable and despite the best efforts of the commandos, paratroopers and 51st Highland Division, the Germans held on, giving ground reluctantly and at great cost to themselves and their attackers. Even by the start of Operation GOODWOOD on 18 July, some six weeks after D-Day, the British front line extended no further south than Bréville and GOOD-

WOOD itself moved the line forward only to the southern edge of the Bois de Bavent, which is passed later on this tour.

The capture of the high ground on which Bréville and the other villages such as le Plein, Hoger and Amfréville sit, was one of the tasks set for the 6th Airborne Division and General Gale allocated it to Brigadier James Hill's 3rd Parachute Brigade. The ground, and the bridges across the Orne which it overlooked, controlled German routes into the landing bridgehead from the east. It was vital, therefore, that it was quickly captured and then held.

On D-Day, after completing their primary tasks, the 9th Parachute Battalion (whose first task was to destroy the Merville Battery) and the 1st Canadian Parachute Battalion (whose first task was to destroy bridges over the River Dives) headed for the high ground. (See map 10.) 9th Battalion got to Hoger, which you passed earlier, and the 1st Battalion reached le Mesnil, which you pass later. Meanwhile No 4 Commando dug in at Hoger and No 6 established themselves between le Plein and Bréville. The Germans held Bréville. It was a patchy situation. The German defence was cellular, strong here and weak there, and this, combined with the independent nature of the specialist commando and airborne forces moving against them, produced a confused and irregular battlefield with opposing forces jumbled together.

The German formations in this area were the 346th and 711th Infantry Divisions and for three days after D-Day they mounted heavy counter attacks against the lightly equipped airborne forces on the high ground. General Gale knew that his forces were tiring, and although the 1st Special Service Brigade had come under his command once they were ashore, he desperately needed fresh troops. But he also had to secure the high ground and to him that meant that he must capture Bréville. The General told Lord Lovat that Bréville must be cleared and towards mid-day on 7 June No 6 Commando supported by the 1st French Commando, under Commandant Kieffer, attacked the village. The No 6 account claims that the village was taken and that a number of field and machine guns were captured and subsequently used by themselves in the defence at le Plein, but it must have been a temporary occupation ended by a German counter attack because on the fourth day after D-Day Bréville was still in German hands.

On 10 June Gale received three battalions of the 51st Highland Division as reinforcements and the 5th Battalion The Black Watch were moved to the château of St Côme to prepare for an assault. The château is some 500yd south-east of where you are down the D376 to your left. It is next on the itinerary. At 0430 hours on 11 June after a preliminary bombardment by five regiments of artillery, the Black Watch set off towards you on their first action in Normandy. It was over very quickly. The Germans opened up a barrage of mortar, assault and anti-aircraft guns and the Black Watch retired with some 200 casualties to where they had started. The morale of the 51st Division at that time was not good and the divisional history admits it. A calculated assessment of British infantry divisions' performance against that of the Germans and the Americans suggests that they were short of combative senior commanders who could inspire and lead. Within two months Major General W.R.J. Erskine, commanding the 51st Highland Division, was sacked by General Montgomery.

General Gale, despite the failure of the Black Watch and being down to his reserve formation, the 12th Parachute Battalion, determined to try again. He strengthened the paratroopers with a company of the 12th Battalion the Devonshire Regiment and a troop of Sherman tanks of the 13th/18th Hussars and ordered an attack for 2200 hours on 12 June. So confused was the general situation that accounts of the attack cannot agree upon whether it was 'B' or 'D' Company of the Devonshire Regiment that was involved. The mixed formations gathered around and in the church in Amfréville (where you were earlier, some 750yd north-east up the D376 to the right) and awaited the preliminary bombardment by the five field and one medium artillery regiments in support. At about 2100 hours the barrage began, but not all of it reached Bréville where you are. Some fell short onto Amfréville near Bernard Saulnier's farm and it seems highly likely that the shell burst that injured Lord Lovat was one of our own. Also injured by a shell at about the same time was Brigadier Hugh Kindersley of 6th Airlanding Brigade of which the 12th Devons were part.

The paratroopers and the Devonshire Regiment pushed on through the commandos holding Amfréville and advanced astride the D376 towards you. This time resistance was less determined but still heavy. Artillery had devastated the defenders and their defences. Damaged German equipment and dead and wounded soldiers were mixed amongst the carcasses of animals killed and left unburied over the last week. A pall of smoke hung over all and the flames from burning houses licked the gathering darkness into a scene of overwhelming horror.

As the paratroopers and the Devons captured and then conferred in the village to co-ordinate their defences, the bombardment began again. The Royal Artillery repeated their earlier barrage, churning the area where you are into a shapeless mass of earth and rubble and destroying churchyard and church. The codeword to start the barrage had been

Memorial to the 12th Parachute Batallion and the 12th Devonshire Regiment, Bréville

confused with another over a crackly radio. It was what those present called 'a bloody shambles'. But Bréville was captured though the price was a high one — the Devons had had heavy casualties as they formed up to attack, possibly from our own artillery, losing thirty-five soldiers and their company commander. The paratroopers lost their CO, Lt Colonel AP Johnston, seven officers and 133 soldiers. The next day the small force handed Bréville over to the 1st Battalion Royal Ulster Rifles.

On the corner opposite the church is the memorial to those who died here, English and French. It reads:

6th British Airborne Division.
In Memory of the Inhabitants of Bréville who died in 1944 and also to the men of the 12th (Yorkshire) Parachute Battalion, the 12th Battalion the Devonshire Regiment and other detachments who on the evening of 12 June 1944 assaulted Bréville through the 1st Commando Brigade positions from the direction of Amfréville and drove out the German force.
162 men of the Division died. They lie in the Ranville Military Cemetery.

On the wall of the churchyard opposite is the small white on green Commonwealth War Graves Commission sign that is placed on civilian

9th Parachute Infantry Battalion Memorial, Château St Côme

cemeteries where British and Commonwealth soldiers lie buried. Inside is a headstone for Captain H.W. Ward of the 53rd (Worcestershire Yeomanry) Airlanding Light Regiment RA who was killed on 12 June 1944.

Turn left and continue south on the D375 for about 500yd and stop at the small track that leads to the Château St Côme.

9th Parachute Infantry Battalion Memorial
The Canadians, part of 3rd Parachute Brigade, dropped at DZ 'V' in the area of Varaville, some 5 miles to the north-east of here. Their main task was to destroy the bridges over the River Dives in the region of Varaville and Robehomme. Despite being scattered over a wide area the Canadians blew the bridges and then moved as shown on map 10 through Château St Côme to a position at le Mesnil which is next on our route.

The memorial here records in English and French what it calls the 'Battle of the Bois des Monts and the Château St Côme 7-13 June 1944', and describes the actions of the 9th Parachute Battalion, the attack by the Black Watch on Bréville and the involvement by the 1st Canadian Parachute Battalion until the force was relieved by the 52nd Battalion Oxfordshire and Buckinghamshire Light Infantry.

Continue to the junction with the N813. Turn right.

After 250yd is the area of le Mesnil, a rendezvous point for the 1st Canadian Parachute Battalion and other elements of 3rd Parachute Brigade whose task was to destroy bridges to the east around Varaville.

Continue to the next village, Hérouvillette, and after the church turn immediately left onto the 'Rue de la Libération'. Continue 100yd to the new cemetery entrance and stop.

2nd (Airborne Battalion) Oxfordshire & Buckinghamshire Light Infantry Memorial (52nd)

On the left of the entrance is the CWGC 'Tombes de Guerre' (War Graves) sign and on the right a deteriorating stone memorial dedicated on 6 June 1987 which says in English (and then in French):

In Memory to those who fought at Pegasus Bridge, Escoville, Hérouvillette, Bré-ville les Monts and to the Seine and to the many brave French who helped us.

In the new cemetery are twenty-seven graves of airborne troops including Army Air Corps, RASC, the 12th Parachute Battalion and men of the Oxfordshire and Buckinghamshire Light Infantry.

This village was captured by the Oxfordshire and Buckinghamshire Light Infantry and the 1st Royal Ulster Rifles on the 7 June. They then went on the same day to attack Escoville, which is passed next, but were unsuccessful. Two days later the 21st Panzer Division counter-attacked Hérouvillette, but were driven off, after losing forty dead and four tanks and armoured cars.

Return to the N813, turn left and at the end of the village turn left again onto the D37 signed Troarn. Continue through Escoville and some 250yd after the junction on the left with the D37b is a track leading left to the Manoir du Bois. Stop. 50yd further on beside the road on the left is a memorial.

8th Parachute Battalion Memorial

The memorial is a simple polished stone that says:

In memory of all ranks of 8th Parachute Battalion 6 June-August 1944.

The 8th Battalion had an unfortunate arrival. One of the pathfinder parties was dropped on DZ 'N', three miles north of here, instead of being on DZ 'K' a mile west. Thus the main body, which arrived at about 0050 hours was split between the two zones. On DZ 'K' the battalion commander gathered about 160 men and formed a firm base. On DZ 'N' Major J.C.A. Roseveare RE, who commanded 3rd Parachute Squadron Royal Engineers, gathered a force of about forty sappers and RE officers and some thirty paratroopers (who were reluctant to take orders from a non-paratroop officer). Collecting six trolleys, high explosives and a jeep Major Roseveare set off at about 0230 hours towards the bridges at Bures and Troarn that were his target. He followed the route which you have driven via Hérouvillette and Escoville. At the road junction of the D37 and D37b, just short of the 8th Parachute Battalion Memorial he stopped. It was 0400 hours. There the paratroop infantry were left to form a defensive position. The main body of sappers was sent off to blow the Bures-sur-Dives bridges (both were blown by 0930 hours), and Major Roseveare plus one other officer and seven sappers jumped into the solitary jeep and, with a trailer of demolition equipment, set off for the bridge at Troarn.

Continue on the D37 to the junction with the N175. Turn left into Troarn and continue to the Syndicat d'Initiative (Tourist Office) on the right. Park in the square behind the office. The square is named after Resistance hero Paul Quelbec.

Troarn

Major Roseveare drove exactly the route which you have followed. At that time the D37 crossed a railway line before the town and the jeep ran into a barbed wire knife rest guarding the crossing. The guard fired one shot at them and disappeared. It took twenty minutes to get free. At the N175 junction they met and shot a German soldier on a bicycle which roused the town. All the party then jumped into the jeep and trailer and Roseveare drove as fast as he could through the town. At about where the tourist office now is, in Major Roseveare's words, 'the fun started, as there seemed to be a *Boche* in every doorway shooting like mad'.

The sappers returned fire with their sten guns and one man in the trailer acted as rear gunner spraying the street with his Bren gun as jeep and trailer swung violently downhill. The bridge that they were to destroy (over the Dives on the N175 to St Samson), was found to be unguarded but they discovered that they had lost their Bren gunner. Five minutes later they had blown a 20ft gap in the masonry structure. It was not yet 0500 hours. Roseveare ditched the jeep north of Troarn and the party navigated their way on foot to le Mesnil which they reached at 1300 hours.

The memorial to the 3rd Parachute Squadron Royal Engineers is a plaque on the wall of the Syndicat d'Initiative behind the Poilu (French World War I soldier) statue which surmounts the town war memorial. The 3rd Squadron memorial was 'Erected by the people of Troarn in honour of the officers and men of 3rd Parachute Squadron Royal Engineers who acting on information obtained from the Resistance destroyed the bridges over the Dives to protect the left flank of the dawn landings of 6 June 1944'. There is also a plaque to civilian victims of the war.

Return along the N175 past the D37 junction where Roseveare's men shot the German cyclist and continue on the N175 to the next village of Sannerville. Turn right at the junction with the D266/D267 and continue on the D277 to Touffreville. Turn right at the second turning after the church and fork left for some 300yd up a farm track to a memorial.

*Memorial to Arthur
Platt, Touffreville*

Private Arthur Platt Memorial

The memorial marks the spot where the body of Private Arthur Platt of 8th Parachute Battalion was found with a comrade on 10 June 1944. In 1976, his son, William J. Lewis (Private Platt's wife married again) himself a paratrooper with the 2nd Battalion from 1958 to 1969, began a quest to find out what had happened to his father. With the help of the 8th Battalion Association and the wife of the Secretary of the Anciens Combattants' Association in Touffreville he established the place of his father's death. He also discovered that Private Platt had been shot in the back of the head and probably while a prisoner of war of the SS. The commune of Touffreville raised the memorial and it was inaugurated on 6 June 1988. Private Platt is buried in Ranville Commonwealth War Graves Commission Cemetery.

End of the tour.

TOURIST INFORMATION

TOURIST OFFICES

Cabourg
Jardins du Casino. This is the largest town near the section. Information on hotels, cultural, sporting and leisure activities.
☎ 31 91 0190.

Merville-Franceville
Local information.
☎ 31 24 2357.

Troarn
Local information.
☎ 31 23 3138.

HOTELS
Strictly speaking there are no towns of any size within this section so see Caen or Ouistreham above, or go to:

Cabourg
Made fashionable by such literary figures as Dumas and Proust, it still boasts some fine hotels, eg
****L Grand Hotel (now owned by PLM)
☎ 31 91 0179
as well as simple hostelleries like:
* Le Champagne (Logis de France)
☎ 31 91 0229
* L'Oie Qui Fume
☎ 31 91 2779

RESTAURANTS
Cabourg, Merville, Franceville and Ouistreham (see above) offer the usual range of gourmet to snack restaurants.

SOUVENIRS/SHOPPING

Pegasus Bridge
Hopefully, the café will once again offer not only coffee, beer and sandwiches during the season, but postcards, books and have on display a unique range of souvenirs donated by returning veterans — the most famous and regular for many years being Major John Howard.

Cabourg and Ouistreham
The nearest shopping centres.

OTHER ATTRACTIONS

Cabourg
Offers casino, night club, musical bars, restaurants, concerts, yachting, fishing, windsurfing, golf (18-hole), riding, tennis, etc.

Houlgate
Assembly point for William the Conqueror's invasion fleet in 1066. Commemorative pillar. Historical market halls.

Route des Marais
Picturesque itinerary through marshy areas around the River Dives, via Troarn.

10
CAEN

C aen was the ambitious D-Day objective of the 185th Infantry Brigade Group of the 3rd British Division, which was not achieved on 6 June. Caen was not taken by the Allies until 9 July. It was a fearsome and costly period for the citizens of Caen.

Air raids continued spasmodically throughout the month of June and into the next, until the dreadful climax of Operation CHARNWOOD 7-9 July. It was the final battle for Caen, preceded by a literally murderous attack on the night of 7 July by Lancaster and Halifax bombers.

Monsieur Poirier, the deputy mayor whose D-Day memory appears on pages 230-1, estimated that there were more than a thousand planes and that the raid lasted 45 crushing minutes. The dead and wounded reached unbearable and untreatable proportions, and many were buried, alive and dead, in the shattered buildings.

During 8 and 9 July the Germans withdrew and in the afternoon of 9 July Canadians of the 3rd Division who, of course, spoke French, and their tanks, were cautiously filing into the city, followed by the British of the 59th and 3rd Divisions. They offered cigarettes and chocolates to the citizens, who came out of their ruins, waving their battered Tricolores. 'The women kissed them, the men saluted them, but with dignity, without mad exaggeration. We have all suffered too much for our dearest ones to acclaim excessively those who have been forced by the necessity of war to do us so much harm', commented an exhausted Monsieur Poirier.

Many Allied 'liberators' were appalled at the carnage and destruction as they entered the shattered city. Some seemed oblivious to the extent of the damage.

Monsieur Poirier, who had received the first German officer to enter the town on 18 June 1940, was now greeted by a British officer. They shook hands at length, both had tears in their eyes, and they had a long conversation about the basic needs of the Caennais. Finally, the officer asked if Monsieur Poirier could direct him to a good hotel where he could get a hot bath. 'Brave Major H', commented the deputy mayor, and explained that three-quarters of the city was razed to the ground. Although the worst was past, the fighting raged around the city until on 15 August, after sixty-five days, the bloody battle for Caen was over.

What to See and Do In and Around Caen
For practical information see 'Tourist Information' on page 186.

Many memorials exist today as a tragic reminder of the civilian suffering. The Caennais are faithful in their memory to their own dead and to their liberators. Each 6 June and 9 July, ceremonies of remembrance and thanksgiving are held, when allied veterans and war widows are warmly welcomed. Memorials include:

Mémorial: Un Musee Pour la Paix (A museum for peace)
Esplanade Dwight-Eisenhower. Off the ring road (*Périphérique*) N13, to the north in the new la Folie Couvrechef district. Well signed. Not surprisingly, after their June and July 1944 suffering, the Caennais wished their magnificent new museum to be a symbol for peace. It was opened on 6 June 1988 by President Mitterand, in the presence of French and Allied veterans, 150 children of Caen, ten from the USSR, ten from Hiroshima and ten from each of the thirteen countries who fought in Normandy in 1944, whose official representatives laid thirteen symbolic memorial stones in the forecourt. The countries involved were Britain, USA, Canada, Belgium, Greece, Czechoslovakia, Poland, Holland, Norway, Luxembourg, East and West Germany and France. The vast building (70m (230ft) long, 55m (180ft) wide, 12m (40ft) high) is on three levels and as well as a cinema to seat 170 houses the following:
The Main Hall. Reception area, well-stocked shop, ticket office, cloak rooms, kindergarten, rest area, telex which constantly records any acts of war throughout the world, a World War II Typhoon.
First Floor. Historical journey with milestones of history on a huge cylinder, from ancient times to the present day, with particular emphasis on the pre-war years, the occupation, World War II, the landings, the resistance and the reconstruction. There are several films, including original World War II material and finally a film whose subject is 'Hope' for freedom and human rights.

There are also cafeteria, restaurant, *bureau de change* and ample parking. The museum uses the most up-to-date audio visual and computer technology and was funded by fund-raising committees, notably in the USA, and in Britain, Canada, Norway, Germany, and France, supported by the City of Caen and the Comité du Débarquement.

Around it are Memorial Valley, Memory Garden and the memorial to those who were shot by the Germans in Caen prison.

A D-DAY MEMORY

Monsieur Poirier, Maire-Adjoint, responsible for the passive defence of Caen and the efforts of the citizens to survive June-July 1944.

(Permission to reproduce extracts from his moving and graphic account, (reprinted with other, anonymous memories by the Mairie of Caen in 1984) has been given by the Documentation Centre of the Memorial Museum of Caen.)

"6 June I was woken up at about two in the morning by the dull, distant yet deafening sound of a bombardment. What is it? There's no doubt whatsoever. Something's up on the coast. Is it the coastal batteries firing? Are they far off bombs? Could it be the landings? Aeroplanes prowl and sirens sound the alert. It is the 1,020th alert. It's never going to end .... I get up and report to my Passive Defence Command Post in the Central Commissariat's shelter. I call up the sectors, who in turn call their outposts. Everyone's at their post. The wakening population besieges the bakers .... It's the landings we've all been waiting for!

The Boches are taking off. Already! Really one has to smile — we're imagining that it's all going to happen without any pain. About 7 o'clock some bombs drop beside the station. I'm informed of one killed and two wounded. The morning passes calmly, but in the distance is still the bombardment of hundreds of artillery pieces from allied war ships. I lunch hurriedly, because I sense that something new is about to happen.

English planes prowl ceaselessly above the town and at 1300 a large formation of bombers release their bombs on the centre of the town. It is the first air raid of such unprecedented violence. The Caennais [citizens of Caen] are stunned. An unbelievable number of bombs fall ... my sectors report to me on my special telephone, but already three lines are cut .... Red Cross emergency teams rush to the stricken regions. There are many dead and wounded, and general consternation at the

This impressive, highly technical museum is a must, but requires at least two hours for a thorough visit. See page 187 for opening times.

To visit the following memorials, pick up a town plan from the Tourist Office at Place Saint-Pierre.

Boulevard Bertrand

Plaque to the first Canadian soldier (called Hill) killed in Caen, is on the wall of the Prefecture garden.

suddenness of the attack. A crowd of terrified people flock into the Command Post and the shelters in the Town Hall cellars. They bring in the wounded and I send them to Bon-Sauveur [a convent], and already atrociously mutilated bodies are brought in .... The raid only lasted about ten minutes but the damage is enormous. The Monoprix shop is in flames and there are more than ten homes on fire in the centre.

At 1625 another short raid, but as violent as the 1300 one. Bombs fall in the Rue de Caumont, annihilating the annexe to the Prefecture ... old St Etienne is hit ... Rue de Carel, the bus depôt for Courriers Normand, and all the coaches in it ... the undertakers where we had stored 500 coffins 'our supply for serious emergencies' — reduced to ashes. We won't have a single coffin to bury the dead. Two wards receive fifteen or so one- and two-ton bombs, burying eight nuns and thirty patients under the debris: one of the Sisters and five patients are killed outright. The St Jean Hospice is destroyed. An ambulance driving over the Vaucelles bridge is hit by a bomb, the young Red Cross driver killed and her body thrown into the Orne. Our No 1 first aid post takes a bomb which totally destroys it. Dead and wounded everywhere. Already the Red Cross and other voluntary workers are insufficient for the task. There aren't enough ambulances, not enough stretchers, two first aid posts are out of action. In spite of prodigious acts of devotion, the medical corps cannot look after or operate quickly enough on the wounded that are being constantly brought in.

The fires multiply, a quarter of the town is in flames .... During the entire evening we hear the roar of aeroplanes. Doubtless they are observers who are coming to take stock of the results of the raids. The teams of helpers work relentlessly in the rubble to pull out buried survivers who are calling out.

There are so many sad victims that we won't be able to save because of lack of adequate tools and lack of enough helpers."

Place de la Résistance
Monument to the *Déportés* (French deported by the Germans during the war).

Rue de la Délivrande
On the left-hand side, opposite the 'LTE' building, a calvary remembering those who died in the liberation.

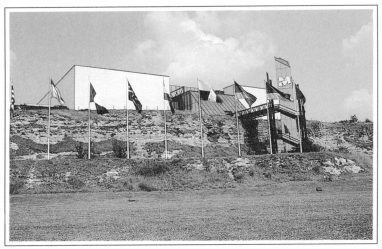

The new Memorial Museum, Caen

Fosses St Julien
Ruins of the famous church, destroyed in the bombardment, with a great modern wooden cross marking the site.

Place de la Gare
At the railway station is a plaque to the railway workers killed during the occupation, the landings and the bombardment.

Crossroads of Pont de Vaucelles (over the Orne) and Quai Meslin
Monument describing the collaboration of the Resistance workers with the Regina Rifle Regiment.

Place Monseigneur des Hameaux
Plaque commemorating the raising of the Tricolore and the Cross of Lorraine on 9 July, beside the Abbaye aux Hommes, in which 10,000 people took refuge during the battle for Caen.

Chapel of St George, in the Château
Memorial to the civilian, killed on 8 July, whose ashes are sealed in the wall.

11

MEMORIALS AND WAR GRAVES ORGANISATIONS

THE AMERICAN BATTLE MONUMENTS COMMISSION

The commission was established by the United States Congress in March 1923 for the permanent maintenance of military cemeteries and memorials on foreign soil. Their first task was to build cemeteries for the American dead of World War I.

After World War II, fourteen overseas military cemeteries were constructed, including the St Laurent Normandy Cemetery. They contain approximately 39 per cent of those originally buried in the region, the remaining 61 per cent were returned to the USA.

The ground on which each cemetery is built was granted by the host nation, free of rent or taxes. A white marble headstone marks every burial (Star of David for the Jewish, Latin cross for all others, whether they be Christian, Buddhist, agnostic or of any other belief). Memorials bearing the names of the missing, a non-denominational chapel and a visitor's room containing the register and visitors' book are standard in all cemeteries. All are open to the public daily.

The cemeteries are immaculately maintained by a superintendent (normally American) using local gardeners. He will supply photographs of the cemetery and the individual headstone for the next of kin and arrange for cut flowers to be bought locally and placed on the grave.

For full details of the Normandy American Cemetery and Memorial, see page109. Other Americans who died in Normandy are buried in Saint James, south of Avranches on the N798 to Fougères. Called 'The Brittany Cemetery', it contains 4,410 burials and the names of 498 missing.

The Battle Monuments Commission offices are at:

UNITED STATES	FRANCE
Room 2067, Tempo A	68 rue 19 janvier,
2nd and T Streets SW	92 Garches,
Washington, DC 20315.	France.

CANADIAN CEMETERIES

The Canadian cemeteries at Bény-sur-Mer and Bretteville-sur-Laize are maintained by the CWGC and are described below. Although primarily Canadian they both include some British and other nationalities. Canadians are also buried in Bayeux (181), Ryes (21), Tilly (1), Hottot (34), Fontenay (4), St. Manvieu (3), Brouay (2), La Délivrande (11), Hermanville (13), Ranville (76), Banneville (11), St Charles de Percy (3), and St Désir de Lisieux (16).

COMMONWEALTH WAR GRAVES COMMISSION

The commission has graciously given permission to reproduce in full here their informative *Guide to the Commonwealth War Cemeteries and the Bayeux Memorial Normandy. June-August 1944*. The dedicated work of the commission and its gardeners, who keep the cemeteries so beautifully, cannot be praised too highly. Please make sure to sign the visitors' book, found in the bronze box in each cemetery, and record your comments. Your visit is appreciated by those who tend the cemeteries.

A total of 22,421 Commonwealth war dead are buried in the ceme-

COMMONWEALTH WAR CEMETERIES IN THE CALVADOS
NORMANDY 1944

teries listed below. A further 1,805, who have no known grave, are commemorated by name on the Bayeux Memorial. Details of each burial or commemoration are kept in the register box on each site. In addition to those buried in the war cemeteries there are a few hundred buried in churchyards or village cemeteries throughout the region, and of course there are others who died of wounds in hospitals in the United Kingdom and were buried there.

Bayeux War Cemetery

This cemetery lies on the south-west side of the ring road around the city of Bayeux, 100yd to the east of the junction with route D5 (the road to Littry)

There was little fighting in Bayeux, and the cemetery, the largest of World War II in France, contains 4648 burials brought in from the surrounding districts and from hospitals that were located nearby. By countries they comprise:

United Kingdom	3,935
Canada	181
Australia	17
New Zealand	8
South Africa	1
France	3
Czechoslovakia	2
Italy	2
Russia	7
Germany	466
Poland	25
Unidentified	1

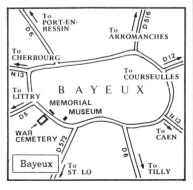

The Bayeux Memorial

The memorial stands opposite the cemetery and was, like the war cemetery, designed by Philip Hepworth. On it are engraved the names of 1,805 of the Commonwealth forces (1,534 British, 270 Canadian and 1 South African) who fell in the Battle of Normandy and the subsequent advance to the Seine, and have no known grave.

The connection with William the Conqueror is recalled in the Latin inscription on the frieze of the memorial:

'NOS A GULIELMO VICTI VICTORIS PATRIAM LIBERAVIMUS [We, once conquered by William, have now set free the Conqueror's native land]'.

The 'Battle of Normandy' Museum lies 200yd east of the memorial.

Ryes War Cemetery, Bazenville

The hamlet of Bazenville lies 3km (2 miles) south-east of Ryes.

Leave Bayeux on the D12 to the east; at the village of Sommervieu carry straight on, following the D112, and after 3km (2 miles) turn right on to the D87. After climbing round a bend to the left the cemetery will be found on the left-hand side.

From Arromanches, take the D87 southwards; after passing through Ryes and crossing the D112, the cemetery will be found on the left of the road a little before the hamlet of Bazenville.

From Caen, take the D22 north-westwards; after 16km (10 miles) and

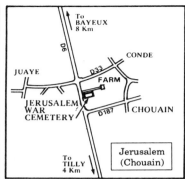

passing through Creully, turn west-wards on to the D12 towards Bayeux. After 2km (1¹/₄ miles), at the end of the village of Villers-le-Sec, turn right on the D87, towards Bazenville and Ryes. After 2¹/₂km (1¹/₂ miles) the cemetery will be found on the right-hand side.

Inland from Arromanches, where the 50th Division landed on 6 June, this cemetery contains some burials made just two days after the landing. The total of 979 is made up of 630 British, 21 Canadian, 1 Australian, 1 Polish and 326 German dead.

Jerusalem War Cemetery, Chouain

This is one of the smallest Common-wealth War Cemeteries, containing 47 British burials.

From Bayeux take the route D6 south-east towards Tilly-sur-Seulles. The cemetery will be found after about 8km (5 miles) on the left-hand side of the road at the bottom of a down hill stretch.

Jerusalem is the name of a tiny hamlet near the village of Chouain. This area was the scene of bitter fight-ing when a German armoured column sought to re-take Bayeux early after the British occupation; the cemetery

was begun on 10 June when three men of the Durham Light Infantry were killed, and about half of those buried here served with that regiment.

There is one Czech burial in here. (A battle group of Czech armoured units with field artillery and a motor battalion served with 21st Army Group from September 1944 onwards.)

Tilly-sur-Seulles War Cemetery

From Bayeux, take the D6 south-east-wards. Tilly-sur-Seulles lies at about 12km (7¹/₂ miles) in the centre of the town, turn right (westwards) on to the D13. The cemetery will be found after 1km (⁵/₈ mile) on the left-hand side.

From Caen, take the D9 west-wards. After about 12km (7¹/₂ miles) fork right on to the D13, and after passing through Tilly-sur-Seulles, the cemetery will be found on the left-hand side of the road.

There was heavy fighting here im-mediately after the landings, involving chiefly the 49th and 5th Divisions, and the 7th Armoured Division. Tilly was not taken until 18 June 1944, and fight-ing continued nearby until mid-July.

There are 1,222 burials, of which 986 are British, 1 Canadian, 1 Austra-lian, 2 New Zealand and 232 German.

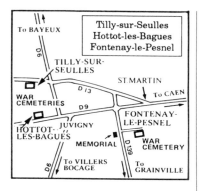

Hottot-les-Bagues War Cemetery

This cemetery can be reached from Bayeux by taking the D6 south-eastwards. After about 13km (8 miles) and after passing through Tilly-sur-Seulles, turn right (westwards) at Juvigny on to the main road, (the D9) that runs from Caen towards Caumont l'Eventé. The war cemetery will be found after a few hundred yards on the right-hand side on rising ground.

From Caen, take the D9 westwards towards Caumont l'Eventé. After 18km (11 miles) and just after passing the junctions with the D6 (Bayeux-Villers Bocage) the cemetery will be found on the right-hand side of the road on rising ground.

There are 1,137 burials, of which 965 are British, 34 Canadian, 3 Australian, 2 New Zealand, 1 South African and 132 German. Most of those who lie here were brought in from the surrounding district, where there was much heavy fighting during June and early July 1944, as the British forces tried to press forward in an encircling movement to the south of Caen.

Fontenay-le-Pesnel War Cemetery

The village of Fontenay-le-Pesnel lies 16km (10 miles) west of Caen on the main road (the D9) towards Caumont l'Eventé, just after the junction with the D13. The war cemetery is 1km ($^5/_8$ mile) south-east of the hamlet of St Martin (on the D139 to Grainville); on reaching a large memorial to the 49th (West Riding) Division, turn down the track opposite the memorial which leads directly to the cemetery.

This war cemetery contains the graves of those who died in the fighting to the west of Caen in June/July 1944. Units with particularly large numbers of graves are the South Staffordshires, the East Lancashires, the Royal Warwickshires and the Durham Light Infantry.

Here are buried 456 British and 4 Canadian soldiers, 1 British airman and 59 German soldiers.

St Manvieu War Cemetery, Cheux

This cemetery is reached from Caen by taking route D9 westwards; after about 8km (5 miles) passing first through an industrial area, with Carpiquet airfield lying on the south side, the road by-passes St Manvieu village, while Cheux lies 2km (1$^1/_4$ miles) to the left. The main road, which has been winding, now straightens out, and just at this point you will find the

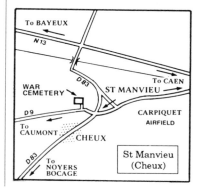

War Cemetery on the right-hand side.

Here are buried 2,183, of which 1,623 are British, 3 Canadians, 1 Australian and 556 German who died in the fluctuating battles from mid-June to the end of July, in this region between Tilly-sur-Seulles and Caen.

Brouay War Cemetery

The village of Brouay lies about 1½km (1 mile) south of the main road between Bayeux and Caen, and half way between the two.

From the main road (the N13), turn south-west on the D217. After crossing the bridge over the railway, fork right on the D94 towards Brouay village; at the village centre turn right, follow the road under the railway arch until you see the church ahead. Go through the churchyard and behind the church on the north side are the steps to the war cemetery entrance.

The 377 buried here lost their lives for the most part in heavy fighting during the efforts to encircle Caen towards the south. Except for two Canadian soldiers, all are British.

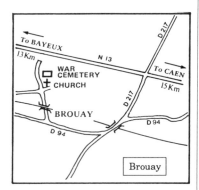

Brouay

Secqueville-en-Bessin War Cemetery

From Bayeux take the N13 towards

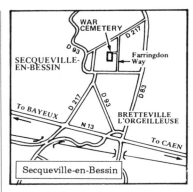

Secqueville-en-Bessin

Caen. After about 12km (7½ miles) turn left on to the D217, and the village of Secqueville will be found about 2km (1¼ miles) to the north. Turn right in the village, and after a few hundred yards take the track to the left, sign-posted Farringdon Way. The war cemetery will be found in open fields on the left-hand side.

Secqueville village can also be reached from Caen. Take the N13 towards Bayeux; after about 10km (6 miles) the village of Bretteville l'Orgueilleuse will be found on the right-hand side. From Bretteville take the D93 northwards and Secqueville-en-Bessin will be found at 2km (1¼ miles) distance; then take the Farringdon Way as indicated above.

This is a battlefield cemetery, containing the graves of men killed in the advance to Caen early in July 1944, with some from subsequent fighting up to the end of that month. Here are buried 97 British and 18 German soldiers, one British airman and one unknown Allied soldier.

Bény-sur-Mer Canadian War Cemetery, Reviers

Reviers is a village lying 18km (11 miles) east of Bayeux, 15km (9 miles)

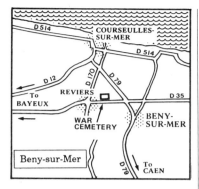

north-west of Caen and 4km (2½ miles) south of Courseulles-sur-Mer. The cemetery lies on the north side of the main road 1km (⅝ mile) east of Reviers.

From Courseulles turn left from route D12 on to route D79 just south of the town; after 3km (2 miles) turn right on to the D35 and the war cemetery will be found after 1km (⅝ mile) on high ground on the right-hand side.

From Caen, take route D79 north towards Courseulles; then, after passing through the village of Bény-sur-Mer, take the next road to the left, where the cemetery will be found after 1km (⅝ mile) on the right-hand side.

The 2,049 buried in this war cemetery are mainly those of the 3rd Canadian Division, who lost their lives either on 6 June, when 335 of the division's officers and men were killed, or during the early days of the advance towards Caen, when the main German force engaged was a battle group formed from the 716th Division and the 21st Panzer Division.

The village of Bény-sur-Mer was taken by the Canadians in the early afternoon of 6 June.

Also buried here at Bény are three British soldiers and an airman, and a French soldier.

La Délivrande War Cemetery, Douvres

Take the main road northwards from Caen, the D7 to Langrune-sur-Mer. After about 12km (7½ miles), the war cemetery will be found on the right of the road, a few hundred yards before reaching la Délivrande crossroads and its twin-spired church.

This cemetery contains 1,123 burials, of which 927 are British, 11 Canadian, 3 Australian, 1 Polish, 180 German and one unidentified. They date from 6 June 1944, and the landings on Oboe and Peter beaches; others were brought in later from the battlefields between the coast and Caen.

Hermanville War Cemetery

Hermanville-sur-Mer lies 13km (8 miles) north of Caen on the road to Lion-sur-Mer (the D60). To reach the war cemetery go northwards right through Hermanville; after leaving the Mairie (town hall) on your left, turn right. The gates to the war cemetery will be found after 330yd where the lane swings north again towards the coast.

The village of Hermanville lay behind SWORD Beach and was occupied early on 6 June by men of the 1st Batallion South Lancashire Regiment.

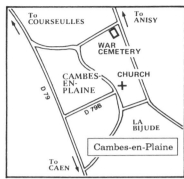

Later the same day, the Shropshire Light Infantry, supported by the armour of the Staffordshire Yeomanry, managed to reach and hold Biéville-Benville, 4km (2½ miles) to the south of Hermanville.

Many of the 1,005 buried in this cemetery died in the fighting in these parts on 6 June and the first few days of the drive towards Caen. There are 986 British burials, 13 Canadian, 3 Australian and 3 French.

Cambes-en-Plaine War Cemetery

The cemetery lies on the north side of Cambes-en-Plaine village; take the road from Caen towards Courseulles-sur-Mer, the D79, and turn off to the right 6km (3¾ miles) north of Caen on the D79B. This will bring you to the village centre of Cambes-en-Plaine opposite the church. Turn left towards the north side of the village and turn right after 550yd. The war cemetery will then be found after 380yd on the right-hand side.

The cemetery may also be reached by taking the road north from Caen towards Langrune (the D7). When La Bijude is reached 4km (2½ miles) north of Caen, fork left on to the road to Anisy; after 1½km (1 mile) turn left and the cemetery will be found immedi-

ately on the left-hand side.

More than half of the 224 burials in this war cemetery are of men of the South Staffordshire and the North Staffordshire Regiments, from bitter fighting on 8 July and 9 July 1944 respectively, during the final attack on Caen. The greater part of that city was captured on 10 July.

Ranville War Cemetery and Churchyard

Ranville is best reached by taking the D513 north-eastwards out of Caen, through the suburb of Colombelles, and after about 9km (5½ miles) turning left at Hérouvillette. Go north for 1km (⅝ mile), and then turn left into Ranville

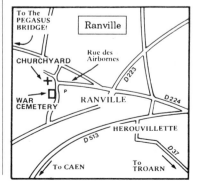

village; the war cemetery and churchyard are approached by taking the Rue des Airbornes.

The name of Ranville will always be linked with the landing by parachute and glider of the British 6th Airborne Division, many of whose dead rest here. Their task was to seize the vital bridges over the River Orne and the Caen canal. The cemetery contains 2,563 burials, of which 2,153 are British, 76 Canadian, 1 Australian, 3 New Zealand, 5 French, 1 Polish, 1 Belgian, 322 German and 1 unidentified.

In the adjoining churchyard 47 British soldiers are buried around the perimeter wall. All landed by parachute or glider and died on 6th/7th June 1944.

Pegasus Bridge, with its interesting museum, lies west of the village.

Banneville-la-Campagne War Cemetery

This cemetery lies 100yd south of the main road (the N175) between Caen and Pont l'Eveque, about 8km (5 miles) east of Caen and 3½km (2 miles) west of the village of Troarn.

It contains, for the most part, men killed in the fighting from the second week of July 1944, when Caen was captured, to the last week in August when the Falaise Gap had been closed and the Allies were preparing their advance beyond the Seine.

There are 2,175 burials, of which 2,150 are British, 11 Canadian, 5 Australian, 2 New Zealand, 5 Polish and 2 entirely unidentified.

Bretteville-sur-Laize Canadian War Cemetery

This lies on the west side of the main N518 from Caen to Falaise about 14km (81/2 miles) south of Caen and just north of the village of Cintheaux. The village of Bretteville lies 3km (2 miles) south-west of the cemetery.

Buried here are those who died during the later stages of the battle of Normandy, the capture of Caen and the thrust southwards — led initially by 4th Canadian and 1st Polish Armoured Divisions — to close the Falaise Gap, and thus seal off the German divisions fighting desperately to escape being trapped west of the Seine. Almost every unit of Canadian 2nd Corps is represented in the cemetery.

There are 2,958 burials: 2,872 Canadian, 80 British, 4 Australian, 1 New Zealand and 1 French.

On this same main road, 4km (2½ miles) further to the south, lies the Polish War Cemetery at Langannerie.

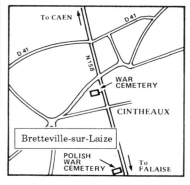

Banneville-la-Campagne

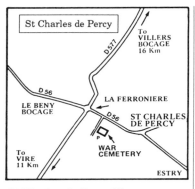

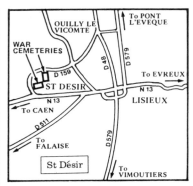

St Charles de Percy War Cemetery

The furthest south of the war cemeteries of the Normandy fighting, St Charles de Percy can be reached, whether from Bayeux or Caen, by going through Villers Bocage. Take the N175 southwestwards then out of Villers Bocage; after 5km (3 miles) take the left fork, the D577, towards Vire. After winding for a further 15km (9 miles) the road descends on the long straight approach to Vire. At this point it goes through the little hamlet of La Ferroniere'. Turn left here on to the D56 and right again after a few hundred yards. The war cemetery will then be found on the left-hand side and on its further boundary there is an ample parking area.

This cemetery contains 799 burials, of which one soldier and 3 airmen are Canadian, and the remainder are all British. They mostly died in the major thrust made by British Second Army from Caumont l'Eventé towards Vire, in late July and early August 1944, to drive a wedge between the German 7th Army and Panzer Group West.

St Désir War Cemetery

St Désir is a village on the N13 to Caen, 4km (2¹/₂ miles) west of the cathedral city of Lisieux, dominated by the basilica of St Thérésa. The war cemetery is about 1km (⁵/₈ mile) west of the village and lies on a secondary road, the D159, which winds northwards towards Ouilly-le-Vicomte.

The war cemetery contains 598 burials of World War II. 569 are British, 16 Canadian, 6 Australian, 1 New Zealand, 5 South African and one from the United States. Most of them died in the final stages of the Normandy campaign, in pursuit of the German forces towards the Seine.

Four soldiers from World War I, whose graves could no longer be satisfactorily maintained in their original place of burial, have been re-interred in this cemetery.

A little further up the same lane lies the German War Cemetery of St Désir (3,735 burials).

POLISH CEMETERY

The poignant Polish cemetery at Grainville-Langannerie, on the N158 south of Caen, contains 650 burials. It is maintained by the French Ministry of Anciens Combattants, rue de Berey, Paris 12.

There are also Polish burials in Bayeux (25), Ryes (1), La Délivrande (1), Ranville (1) and Banneville-la-Campagne (5). See the CWGC listing, pages 234-42.

VOLKSBUND DEUTSCHE KRIEGSGRÄBERFÜRSORGE

(The German War Graves Welfare Organisation)

The organisation is similar in function to the Commonwealth War Graves Commission and the American Battle Monuments Commission in that it maintains the war cemeteries and memorials to the German dead from World War I onwards.

In 1956, the organisation, with the help of volunteer students, started re-interring the German war dead, then buried in 1,400 sites in Normandy, into the six large cemeteries which exist today.

La Cambe in Chapter 6, is described in detail on page 89. Other German cemeteries in Normandy are:

Champigny-St André, between Evreux and Dreux, 19,795 burials.
Huisnes-sur-Mer, near Mont St Michel, 11,956 burials.
Marigny-la-Chappelle, near St Lô, 11,169 burials.
Orglandes, near Valognes, 10,152 burials.
St Désir-de-Lisieux, 3,735 burials.
There are also German burials in many CWGC Cemeteries.

The address of the organisation is
Volksbund Deutsche Kriegsgräberfürsorge EV,
Werner-Hilpert-Strasse 2,
3500 Kassel,
West Germany.

12

ORGANISATIONS FOR EX-SERVICEMEN AND REMEMBRANCE

EX-SERVICEMEN'S ORGANISATIONS

As the veterans of the Normandy campaign reach retirement age and have more time to spend on meeting old comrades and on thinking back, membership of veterans' associations is growing. They include:

The American Legion
They also have information about the many strong American divisional and other ex-servicemen's associations.
Head Office: PO Box 1050 Indianapolis, IN 46206, USA.
49 rue Pierre Charron, Paris 8ème, France.

Airborne Assault Normandy
A trust to preserve the history of 6AB's assault into Normandy. Membership open to veterans and interested associate members.
Regimental Headquarters, The Parachute Regiment, Browning Barracks, Aldershot, Hants, GU11 2BU, UK.

D-Day and Normandy Fellowship
Formed in 1968, this is open to men and women of all armed forces and merchant navies who took part in the D-Day and subsequent operations in Normandy, to their relatives and those closely associated with or interested in the events of 1944.
It is planned to unveil a commemorative window to Normandy veterans in Bayeux Cathedral on the 45th anniversary of D-Day (similar to the window unveiled by the Queen Mother in 1984 in Portsmouth Cathedral). Contributions are invited.
Contact: Mrs L.R. Reed, 9 South Parade, Southsea, Portsmouth, Hants, PO5 2JB.

Moths (Memorable Order of Tin Hats)
Similar to the RBL, one has to have seen active service to belong to this

organisation which was started in South Africa after World War I. They have several 'Shell Holes' (branches) in the UK and have many Normandy veterans amongst their members.

Contact: Mr Harry Turner (Senior 'Old Bill'), 33 Millicent Fawcett Court, Tottenham, London N17.

The Normandy Veterans Association

The association was formed in April 1981 in Grimsby by thirty-four dedicated Normandy veterans, whose energetic committee, with publicity officer Arthur Flodman, wrote to every local newspaper in Great Britain. By May, sixteen other local branches had been formed. Arthur Flodman became the first national secretary, but sadly died in 1985. By 1988 there were seventy-one active branches, (with about 8,000 members) including international branches in Holland, Belgium, New Zealand, Nova Scotia, Australia and West Germany. The members of the 68th branch, 'Calvados', fought with the Maquis.

Representatives from the ten British regions form a national council. Funds are raised for the benevolent and welfare section through the sale of the NVA's own Commemoration Campaign Medal and other items.

The president is General Sir John Mogg, GCB, CBE, DSO, DL and the Duke of Gloucester, KCVO is the Royal Patron. The association has its own chaplain and national standard. Parades and services are held each year on the Sunday after 6 June and the association parades on Remembrance Sunday at the Cenotaph. Many branches run pilgrimages to Normandy each 6 June.

The purpose of the association is 'comradeship' and membership is open to all who took an active part in the assault on the beaches of Normandy.

Contact: Mr E.S. Hannath, Hon Gen Secretary, 53 Normandy Road, Cleethorpes, South Humberside, DN35 9JE.

Royal British Legion

Their benevolent department arranges pilgrimages for war widows to CWGC cemeteries in Normandy. Their head office is RBL, Pall Mall, London SW1.

ORGANISATIONS FOR REMEMBRANCE

Association France-Grande Bretagne
Comité de Caen, 9 Place Jean-Letellier, 14000 Caen.
Contact: MMe Joan Boyer.
This extremely helpful association has been providing assistance for many years to Royal British Legion pilgrims and others wishing to visit the CWGC cemeteries around Caen, but who have no transport.

Comité du Débarquement (D-Day Commemoration Committee)
After the landings, the first 'Sous-Prefet' to be appointed in France was Monsieur Raymond Triboulet, OBE. He operated from Bayeux, the first French city to be liberated, and became Ministre des Anciens Combattants in 1958. He was also appointed Chairman of the 'Comité du Débarquement', set up in May 1945, which is dedicated to preserving the sites and the memory of the invasion and the landing beaches. The Comité is responsible for the siting of ten 'Monuments Signaux' — great stone markers commemorating the landing at, or Liberation of, Bénouville, Ouistreham-Riva-Bella, Bernières, Graye, Port-en-Bessin, Les Moulins (St Laurent), Isigny, Carentan, St Martin de Varreville and Ste Mère Eglise, as well as other memorials.

It also set up, or supports, the museums at Arromanches, Bénouville, Ste Mère Eglise, Cherbourg, Ste Marie-du-Mont (UTAH), Ouistreham, Merville Battery and the Memorial Museum at Caen. The Comité liaises with British regimental and ex-servicemen's associations to participate in ceremonies of remembrance in Normandy.

Its head office is at Place aux Pommes, Bayeux.

Souvenir Français
This association was founded in 1872, after the Franco-Prussian War. Its aim is to keep alive the memory of those who died for France, to maintain their graves and memorials in good condition, and to transmit 'the flame of memory' to future generations.

The Head Office is at 9 rue de Clichy, 75009 Paris.

Major and Mrs Holt's Battlefield Tours
They run well-organised, well-researched guided battlefield tours and pilgrimages to Normandy (and other battlefields around the world) for veterans and others interested in military history.

Their head office is at the Golden Key Building, 15 Market Street, Sandwich, Kent, CT13 9DA, UK. ☎ 0304 612248.

BIBLIOGRAPHY

Ambrose, Stephen E. *Pegasus Bridge* (George Allen & Unwin, 1984)
Belchem, Maj.-Gen. David. *Victory in Normandy* (BCA, 1981)
Benamou, Jean-Pierre. *Normandy 1944* (Heimdal, 1984)
Boussel, Patrice and Florentin, Eddie. *Guide des Plages du Débarquement et des Champs de Bataille de Normandie* (Presses de la Cité, 1984)
Citizens of Caen. *Témoignages, Récits de la Vie Caennaise 6 Juin-18 Juillet 1944* (Ville de Caen, 1984)
Edwards, Cdr. K.E. *Operation Neptune* (Collins, 1946)
Ellis, Maj. L.F. *Victory in the West. The Battle of Normandy* (Official History, 1960)
Essame, Maj.-Gen. H. *Normandy Bridgehead* (Macdonald, 1970)
Golley, John. *The Big Drop* (Jane's, 1982)
Harrison, G.A. *US Army in World War II. Cross-Channel Attack* (Office of Chief Military History Dept of the Army, 1951)
Hastings, Max. *Overlord* (Michael Joseph, 1984)
Haswell, J. *Intelligence and Deception of the D-Day Landings* (Batsford, 1979)
Holt, T. and V. *Holts' Battlefield Guides. Normandy — Overlord* (TVH, 1987)
Jacobsen, H.A. and Rohwer, J. *Decisive Battles of World War II: The German View* (André Deutsch, 1965)
Jewell, Brian. *Conquest and Overlord* (Midas Books, 1981)
Johnson, G. and Dunphie, C. *Brightly Shone the Dawn* (Warne, 1980)
Liddel Hart, B.H. *History of the Second World War* (BCA, 1973)
Maule, Henry. *Caen* (PBS, 1976)
Messenger, Charles. *The Commandos. 1940-1949* (William Kimber, 1985)
Montgomery, Field Marshal. *Normandy to the Baltic* (Hutchinson)
Morgan, Kay Summersby. *Past Forgetting* (Simon & Schuster, 1975)
Partridge, Colin. *Hitler's Atlantic Wall* (D.I. Publications, 1976)
Ramsey, Winston. *After the Battle*, Nos 1(1973), 34(1981), 45(1984)
Rapport, L. & Northwood, A. *Rendez-vous with Destiny* (101st Airborne Division Association, 1948)
Ruge, Friedrich. *Rommel in Normandy* (Presidio Press, 1979)
Tute, Warren Costello, John and Hughes, Terry. *D-Day* (Pan, 1975)
Valavielle, Michel de. *D-Day at UTAH Beach* (OCEP, 1976)
Wheldon, Sir Huw. *Red Berets into Normandy* (Jarrold, 1982)
White, Sir Bruce. *Mulberry* (White, 1980)
Wilmot, Chester. *The Struggle for Europe* (Collins, 1952)
Unattributed:
    By Air to Battle (HMSO, 1945)
    German Order of Battle 1944 (Arms & Armour Press, 1975)
    Royal Engineers Battlefield Tour: Normandy to the Seine (BAOR, 1946)

INDEX

MUSEUMS

MEMORIALS

In addition to those below, many streets, roads and squares are named as memorials to individuals and units who took part in the landings and the Battle for Normandy; a number are mentioned in the text.